From Venice to Rome with Two Stops Between

by

Sābra Hunter

～ Chapter 1 ～

I don't know about other work environments, but weird things always happen inside airports whenever there's a full moon overhead. People act nuts; they say and do things that are totally out-of-character: nice people become nasty; respectable people act disrespectfully. Rudeness gets worse. Even those of us working in the airline business have been known to exhibit behaviors contrary to the public faces we're expected to present. And while it's true these lunar transmutations don't affect everyone equally—and yes, I know they happen monthly—every year there's at least one of these mega moon's (the infamous Blood Moon) with noticeably stronger effects than during times of plain old full moons. Take last month for example.

The fifteenth marked the beginning of one of those standout lunar cycles. I knew it the minute I spotted that huge reddish globe hovering overhead while driving home from work. It looked electrified against the otherwise blackness of the night sky, with contrasting landmasses appearing so close at hand they looked as though I could reach out and touch them. The lunar attraction was so strong, in fact, that I pulled over to the side of the highway just to admire the sheer beauty of it. Then a wary breath of anticipation hit. This heavenly body, gorgeous as it was, was about to screw up work for at least the next week to come. I just knew it.

How right I was. The very next day sickouts hit a record high, putting those of us who did show up in bad moods at the promise of double-duty. Our sullenness showed by ignoring Supervisor Noggin's as he read the daily briefing notes in his usual grating monotone, stumbling over the words like a fourth grader. Why listen anyway? The information had been posted for days on the company web page, so reading it to us was both demeaning and a waste of time—time that could have been better spent standing in line at Mickey D's waiting to begin our shift with a cup of caffeine.

"Enough already!" someone finally yelled from the back of the room. "Just take attendance and be done with it!"

Not a single head turned to see who the brave voice belonged to.

"All we want to know is who gets an assist and who's stuck working alone," said another. Tentative nodding accompanied the voice.

"Is my flight going to cancel?" added a third in a nervous soprano, sounding like so many of our passengers. Snickers followed.

"What about me? Am I overbooked?" came from what sounded like the far corner, near the TV.

"They're all overbooked. They're always overbooked," said a voice from somewhere up front.

More muffled laughter rippled across the room. The more experienced of us stole commiserating glances at the guilty parties. We were well-aware that if there was one thing Richard Noggins didn't like, it was being interrupted while he was holding court during our daily shift briefing. It was the one thing he never missed. It was just about the only real work he did all day long.

Four leftover bodies from the day shift sat sprawled in front of the TV, their feet lined up beside each other on the coffee table like bowling pins. I couldn't see their faces, only the backs of four immobile heads all facing *Gunsmoke*. They were either engrossed or asleep. From my vantage point it was hard to tell which.

"Hunter," Noggins announced, forcing my attention back to his pot-bellied stance. "You and Bonano need to go help out in baggage service."

"Why me?" I complained before I could stop myself.

The rest nodded in solidarity, though I knew every one of them was secretly relieved they hadn't been chosen for this unpopular chore.

But Noggin's wasn't in a negotiating mood. "I said you, Hunter. I meant you. You think you're too good to pull bags?"

"No, but I do think that as senior agent on this shift, I should have something to say about where I'm assigned to work."

"Not today you don't. If you can't do the job, Hunter, then maybe it's time you give some serious thought to doing something else for a living."

I opened my mouth with a ready retort, but held back at the last minute. What the hell did he mean by that? Foolhardy or just plain dumb, I held hope that negotiating might still be an option. "Don't you think it would be more efficient to put some guys with muscles on bag detail? Those international bags are monsters and I, for one, don't want to get hurt wrestling with them. You know how there's always a ton of OJI's during full moons."

That meant paperwork, and paperwork was something Noggins religiously avoided.

"We have guys with muscles here?" Bonano mumbled just loud enough for those sitting close to her to hear. She looked around the room. Her eyes settled on the *Gunsmoke* gang, and lingered.

"Like I said, if you two can't do the job, then you better figure out a way to do something else." Noggins pursed his lips and frowned at Maya. "Bonano, I don't want to have to remind you to put your hair up before you leave this room. Even a teenybopper ponytail would be preferable to that bedroom hair you're wearing today." His smile turned to a sneer. "On second thought, you're too far past your twenties to get away with a ponytail." As an afterthought, he added, "You know the rules. Company policy dictates you either wear it up or cut it short. Do you need me to cut it?"

Bonano had the good sense to keep her mouth shut, though I could tell by her flushed face that she was seething.

For some reason I refused to accept Noggin's assignment without a fight, even though I knew I'd pay a price by way of continued crappy assignments for the rest of the week because of it—maybe the rest of the month. "If I wanted to work baggage, don't you think I would have bid baggage?"

Emboldened, Maya joined in. "Yeah, I bid gates this bid because I wanted to work gates. You know, as in **be** a gate agent. Now you're farming me out to bags, so I don't even get near a gate? That's so not fair!"

"Why didn't you call my cell and let me know you were sending me out front?" I asked. "Why did you let me walk all the way out here, punch in, then wait for this bad news briefing just to tell me just I get to walk all the way out front again? You have our phone numbers. You could have saved me a lot of time and trouble by letting me punch in at the ticket counter. I don't think that was very fair either."

All heads nodded in agreement although no one had the courage to speak up in our defense, either. It wasn't that long ago Noggins requested everyone's cell number. Those requests evolved into demands, complete with retaliatory assignments until the information was handed over. Afterward, few of us escaped Noggins after-hours calls to second-guess gate malfunctions, flight delays, or to investigate inter-office slights and petty accusations. I ended up blocking him. I live in a rural area, so I always pleaded awful service as the reason I could never be reached. I knew he'd never call to do something nice. So far, he hasn't figured it out.

"Tough," was all Noggins finally said, ending the briefing by turning and retreating to his office, slamming the door shut behind him.

"Dickhead," I muttered, following Bonano out the door to re-trace the twenty-minute excursion to the front of the building. "How in hell does he expect the two of us to handle a hundred plus international bags the way a couple of guys could?"

"Especially when one of them is as old as you," Maya wisecracked, jockeying ahead of me at the top of the escalator.

I didn't comment. The truth hurt.

Downstairs, only one train was running, same as my earlier trip out to the concourse. This time the sign overhead flashed: *'Out of service for scheduled security checks.'*

Maya pointed to the sign and laughed. "The traveling public wouldn't dare complain about *security checks,* would they?"

I made a face at the sign. "Security checks my ass. One of these trains is always out of service. This airport's just trying to save on electricity. They think no one will notice."

Bonano laughed and removed the elastic band holding her ponytail, shaking the long black strands free with both hands. "I read somewhere the airport CFO claimed it was her duty to influence better health habits among the traveling public. That would explain why she shuts one side down a couple of times each day."

I agreed, watching a dozen or so people standing nearby, fidgeting, looking at their watches, trying to decide whether to wait or walk for health. "They should send her to California and let her do her social engineering there. She'd fit right in."

Maya shrugged. "Oh well, it is what it is."

"Thank God I only have to put up with his shit for another week," I said just as the train showed up and the doors slid open.

"Another week?" Maya said, side-stepping the crowd of arriving passengers, glancing backwards at me. "Don't tell me you are retiring?"

"Not yet," I said, laughing. "Vacation." Suddenly an idea struck. I grabbed Maya by the arm and pulled her away from the open train door. "To hell with this, let's just walk. We're not in a hurry to get there are we?"

"We're not?" she asked, sounding confused at being coerced into a fifteen-minute walk instead of a four-minute ride.

Our steps synchronized as we began the mile-long trek to the terminal. "So, you going anywhere special?"

"Not this time. This one is a working vacation at home. No fun. No rest, either."

Maya shifted her backpack purse, wincing while pulling her hair out from under one of the straps. "Working? Doing what?"

"I had a new fence put up this summer. Now I have to paint it. Which means either I pay someone to do it for me, or I save the money—a lot of money in this case—and do it myself." I paused to catch my breath. "Slow down, Maya. This isn't a race."

She laughed. "Right. I remember: we are not in a hurry to get to baggage."

"I can't wait to get away from this place right now. Every time you turn around there's another security issue. I can't keep all the new rules and regulations straight, especially when some of them contradict previous rules and regulations."

Maya agreed. "I could use a break from here, too. I haven't been anywhere for months." She stopped and turned to face me. "You know what? We should put some kind of itinerary together and plan a little getaway. Just the two of us."

"Our timing might look bad after this morning, though," I said, thinking of the difficulties we'd now face to get Noggins to approve any of our time off requests.

"What do you . . .? You mean because of stepping into his crosshairs during briefing?"

I nodded. "He'll have plenty of time for revenge. On the other hand, we'll probably need a vacation by the time he's finished harassing us and turns his attention to someone else."

"What are you worried about? You won't be here next week. You'll miss most of the fallout."

"So where should we go?" I asked, changing the subject.

"I keep saying I want to do Venice. I should just pack up and go there by myself before our service stops for the winter," Maya said. "I don't know why I keep putting it off."

"I can't believe you haven't been there yet. Especially since you already speak the language. That's half the battle, in my opinion."

Maya nodded. "I know. But Venice maps are really confusing."

"Confusing? How? It's an island, and it's round—more or less. Walk long enough and you'll end up back at the main plaza again. It's the street addresses that are confusing. They're impossible to find over there. That's why I finally stopped booking hotels on the island."

Maya looked over at me with renewed interest.

"My last couple of trips there I just stayed in Tessera near the airport and took the city bus in. It's a short hop straight from the airport to the island and back with a quick stopover near the hotel. So much easier than hauling luggage over Venice cobblestones. Not to mention multo cheaper."

"Last couple . . . how many times have you been there?"

I laughed. "Too many to count. I have to find somewhere new. Maybe Rome—that's the one city I keep putting off visiting. I keep saying I'm saving it for retirement. Not that I see that happening anytime soon. The more Noggins insinuates I should retire, the less inclined I am to go."

"I'm serious," Maya insisted. "We should do it. I know Rome, you know Venice. It's perfect! We can tour guide each other. Let's put in for some time off after you get back from vacation. Hopefully Noggins will have forgotten about us by then.

"Sure, I guess. In that case though I'll need to get back to my language tapes. You're native Italian, but I'm just a beginner. I always end up reverting to Spanish and hope they understand me. Sometimes they do. Mostly they just frown and say, '*No capito*.' It's so frustrating."

Maya snorted back a laugh. "Didn't you start those language tapes over a year ago? I remember you talking about listening to them on your drive to and from work."

I shrugged. "They were great for vocabulary, but once they started asking me questions and expecting answers, I got stuck. They go so fast I can't keep up."

"*Gli italiani sono famosi chiaccieroni velociI*," she said, using a free hand for emphasis.

I nodded. "Easy for you to say. To you it only sounds fast. You capish all of it. To me it sounds like some of our speed-demon gate agents—native English speakers yet no one can follow them."

"Seriously, what do you say?" Maya asked as we stepped on the escalator leading upstairs to the baggage level. "We could go late September to mid-October while the weather's still nice, and after all the college kids have returned to school."

"Okay. Sure. Why not. Today, meanwhile, I am following Dickhead's fine leadership example. I plan to stay as busy as he does; regular trips to Starbucks, alternating with runs to the bathroom, a few visits to the other airline baggage offices to see if they're holding any of our bags, not to mention a side trip or two upstairs to check out the ticket counter traffic. Hell, if I smoked, I'd head out back to the loading dock and suck down a few. Screw that oversized idiot. Today I'm doing just like Dickhead by making myself scarce until this shit assignment is over."

"You better be careful about calling him that, Sābra. One of these day's you'll let it slip while you're talking to him. Then what will you do?"

"Oh, I'll just pretend I was talking about someone else," I answered over my shoulder as we stepped onto the ground floor landing and into the baggage claim area.

Our spirits sank as we made our way toward the baggage carousel. Even from a distance we could see a steady stream of oversized bags popping up out of the conveyer chute and tumbling down onto the rotating carousel. Bags that big could only have arrived from our latest international arrival. Most of their owners, more than likely, were still out on the concourse, standing in line at the security exit outside of customs. That left Maya and I to offload all these heavy suckers and line them up for their weary owner's eventual arrival. Preferably undamaged.

"I can see why they have to send someone out here to deal with this mess," Maya commented as we approached the loaded carousel. "One more trip around and these bags will be two layers deep."

I surveyed the never-ending parade of bags. "Maybe we should just let them jam up. We'll just tell Dickhead we couldn't keep up."

Maya looked at me in wide-eyed fear. "That's what he wants, Sābra. Besides, won't a bag jam with this many bags mess up the whole belt system?"

I grabbed a handle of the nearest bag and tugged, but the bag didn't budge. "What do you mean that's what Noggins wants?"

"Think about what he said in briefing," Maya began, latching onto a bag and trotted alongside it before managing to drag it over the conveyor lip and onto the floor. She took a deep breath then reached for the next bag. "I think he was hinting that . . . after a certain age, well . . . that maybe we . . . er, you . . . should consider retiring."

I nodded. "You do know that age discrimination is illegal, don't you?"

Maya just laughed. "But does he?"

"It's just so insulting to have that lazy bozo judging me to be so over-the-hill that I need steering out the door. My God, you'd think I was seventy-five years old!"

Maya chose a smallish bag and flipped it onto the floor, then reached for another. She lunged for its handle and hung on in spite of the fact it only moved an inch or two before it became tightly wedged between two neighboring bags. She let go and came back to stand beside me.

Both of us silently stared at the still growing pileup of bags revolving around in front of us. "Think about it, Sābra. If Noggins assigns you tough, physical jobs, you either have to keep up or get out."

"Doesn't mean I have to like it."

Maya gave me a look of sympathy. "Don't take it personal. I think all businesses do it once you hit a certain age . . . " She corrected herself, adding, "Once you're over fifty. Or sixty. Maybe he was just trying to be polite."

"Polite? He was being illegal," I stressed. "And why wouldn't I take it personal? I'm as accomplished and as productive as anyone else out here." To prove my point, I lurched forward and wrestled another monster bag onto the floor.

"Well, you can always tell Noggins that you . . . that we couldn't manage this assignment and see what he does."

Did Maya's voice sound a little bit hopeful? After all, my retirement would pave the way for another full-time vacancy. She'd move up another notch on the seniority ladder. In the end I shook my head and pushed the thought aside.

"Maya, if I tell Noggins I can't do it, then I'll wind up here all day every day for weeks to come. Trust me, he'll see to it. I sure don't want him thinking I'm old and feeble." I grabbed another bag and flipped it, watching as it bounced over the carousel and onto the floor where it landed with a thud. I stretched my aching back to work out a beginning kink and looked at the mountain of bags yet to be dealt with, trying not to feel overwhelmed.

"What kills me is that people like Noggins have ruined everything that used to be good between agents and management," I explained. "We're non-union, so there's no reason why these lazy supervisors can't get out in the trenches alongside us once in a while and help out with the overload. Our so-called 'leaders' have taken laziness to a new level by exempting themselves from all public contact. They don't bother coming out of their office long enough to assess the operation, so they have no idea what the hell we're dealing with."

As I ranted, I swept my arms out toward the endless pile of bags on the carousel. "This is a prime example. Why would you purposefully assign a pair of females to a job like this? A sensible leader would assign tasks with an eye on what's best for the company. Ultimately that means our customers."

Maya nodded in agreement but said nothing.

"Some of these bags weigh more than you do!" I continued. "So why assign you here at all? Is it any wonder so many agents get injured or that so many bags get damaged? You tell me, how is that effective leadership?"

Maya snorted. "How can they be effective when they're not here. They're all out on the golf course or something. By the way, nowadays it's called 'servant leadership.'"

"What a crock."

Again, we paused to survey the carousel. Some bags were so embalmed with plastic wrap that not even a hint of a handle stuck out. Most were overstuffed. With my luck any one of them could end up exploding open the minute it slammed onto the floor. The next one coming round the bend, in fact, had already ruptured at its mid-section zipper. Clothes and plastic bags of God-only-knew-what trailed behind it as it made its way around the track.

My heart sank as a third tier of bags began piling on top of the first two. "You know what really hurts?" I said to Maya. "That the company doesn't care about experience and job knowledge anymore."

Maya looked over at me. "That's because those things mean *old*. They'll never admit it, but what they want is young."

"Young and cheap. Sounds like China. Over there, the minute you hit thirty-five you're over-the-hill. Time to get out and make way for the next crop of comrades." I shook my head and clamped my mouth shut. I didn't want to discuss it anymore.

Poor Maya, she was a head shorter than I, so she wasn't able to get enough leverage to lift a bag, much less flip it off the carousel. There's a trick to flipping a moving bag by using your body weight to gain enough momentum to lift it over the carousel edge and onto the floor without looking like you're purposefully manhandling it—or without getting a hernia in the process. I watched Maya fumble with yet another bag, managing only to get her hand stuck in the handle.

"Maya," I moaned, watching her tug while quickstepping alongside the bag. "Let go of the damn thing before you hurt yourself."

She tried, but it took another dozen or so steps before she managed to get her hand free. "Is there some trick to this that I don't know about?" she asked, returning to my side while massaging her wrist.

"Pay attention," I said, setting my feet as I grabbed the next handle that came into reach.

Unfortunately, the bag I grabbed was the size of a mini-car and weighed about as much as Dickhead, who was by now no doubt parked on his backside with his feet up on his desk. I could just see him, keyboard in his lap, engrossed in a lengthy FaceTime chat. "Bastard!" I muttered, letting go of the handle rather than hold on while running alongside the moving carousel and make a public spectacle of myself.

"Who?" Maya asked, laughing at the sight of my undignified lurch and release. "Noggins or the bag?"

"Both," I answered. "First rule: don't get hurt messing with one of these travel elephants. Dumbass people want to check hundred-pound bags, they deserve to pick 'em up themselves."

"What happens if someone does get hurt while they're lifting them?"

"Call Dickhead. He'll have to come all the way out here and fill out a report."

Maya twisted from side to side, massaging the small of her back. "Wouldn't it be faster if we just called for an ambulance ourselves?"

"Faster, yes. But we don't make decisions. Not us. No-sir-ee. For that you call Dickhead. Official reports are a function of leadership." With that I turned and headed upstairs toward the restrooms.

I detoured past the ticket counter afterward. That's where I spotted the Chanel 5 newscaster. Alongside him stood a lone cameraman with a monster camera—complete with a large telephoto lens balanced on his shoulder. They stood side-by-side, engrossed in a muted conversation while, at the same time, keeping an eye on the growing crowd of passengers lining up in front of a row of seated ticket agents. The red lit sign overhead proclaimed: "International Check-In."

I turned and made a beeline for the exit in order to avoid the newsy pair. No way was I getting trapped into a conversation with either of them. I reentered the building at the next set of doors via the revolving door located directly in front of the escalator leading down to baggage claim. That's when I spotted Maya, walking right past the news team. I froze, and groaned at the sight.

"Hi guys," I heard her say. "What's up?"

The one with the microphone turned and took a couple of strides her way. Before she had time to get away, he shoved the microphone in her face. At the same time his partner swiveled into position in front of her. It appeared to be a well-practiced ambush.

I raced over in Maya's direction with no plan other than to prevent her from getting suckered into talking on camera, which would surely get her into trouble. We agents are never to be seen or heard on-camera. That means no public comments about company policies. No public babbling at all, in fact. I wove my way through the crowd, all the while conscious of remaining out of camera range. After this morning, the last thing I needed was to be seen on camera in front of the ticket counter instead of wrestling in baggage.

The newscaster still had his microphone pointed at Maya's face. "What can you tell me about Omega Air's new policy prohibiting passengers from carrying laptops onboard your international flights?" Even at a distance, I could see the green light blinking from the lower front of the camera. Green meant recording.

"Really?" I heard Maya answer, sounding sincere. "When does that start?" The sound of her nervous giggle after the comment made me wonder if she did realize she was being filmed.

My focus bounced between the blinking green light and the tanned face smiling down at Maya. I knew better than to say anything while that camera was recording. Question was, did she? Protocol dictates that we refer inquiring parties to corporate, which is pretty much what I heard Maya tell the pair before she turned and escaped back downstairs to baggage.

I let out a breath of relief and followed. Back to work.

"It was announced this morning," I heard the newscaster shout behind me, along with an insult about how employees in this city—those of us working for Omega Air specifically—always seem ignorant of the latest and greatest government issued security policies.

Ignorant? Who was he calling ignorant? I said to myself, stopping dead in my tracks. I clenched my jaw and turned, surprised to see that he was right behind me.

"That's right, go ahead and lob insults when you can't trick us into giving you a quote on camera," I hissed. "You know we can't talk to you. Or are you intentionally trying to get us fired?"

"I did not mean to insult . . . "

"Yeah, right. I heard you say 'Once again Omega Air fails to brief their agents.' Are you denying it?"

"I wasn't insinuating incompetence," he said lowering his microphone.

"No, just noncompliance. You guys are always out here trying trip us up. Either that or you're busy putting words in our mouth. Why don't you go ask one of our members of leadership instead? Go ahead . . . but guess what? You'll have to find 'em first. They're not out here! They're too well hidden for that. That's the real story here. Go try to find one of our overpaid prima-donnas. They're all holed up fielding email jokes to each other from behind closed doors, or else ducking out the side door to go home early. You and your megapixel recording partner should use your investigative talents to go research that instead of lying in wait to trip up one of us frontline worker bee's." That's when I noticed the camera. It was pointed at me from about six feet away. Worse, the green light was blinking.

I looked at the camera. "I asked you to turn that damn thing off!" But the light remained blinking.

"Let me make this perfectly clear," I began, pointing my finger at the newscaster. "I am not giving you any quotes. I am not answering any of your questions. None! You got that?" With a final glance at the camera, I turned and fled.

I was breathing hard by the time I reached the escalator. Unbelievable as it seemed, I could hear heavy steps following me.

"Miss . . . Miss . . . " the voice belonging to those steps insisted. "I just need another a quick moment of your time."

"Yeah, well fat chance of that," I muttered, glancing over my shoulder as I leaped for the second step of the escalator.

Two women stood talking at the landing below, blocking the way, oblivious that others were about to cannonball into them.

I hit the bottom step and dodged around them with a quick "coming through," before fast-walking over to the carousel, which was holding steady at three layers deep.

"What the hell . . . " I heard someone in the distance yell. A backward glance confirmed that the cameraman had toppled into the two women.

"That's right, Ladies, just stand there! How could you possibly be in anyone's way?" I heard him shout while picking up his camera.

I rushed over next to Maya and grabbed a bag, setting it next to the neat and orderly lineup she had begun.

"Did you get caught by those two?" she asked, nodding her head toward the newsy twosome, still in heated conversation with the two idiot women. One of the women was still on the ground, but at least now they were all clear of the escalator's landing.

"Sort of," I said, shrugging. "Did you hear any briefing items about international passengers no longer being allowed to carry laptops this morning?"

Maya shook her head. "They asked me about that, too. Wasn't in our briefing, I know that much. When does it start?"

"Yesterday, by the sounds of it. Can you imagine the fallout of business passengers being prohibited from carrying laptops onboard? Next thing they'll boycott Kindles and iPads, too."

Maya gave a sideways glance at the news crew again. Suddenly she did a double take and let go of the handle. "Oh my God . . . I knew he looked familiar!"

"What?" I followed her look at the dynamic duo.

"I just realized who that is!"

"Who? Which one?" I answered, my attention claimed by a stubborn bag that refused to budge. It must have weighed a hundred pounds.

"The Chanel 5 guy!"

"They're *both* Chanel 5 guys, Maya. But no, I don't have a clue. What's more, I don't care. I never watch them anymore. Too many lies. They misrepresent everything. We get enough of that from our frequent flyers, thank you very much. Last thing we need out here today are a couple of nosey newscaster dirt bags."

"You really don't know who that is?" Maya couldn't disguise her disbelief.

I glanced over at the two again. "Nope." I shrugged and shook my head. "Enlighten me."

"The one with the microphone . . . "

"The dark-haired one?"

Maya nodded, waiting for me to see what she saw.

"He looks to be about the same age as my son."

Maya frowned in irritation. "The hunk, Sabra! That's Bryce Williamson!"

"Who?"

"You know! THE Bryce Williamson. The Channel 5 hunk who was married to that loud mouth frequent flyer of ours with the bright purple-red hair. They owned the Cowboy Club downtown."

I shook my head in ignorance. "Never heard any of this before."

"You must have had dealings with her. You know, big mouth, big boobs . . . she's out here all the time. Always complaining. Always demanding upgrades as compensation for every one of her perceived inconveniences. Anyway, he caught her in bed with someone else—in their house . . . maybe it was the other way round, I don't remember. But she threw him out. Problem was, he owned the house. So, then he got her evicted. She refused to go. They both hired lawyers. She sued him for custody."

"Of the house?" I asked.

Maya nodded. "The business and the house. He won. He gave her the big kaputsky. Their divorce was loud, long, and messy. They had to sell the Cowboy Club—it closed down during their lawsuit. I can't believe you didn't hear anything about it—it was all the local news people talked about for months."

"Commiserating with one of their own, no doubt."

Maya waited for my next comment. I reached for a bag instead. "All I know is that he tried to corner me for a statement while the camera was running. I told him no, but I'll bet I still make the five o'clock news. Which means I'll get called in for a private chat with Noggins as soon as I clock in tomorrow. Won't he have fun with that?" I heaved the bag off the belt and sent it flying alongside the others in the lineup.

"What did you say to him?" Maya looked back and forth between the Chanel 5 guys and me, a worried frown on her face.

"I don't know, I don't remember . . . something about not liking his claims that we aren't current with international security procedures . . . or that if we know about them, we're not implementing them. Words to that effect."

"You said that?"

"Not me—he did! I clearly told the camera 'No comment.' Twice, I think."

"So, if you didn't give them a quote, what's the problem?"

"You think that'll matter to Noggins?"

I offloaded another half dozen bags before I walked over to where our tidy lineup of bags once stood. Arriving passengers had claimed many of them, leaving the remaining bags a cluttered jumble. I reached the end of the line and began organizing, turning bags upright, setting them side-by-side, glancing around in the process. That's when I spotted Maya, all the way on the other side of the room by the escalators, involved in a conversation that included much Italian-style hand waiving, with none other than . . . guess who?

"Oh God, Maya," I mumbled to myself. "That's right, flirt with danger." I took a deep breath and turned back to the job at hand. I refused to rush in and help a second time.

Later, after the last bag had been offloaded, I wiped the sweat off my brow with the cuff of my sweater and twisted the kinks out of my sore back. I looked around for Maya but she was nowhere to be seen. Unlike the Channel 5 team.

"Oh shit," I grumbled as Mr. Newscaster himself came walking toward me.

Maya's hunky heartthrob extended his hand. "It's Sābra, isn't it? Hi, I'm Bryce. Look, I'm sorry we got off on the wrong foot earlier. Your teammate explained to me the ramifications of agent statements without prior approval."

I shook his hand, but said nothing. He knew the rules as well as I did. Better, no doubt. There was no such thing as 'prior approval' and we both knew it. No way was I getting tricked into saying something I might yet regret. A quick glance sideways confirmed that the cameraman had remained behind, safely out of recording distance. And even though the camera remained perched on his shoulder, I saw no blinking green light, at least.

"What do you want?" I finally asked.

"Well, it's pretty embarrassing to have to admit this, but I walked away from your colleague without getting her name. She's a pretty convincing young lady . . ."

"Yeah, a real Italian spitfire."

He smiled. "Now if I'd said that, it would have sounded chauvinistic and you'd probably hold it against me."

"Maybe," I countered, trying not to smile. "Probably."

"Tell you what, if you'll be so kind as to give me her phone number, I give you my word that our earlier encounter will be edited out of tonight's broadcast."

"Your word?" I snorted a half-laugh. "What if Maya doesn't want you to have her number?"

"Maya, huh? Her badge said *Bonano.* So, it's Maya Bonano is it? You know, with that information I could do a bit of research and find her number myself. But I'm asking you to help me out and save me some time. Besides, coming from you, she'll be expecting my call. That way she'll have time to prepare. If she's not interested, she can tell me so herself. No harm done. What do you say, Sābra? I give you my solemn promise. No quotes. No broadcast troubles."

In spite of my misgivings, I sucked in a breath and reached for my phone in my back pocket. "I suppose you want her address, too?"

⁓ Chapter 2 ⁓

The lunar effect was in full force the next day. I felt its pull it as soon as I reported to work. For starters, Richard Noggins had already arrived. There he sat, stretched out behind his desk, his office door wide open, ready and waiting to pounce.

I had no more than entered the break room—before I even had time to drop my purse and lunch bag on the table, when I heard his voice. "Hunter. My office. Now."

"Well good morning to you, too," I said, stepping inside his cluttered lair.

"Don't shut the door."

Uh oh, I thought. Job performance issues or flight error discussions are normally discussed in private . . . . i.e., behind closed doors. Open-door discussions like this enable others to bear witness from a safe distance, to freely discuss not just what could have happened, but who else might have been involved. It was a highly successful tactic to maximize impact with minimal effort because word travels fast in an airline city.

In an environment like ours, with rotating assignments of flights and gates, every one of us has "the goods" on someone else at one time or another. It's just the way our business works because spot resolutions constantly occur in such a time-controlled high-stress environment. For the most part, however, these minor infractions are ignored rather than reported. After all, we all do it. We have to. There are exceptions, of course, causing all of us to pause and recall the particular incident and who was involved, in order to focus on who the snitch might be. As with any office environment, the culprit is usually someone from within the same well-known group.

Standing inside Noggin's office, I felt dozens of eyes upon me as agents passed through with the shift change. Throughout it all, I couldn't help but wonder if Mr. Chanel 5 lied to me yesterday.

Noggins didn't beat around the bush or offer any pleasantries. "You'll never guess who I saw on the ten o'clock news last night?"

"Beats me," I answered focusing on a spot on the wall above his head. "I never watch those propagandists anymore."

"It was you, Hunter. Big as life. Up close and personal. There wasn't any sound, but there was no mistaking you. You and your sidekick Bonano."

"Both of us?" My mind raced through the events of yesterday, but came up blank. I couldn't help but wonder when had Maya and I been together during the filming?

Noggins cocked his head, awaiting further comment.

"Don't tell me there's a recorded testament of us manhandling hundred-pound bags?" Better to crack wise than to confess anything this early in the interrogation, especially since I didn't know what other cards Noggins had tucked up his sleeve.

"No, you were pointing a finger at the camera. Snarling, in fact. No sound, as I said, but still, pretty unprofessional-looking behavior if you ask me.

"Which finger?" I joked. But when Noggins failed to respond, I frowned and tried to recall details of the encounter in question. "Snarling you say?"

"Spin it however you want, Hunter. Didn't look good. Not at all."

I shrugged. "What can I say? I didn't see it." It didn't sound like Bonano was involved, I thought, breathing a sigh of relief. That meant we weren't about to play the he-said she-said blame game.

Still, Noggins persisted. "Good thing. You wouldn't have recognized yourself if you had—Bonano either, not with that mop of hair of hers hanging down, half-covering her face. In clear violation of Omega Air's dress code, I might add."

"Was that all?" I was about to say, but stopped, and switched tactics instead. "Yet you recognized her . . . or at least you thought you did?"

Noggins slapped his hand down on his desk, making me jump. "Are you going to tell me what that little encounter with Chanel 5 was all about or not?"

"I'd rather not," I said, looking at the floor wondering where this was headed.

Noggins drummed his fingers on his desktop, waiting for me to answer. "I'm waiting," he finally said. "And I remind you, I've got all day."

That would mean having to put in a full eight-hour shift for the first time in years is what I felt like saying, but I bit back the words. I wasn't ready for a full out battle, since, technically speaking, I was guilty . . . sort of. But I had to give him something.

"Look, they cornered us before we could get away. One of them shoved a microphone in my face and hit me up with some security question. Maya told them exactly what we're supposed to say. You know, get your quotes from corporate. Can I help it if they didn't like our answer?"

"What did they ask you?"

An idea popped into my head, and I paused for effect. "Well, the one holding the microphone asked about the possibility of speaking with my supervisor." On a roll, enjoying the wary look that had crept onto Noggin's face, I continued. "I told him you were out on the concourse, that I was normally a gate agent, but was handpicked by you to come out here and offload international bags so it would take some time for you to come all the way out here to meet with him."

"Then what?"

"He asked what your . . . what my supervisor's name was. I guess that's when I lost my temper—probably the finger-pointing episode you mentioned."

Noggins stared at me for a long moment and then swallowed. "Did you give them my name?"

I bit my lip and frowned. "Maybe . . . I don't think so. I really don't remember. I was pretty stressed out." Let him stew about that one for the rest of the day, I thought, glancing down at my watch. "I really have to get to my gate."

Although Noggins nodded permission, he couldn't conceal a look of preoccupation. "Do me a favor will you Hunter: If you see any more reporters today, duck into the nearest ladies room."

"What if it's a female reporter?" I asked, unable to resist.

"Out," was Noggins only comment, pointing toward the door.

The rest of the day breezed by after that initial scare. I was still paying a price for my earlier Noggins transgression by being assigned to work four oversold flights back-to-back with no assist—unless you count a disinterested, gum-popping college chick with purple streaks through her regulation-length blonde hair as bona-fide help. By the end of the shift, I was exhausted, so much so that the minute the clock struck going-home time, I punched out and speed-walked my way down the concourse.

Less than two gates later a passenger waylaid me. "Excuse me, do you work here?"

"Nope," I answered without breaking stride. I tucked my airport ID inside my blazer, lowered my head and kept walking without a backward glance.

"Hey, what's the big hurry?" I heard a voice behind me ask, but I refused to acknowledge it. Suddenly a shadowy figure fell in step alongside me. I glanced over to see that it was Maya.

"You did agree to doing an Italian run together when we were talking yesterday, didn't you?" She managed to keep up with me, but was out of breath before we passed the next gate.

I shrugged. "Yeah, sure. I guess so. Why not?"

"Your husband will be okay with it, won't he?"

I laughed. "As long as it doesn't involve him doing international standby travel or European shopping, he'll be more than happy to stay home with the dog."

"Good. It'll be a nice change for me. Normally I travel alone . . . "

"Alone?" I said, stopping. "You think that's wise? I mean, considering the political climate these days. Surely that can't be safe."

"Oh, jeez, now you sound like my mother. I never worry about that kind of stuff. Besides, I've been doing it for years and nothing bad has ever happened. It's easier traveling alone: I can do what I want, when I want, and go where I want without dragging someone along against their will."

"So why take on a travel companion now?" I asked, curious. Especially one who sounds like her mother? It didn't sound like much of a recommendation.

This time it was Maya who shrugged. "I don't know. Maybe because I've been to Rome so many times, I'm bored with it now. With you along, it'll put a new light on things. Plus, you'll be my guide around Venice, so it'll make it easier for me."

"Mutual convenience, I guess. When do we want to go?"

"I told you yesterday, by mid-October," she said, sounding like a teenager reminding her mother for the umpteenth time. "The flights will still be open, and the college kids will be back in school. So we just need to schedule our time off."

"How about hotels? Do you have any favorites?"

Maya shook her head. "I never book hotels in advance."

My mouth fell open at that bit of news. "You've got to be kidding. I research prices, location, and reviews before I even think about booking. Even with all that information, I check their location on city maps. Takes the surprise out of not being able to find the place once we get there and end up having to spend money on a taxi."

"All on less than a full night's sleep," Maya added, laughing. "Do whatever research you normally do. Knock yourself out. I don't care."

"I'll make sure you agree with everything before I book," I said, sealing the deal.

My drive home that night was not spent on Italian conversation tapes. Instead, I pondered the idea of heading overseas without a single hotel reservation! Was that adventurous or just plain foolish? Should I try living dangerously and do it her way? In the end I shook my head. Nope, I couldn't do it. I'd worry myself sick about what would happen if we got there and couldn't find a decent hotel. Or one that was affordable. Jet lag and credit cards are a dangerous combination. I had to admit that being over fifty make you more cautious. I no longer had the will or the stamina to be that carefree. I vowed to start searching for a hotel in Rome as soon as possible. Venice was a no-brainer. I always stay at the Airport Marriott if it's available . . . or in the same Tessera neighborhood.

I didn't get a chance to do any online searching for the rest of the week, however, because every day was filled with oversold flights, or more trips to baggage. So it was a welcome relief when Super Friday—the last day before vacation—arrived. I preferred a week of insect spray and outdoor painting to any more of Noggins' antics.

A short week later, I returned to work refreshed and well-rested, ready to face my first day back in renewed good spirits. At least until I realized that nothing had changed. My work schedule was the same repeat of oversold flights or international bag detail I'd endured before, thus confirming that I was permanently parked in Noggin's doghouse for the foreseeable future. No doubt about it, it was time for an out-of-town adventure.

For days on end, I spent my lunch break eating in front of a computer, cruising through web sites of Roman hotels, taking notes. Unfortunately, I never found anything interesting enough or affordable enough to book. Not knowing the city layout, I was at a decided disadvantage. Maya's last instructions to me before she migrated to a vacant day shift was, "Find something near the Termini station."

"Why?" I texted.

"Because that's where the bus to the airport leaves from. Rome traffic is God-awful."

I printed a map of the area and concentrated my search on affordable three-stars within walking distance of the station, then narrowed the list by reading customer reviews till I was blurry-eyed.

Maya's move to an early morning shift limited the amount of time we had for face-to-face discussions, forcing us to resort to quick back-and-forth text messages and emails for comments and questions. By mid-week I sent her a list of possibilities, along with short descriptions of each. I ended the message with, "Which one do you like?" Before I sent it, I added the postscript: "Did Mr. Channel 5 call you yet?"

"All too expensive," she replied almost immediately. Not a single word about Mr. Channel 5 on the other hand, not that I really expected one.

Next, I zeroed in on price over location.

"Are we poor or what?" was Maya's quick response. "We want nice AND cheap. Also, use hotels.com and I'll book it using my account. I have a free night coming."

"Normally I use booking.com," I replied. "No free rooms, but I do have a discount status."

"How much?"

"Ten percent," I typed, racing away to punch the clock in time for another of Noggin's painful read-along briefings.

As soon as I found some idle time later in the week, I Googled: *Rome hotels*. That's when I stumbled upon *Hotel Ferrari*. Originally, it was the name that caught my eye. It sounded high-class. And the location was perfect. But then I spotted the photo. It wasn't one of the hotel's main entrance centered behind a welcoming fountain, nor was it the usual scenic shot of Rome's historical skyline taken from an upstairs patio. None of that. This photo was a bird's eye view of one of *Ferrari's* king-sized beds, its covers rolled back to reveal worn and rumpled sheets. I confess it held my attention with some kind of morbid fascination.

Further investigation revealed that *Hotel Ferrari's* unhappy customers were less than impressed with its cleanliness. Naturally, the manager disputed each claim, saying it was due to 'renovations' or 'awaiting upgrades.' Another reviewer complained about the marble floor tiles—specifically how the cracks were wide enough to allow continuous armies of ants inside. One unhappy customer wrote that he had to straddle the toilet in order to even get inside the shower. I continued reading in fascination. My favorite came from an insulted woman who wrote about the not-quite empty box of *Blowtex* left on their room's bedside table . . .

I grabbed my phone and shot off a text. "Hey Maya, what's Blowtex?"

"Italian Trojans," was her immediate reply. Followed by . . . "???"

I returned to the review with renewed curiosity. *Dare I mention my Italian-speaking husband said the package claimed they were tutti-frutti flavored?"* The overall consensus was that Hotel Ferrari was a sub-par crap shoot at best.

I decided to have some fun, so I copied the page and emailed it to Maya with the announcement: "We have a winner!"

"Are you shitting me?" was all she wrote in reply.

"Booked it . . . that very same room," I added, enjoying the prank.

When I next met up with Maya, our topic of conversation naturally gravitated to *Hotel Ferrari.* "Honestly, in all your years of hotel hunting have you ever seen an advertisement with a photo of an unmade bed?" I shook my head in disbelief. "You have to wonder who the hell approved it."

Maya was too busy typing on her phone to reply. Suddenly she burst out laughing and held her phone up to me, revealing the opened link I'd sent her earlier. There it was: the unmade bed. "You goofball! That picture wasn't from any booking site. It was a bitch review left on Tripadvisor. The photo was meant to prove the mattress was a virtual canoe, causing everyone on it to roll down to the middle."

I confessed it was all a joke, then changed the subject. "Did that Bryce guy ever call you?"

"Shhh," Maya said, glancing in both directions to make sure no one overheard. "Yeah, he called." But she hesitated to add anything else.

"Come on Maya, you're killing me. What did he say?"

She blew out her breath. "He asked if we could meet somewhere away from work. I told him I wasn't really interested . . . "

"Not interested?" I answered, my voice rising in surprise. "No way!"

"Well, in the end I told him I'd think about it." It was obvious she wasn't going to disclose anything else by the way she busied herself with the contents inside her shoulder bag rather than continue the discussion of Mr. Hunky Channel 5.

"You just concentrate on hotels. Nice hotels. I have a coupon for a free night, so I'll take care of the booking in Florence."

"Florence?" I asked, confused. Who said anything about Florence?"

"Why not? We'll be right there. I'll book the same place I stayed at last time. It's small, but it's in a great location—just around the corner from the cathedral."

"But we never discussed . . . " My mind raced over itinerary complications; how many extra vacation days did we now need, or do we cut short Rome by a day? Maybe we should cut a day off our Venice time instead?

Maya was still talking. "I guess I forgot to mention it. Sorry. I just figured as long as we're going to be in the neighborhood, we might as well do a quick visit. The trains all go right through there anyway. One day, that's all we need."

I had to agree with her. "It's okay. I love Florence. Sitting in one of those outdoor cafes near the cathedral watching people go by—that alone makes the trip worthwhile."

"My last trip there was filled with museums. It was great, but I have to confess I didn't get to see much of the city because of it. I ran out of time before I even got to see the copy of David."

I didn't realize there was a second David statue, yet I nodded in sympathy. "I know what you mean. There's so much to see, it's hard to fit it all in."

"No museums then, agreed?" Maya stated. "Museums means crowds and long days, and that gets tiring. Besides, all those museum ticket prices really add up fast."

"Just one thing," I insisted. "I want to find Michelangelo's workshop. I couldn't find it last time I was there. I checked online later and they said it's right on the main piazza across from the Duomo."

Maya nodded her agreement. "Get the address."

"As long as we're doing stopovers," I continued, recalling previous co-worker online raves, "how about we do a quick afternoon in Bologna?"

"I don't care. But why? What's in Bologna?"

"The anatomical museum. A friend of mine accidentally wound up in Bologna a couple of years ago and stumbled across it. It's living history, the inside of which sounded incredible."

"How do you accidentally wind up in Bologna?" was Maya's reply.

"I know, I know . . . long story. But her description of it sounded fascinating. It's close to the university."

"This friend of yours accidentally managed to find the university, too?"

I just smiled. I wasn't about to give away who this co-worker might be.

"Sounds more like this friend of yours was in search of something smokeably fragrant, something frequently found on a university campus."

I smiled. "Where better to look?"

"But in Bologna?"

"Milan was the only flight she could get out on, that's all I know. The train she ended up on went through Bologna. It was probably the first stop for food and drink. Anyway, this surgery center she told me about is where medieval medical students watched autopsies. It's a small round amphitheater, with the surgical table front and center, surrounded by wooden walls and carved statues. Doesn't it sound interesting?"

Maya shuddered. "Not at all. Can you imagine what the smell must have been like back in the day?"

"You don't have to do the tour if you don't want to. You can always find a little cafe nearby. Get something to drink while you're waiting for me to go check it out."

Maya held up her hand. "It doesn't sound the least bit appealing. But what the hell, if you want to see it, I'll go with you."

"Another site to see in Bologna are the two towers."

Maya blew out air. "Italy's full of towers. Most of them are about to fall down. You can't even climb inside the majority of them anymore because they're so unsafe."

I couldn't help but recall my motion-sickness symptoms inside the Tower of Pisa on a previous Italian adventure, detailed *in I'd Rather Eat Pizza Than See Pisa*. I sure didn't want to go through that again. On the other hand . . .

"As far as the two in Bologna," I continued, "you can still climb one of them. I just don't remember which one it is."

"I'm sure we'll find out." Maya answered with zero enthusiasm.

By the end of the week preliminary planning had come to an end. We were ready to nail down the details. I shot off a quick text, "So two nights in Venice, agreed?

"Sì," she answered, already switching into *modalità italiana*.

"One or two days in Florence?" I asked.

"*Uno dovrebbe bastare.*" (One should suffice.)

"One bastard," I entered on our preliminary itinerary. "And for Rome, two nights?"

"*Naturalmente.*"

After that she switched back to English, probably to ensure my lousy Italian didn't screw up the plan. "Our last night in Rome should be somewhere close to the airport because Fiumicino is way the hell out in the country. We'll have to take a bus from Termini Station downtown to get there. What with the traffic over there, I don't want to take a chance on getting stuck for hours the same day as our flight home."

The rest of the week we continued bouncing messages back and forth, zeroing in on sights to see, narrowing our hotel lists, and, most importantly, checking standby flight loads. I pulled copies of train schedules. She sent me links to Rome ticket site purchases.

"Spanish steps and Trevi?"

"Both yes. Free but multo crowded."

"Vatican?" I typed.

"Definitely yes."

"St. Peters Basilica. It's free, no?"

" . . . I think so."

"You think? You've been there before and you're not sure?"

Maya didn't seem to take offense. "Pretty sure. It's been a while. Whatever. Have credit card will travel, that's my motto." She ended the message with a yellow smiley face.

"I have a credit card, too, but I'm not comfortable unless I have plenty of cash on hand,"

"There you go sounding like my mother again."

I chose not to answer. I hadn't given much thought to the age difference between Maya and myself, but it was becoming clear that we had distinctly different travel styles. Oh well, we'd work it out in due time. If not, this would be our first and last trip together.

The minute I officially requested the time off, Noggins called me into the office. "You just had a week's vacation, Hunter. Why do you need another?"

"I don't *need* one. I *want* one." I almost told him it was none of his business, but I knew he'd immediately deny my request if I picked a fight, leaving me at the mercy of trading shifts. A future payback day was not something I wanted to do, so I decided to make nice.

"Got the urge to see Rome," I said with a shrug, acting like it was no big deal. "And for once the flights are open, so why not? It is one of the perks of our job, after all."

"My wife's always telling me she wants to see the Vatican," he said, sounding wistful. "I should probably take her over there some time. Maybe when you get back you can give me the lowdown—you know, tell me what's worth seeing and how to do it." Then he snapped his fingers and pointed a finger at me. "Bring me back a bottle of holy water. It'll be a great gift for my wife. And not one of those dinky bottles either."

I nodded, wondering if he was going to offer to pay for it. I wisely decided not to ask. Supervisor Noggins didn't like being put on the spot.

In spite of leaving the office on friendly terms, Noggins denied my day off request for the first day of our trip—a Friday. "I'm shorthanded every Friday," was his curt explanation. "You'll just have to put in to get off early that day and see how it goes. Who knows, maybe the weather will hold up and there won't be any air traffic delays in and out of New York. Never know."

"Yeah, and maybe hell will freeze over," I shot back, walking out of his office.

From the safety of her day shift, Maya didn't have to worry about getting off duty in time for an afternoon flight to New York. Not so for me. Since I worked an afternoon shift, the denied day off meant I'd have to trade shifts with someone. That meant a turnaround from a late night the night before and then back early the next morning, compounded by the fact I'd have to report to work with a packed suitcase in addition to trying to get off early. That was a triple whammy any way you looked at it. Worse, it meant having practically zero rest going into an international flight, where sleep is difficult no matter if you're lucky enough to get a first-class seat or not.

And let us not forget that the latest security procedures for airline employees require us to clear security at the ticket counter, then remain in a public (secure) location prior to boarding. In my case that meant hauling my suitcase from gate to gate throughout my sleepy morning, and then head all the way out to the ticket counter to clear security when and if I was released early, plus still have time to board the flight.

In the end, the shift trade didn't happen. No one was interested. Last minute packing presented no issues since I wasn't taking much. I didn't have a problem wearing the same pair of jeans all week long. A pair of sweats could do double duty as pj's, a couple of shirts—one long sleeve and one short, socks and underwear, a lightweight jacket, and I was good to go.

The flight schedule worked out whereby Maya and I would have four hours in New York before the Venice departure. But you might know, air traffic delays managed to reduce all or leisurely waiting time.

The Air Traffic Control system is unpredictable on its best day, which is why, from a gate agent's point-of-view, it's so difficult working ATC affected flights. Moments after a delay is announced, customers rush the gate agent with inquiries and complaints. Most are a complete waste of time—demanding to know if the delay will be extended is but one. Do gate agents look like fortunetellers to you? How would we know? We simply pass on information the tower gives us. Do you think the flight will cancel? is another. Many a day I'm tempted to just answer, "yes . . . next!"

Nowadays tech-heavy airlines send passengers delay messages long before anyone gets around to advise the gate. Please don't tell me about your connecting flight, either. We already know who has a connection. It's all in our computer. The minute a delay is announced, we begin checking for possible misconnections and start booking backup flights—more than likely the next day if it's an international connection. But that process is slow and tedious, especially with continual interruptions.

As far as delays go, sometimes the ATC Center will levy a long wait between updates. The latter is the scenario I wound up with that Friday.

The first couple of hours into the delay went by quickly, mainly because I was kept busy with a never-ending line of passengers. Noggins, in a rare moment of sympathy, assigned another agent to the flight, thus making me the extra hand for once and not the sole gate agent.

When Maya arrived, she went around to the back of the podium to stow her possessions. That's when I first spotted her suitcase. It was a large soft zip around, with a pregnant bulge in the middle. "Holy crap, Maya, how many clothes are you taking?"

She looked at me with a quizzical expression. "No more than I always take; an outfit for each day, sandals, tennis shoes, socks, leggings . . . "

"Where are you going to put souvenirs? Oh God, don't tell me there's an extra bag inside that monster?"

She winced. "It's collapsible. Don't worry, I probably won't even need it."

"You going to check it, right? Or are you planning on hoisting that thing in the overhead all by yourself?" I doubted it would fit. Or that she would be able to lift it that high without assistance.

Maya just laughed and took a seat in the gate, joining others in watching the clock. "Relax, will you? That's the bag I always use. You just worry about us getting to New York in time for the Venice flight. Me and my bag, meanwhile, will be just fine."

I shrugged. "If you say so." I hoped she didn't plan on asking me to hoist that thing in the overhead. It must have weighed forty pounds.

The next hour crawled by until, at last, we heard magic words from the tower over the radio: "We are good to go—as soon as the crew can be located."

Maya and I both groaned. Typical! The tower finally tells you to board, but first you have to track down the flight crew.

"One time it took me over hour before I found them," I whispered to Maya. "Turned out one of the flight attendants was sound asleep in the lounge. Never heard a single page or her phone ring."

Maya glanced at her phone. "We're down to less than an hour connection time."

Thankfully the crew showed up in record time and allowed us to board almost as soon as they did. Maya laughed. "Whatcha bet they're based in New York? Probably in a hurry to get home."

I stepped behind the desk to make a hurried call to the office for official early-out approval. The answer? A reluctant—a very reluctant—"Okay." Maya stepped behind the gate to help out, giving me time to grab my wheelie and take off to the front of the building, to the ticket counter in order to clear security.

The flight to JFK was one of those regional jets that utilize the valet tags—where you drop your bag at the front door of the plane, then pick it up at the front door (or somewhere inside the jetway) upon arrival. It makes the boarding process much faster, since you're not standing at the back of a slow-moving line, waiting for some dumbass ahead blocking the aisle with repeated attempts to squeeze his oversized bag into a tiny overhead bin all because he or she is too busy or too important to wait three minutes in the jetway on arrival to pick it up.

Maya was standing beside the open jetway door when I showed up. Out of breath, I followed her down the jetway where we dropped our bags and, at long last, walked inside the plane.

Then we sat there waiting, watching the minutes tick by until the airplane finally moved. "Clock is ticking," Maya mumbled, putting her phone on airplane mode. "Hope we make it there in time."

I nodded, wondering if I should have checked for available New York hotels.

Suddenly the aircraft stopped. We sat motionless on the ramp for long minutes. I looked out the window and watched the ramp agents on the tarmac below talking into their headsets, arms waiving. The aircraft gave a slight lurch, indicating the towbar had been re-connected. I groaned and faced Maya just as the overhead speaker crackled to life.

"Ah . . . ladies and gentlemen . . . your Captain speaking . . . New York ground delay program has been reinstated. Rather than . . . burning gas b . . . released by ATC system . . . returning to the gate. You may re-claim your bags . . . gate personnel will advise you of further updates . . . take all your possessions with you . . . exit."

"Shit," Maya said, pulling off her earbuds and unplugging them from her iPad.

"We have time to make the Paris flight," I said, checking the time. "But we'll need to buy discount tickets for Air France from Paris to Venice."

Maya nodded. "We can stop at the service center on the way to the Paris gate and use the computer there. Faster than trying to click our way through Omega Air's website with this God-awful airport Wi-Fi."

Why is it than when you least can afford delays, everything takes twice as long to complete? It took long precious minutes for our bags to be delivered inside the jetway. It was difficult to get into position to claim them, because everyone was jockeying forward in preparation for a quick getaway. I watched as Maya's bag was heaved inside. To my surprise, I saw an elderly Indian male grab it and take off running.

Maya looked at me, then at him. "What the . . . ?" She took off after him just as my bag showed up.

I pushed my way forward to grab it and then took off after Maya. Before I caught up, however, I passed the sheepish-looking (and now empty-handed) Indian returning to join the lineup again inside the jetway. I felt like telling him, "They all look alike, don't they?" But I didn't. Technically I couldn't because I was still in uniform.

Bags in hand, Maya and I took off toward the unmanned service center. We each grabbed a computer. I changed our flight listings from JFK to Paris, while Maya alerted the agents at the Paris gate that the two of us were headed their way. We bought our standby tickets, took screen shots of the receipts with our cell phones, and then took off running with our bags, ignoring the growing line of passengers queuing up in the maze of ropes in front of us.

We stopped running as soon as we were within sight of the Paris gate. The door was open with a line of wheelchairs in front of it. We could hear the jumble of multi-language boarding announcements in preparation for boarding.

"I've got to change my clothes," I yelled to Maya, detouring toward the bathroom. Company policy prohibits the partaking of pre-flight Mimosas or any other alcoholic beverage while in uniform. After the day I'd had, no partaking was not going to happen.

"*Ci vediamo a bordo*," Maya yelled back at me, waiving her standby card in the air so I could see her over the heads of those swarming in front of the doorway.

Moments later she disappeared out of sight.

<h1 style="text-align:center">❧ Chapter 3 ❧</h1>

It had been years since I last flew into Paris. Worse, I had never connected out of there to another international destination, so I had mixed feelings as we descended through the boiling mass of dark skies toward the City of Light. I had a concourse layout map in hand, thanks to the inflight magazine, but since we didn't know what gate we would arrive at, it was impossible to tell how long of a distance we'd need to cover to get to our connecting gate. One rule of thumb never varies no matter what city however: international to international gates are close together, just as domestic—or in this case, inter-EU gates—are also grouped together. It's the distance between the two groups that presents the challenge.

I know, I know . . . navigating through airports is pretty much the same no matter the city as long as you can read signs and follow the arrows. But this was Paris! It's huge! And, let us not forget it has always had the intimidating reputation of not being exactly what you'd call user-friendly.

"God, I feel as dumb as a regular passenger," Maya groaned, watching the buildings wiz past below. "Do we clear customs here? I don't remember."

I shook my head. "Passport control only, I think. Other than that, we'll play it by ear."

Maya snorted. "Like we have a choice."

"Don't let me forget to find an ATM before we leave here," I instructed.

"What for?"

"Euros, remember?"

"Just get some in Venice." Her tone sounded like I was worrying over needless trivialities and that she was tired of hearing about it.

"Yes, but on my last trip to Italy, the ATM's only let me make one withdrawal per day. I went into one of the banks and asked what the

41

problem was. They said it must be my card. I asked my bank about it when I got home, but all they could tell me is it wasn't them, that it must be some kind of weird Italian bank rule."

"Do what I do and just use plastic," Maya said, shrugging, turning her attention to shuffling the contents inside her oversized backpack purse.

I shook my head. "I'm old school, where cash is king. You'll see."

Changing planes turned out to be as easy as connecting anywhere else I'd ever traveled through. We just joined the lineup and mindlessly followed everyone else following the *"Correspondance"* signs, down roughly a half-mile of dirty orange carpeting. The carpeting consisted of replaceable squares in mismatched shades of orange, undoubtedly from years of spills and dirty shoes. Many of the squares had dangerously high peeling corners, a sure indication that more than a few were in dire need of replacement.

Eventually the line slowed, coming to a halt in front of French Passport Control. It's always the same at immigration checkpoints the world over; passengers pause only long enough to glance at the lit signs over inspection booths before sprinting for the shortest line for their nationality. In our case, the signs should have indicated either EU ONLY or NON-EU. But not today. The cause of the confusion was because only two booths were occupied. Worse, all the overhead signs remained unlit.

"Which one do we go to," Maya whispered, a note of frustration creeping into her voice.

"Either one," I instructed, leading the way forward. "If no signs are lit up, then I guess they'll just have to deal with anyone who shows up." A backward glance confirmed that the remaining passengers hesitated to follow our lead. All of them remained huddled together a safe distance away in collective confusion.

"You'd think they'd time the beginning of their customs shifts with the international arrivals," Maya complained, following close on my heels.

I just shrugged. "Wouldn't matter. This is France. They're all union workers. Need I say more?"

We approached the booth and greeted the uniformed official with his characteristic busy moustache sitting inside with simultaneous *"Bonjours, "* while sliding our passports into the concave tray beneath the plexiglass.

This uniformed member of the French douane took a slow sip of what must have been his first cup of espresso of the day before grunting a greeting. Bloodshot eyes rose above his steaming paper cup and he gave our faces a quick once over before he set the cup aside, gave a slow weary sigh and reached for our passports.

Overhead signs must have just switched on, because the sound of footsteps racing forward drowned out any further attempts at conversation.

Two newly arriving immigration officials remained standing outside their "EU Only" booths, engrossed in a nose-to-nose conversation accompanied by vigorous hand gestures. It looked like a budding disagreement to me. I tried to focus on their words, but a recurrent *"Merde!"* was the only thing I understood. A glance backward confirmed the ongoing confusion among the line of EU ONLY passengers. All silently accepted the delay. No one dared complain. I could only guess the repercussions levied against those who misbehaved while dealing with French officialdom.

Maya and I exited through the turnstile and into a hallway. A large *Correspondance* sign led us to the right, where, a short distance later, we entered an open lobby. A ticket counter stretched half the length of the far wall. Above it was proudly showcased the distinctive blue, white, and red diagonal lines representing Air France's logo, itself a play on the colors of the French national flag.

Snaking rows of ropes and stanchions stood guard in the empty bay in front of the counter, ready and waiting for future crowd control. Three uniformed female agents sat perched behind the distant counter, two of them involved in a friendly conversation; the third sat hunched over a short distance apart, intently filing her nails. All three studiously avoided any kind of eye contact with us.

"Crap," heard Maya say from somewhere behind me. "I don't see any more *Correspondance.*"

"Let me ask," I replied, ducking under the outermost rope, heading for the counter. The pair halted their conversation and looked at me with guarded expressions. There wasn't a glimmer of a welcoming customer service smile on either of their faces.

"*Excusez-moi,*" I began . . .

All three stared with silent professional courtesy—a look I recognized, a look that told me I was interrupting, so I'd better make it quick. But before I could get any French words out, one of them pointed behind me, toward an escalator on the opposite side of the room, unnoticed until now. In rapid-fire French she informed me that the N1 shuttle access was downstairs.

"Merci," I said, escaping to where she had pointed. "We should have just followed everyone else," I grumbled after I rejoined Maya.

By now another large group of passengers had arrived. Maya and I fell in line behind them as they turned the corner and disappeared one-by-one down the escalator.

"Hey you two," a woman we recognized from our flight shouted at us before breaking away from her group. "And here I thought you two knew where you were going. How'd I get here first?"

Neither Maya nor I had a ready response to her giddy chatter.

"The way you two charged ahead at passport control led me to believe you were old hands at this." She hopped on the escalator, motioning for us to follow. "And now here I am, leading the way like a regular tour guide. The N1 shuttle, correct? For an EU connection? Or are you taking the train into town?"

"N1," Maya and I echoed.

"Well then, follow me. I myself am headed for the Nice gate." She kept up a steady stream of chatter while we moved downward and forward, periodically turning to look over her shoulder to make sure we were still listening. "I do this trip a couple of times a year. For business. Easier doing it this way than flying into that Godawful mess at New York and going direct, can you believe it? From the first time I came this route, I learned to pay attention and follow everyone else. Crowds have an intelligence of their own, you see."

Maya and I both nodded. We did see. The sign ahead said: CDGVAL. The inter-terminal connecting train stop was well marked, but I still double-checked our progress on my terminal map to be sure I knew where we were.

The escalator dumped us directly into the train lobby. A short time later our train arrived and the doors opened. We surged forward along with everyone else. Maya, however, got stalled in the open doorway when one of her suitcase wheels turned sideways and ended up wedged in the narrow opening between the car door and the landing outside.

"That wasn't so difficult, was it?" the lady said after giving Maya's bag a healthy shove with her foot just as the doors closed and we departed the station.

"Ask us after we find our gate," Maya grumbled.

"I'm Miriam, by the way. I spotted you two on the flight right after we boarded yesterday. Sitting up there in first class no less!" She laughed again. "You looked so carefree; I just figured you must have done this dozens of times before. Which is why I initially followed you. Don't know why, really, because by now I've pretty much got this connection part down pat."

"So, what's happening in Nice?" I asked, changing the subject. Omega Air, like other airlines, frowns on off-duty employees discussing perks of the job while traveling, no matter how hard-earned we thought our benefits were.

Miriam brightened. "Cannes, actually. I'm so excited! Never been there before. I sure hope I see some of the EU beautiful people. You know, international versions of our Hollywood types. Sans makeup, of course."

"Without makeup?" I echoed. "They wouldn't dare!"

Maya chimed in with our laughter while reading the electronic sign as it scrolled around the top edge of the car, first in French, then in English. "Second stop brings us to Terminal 2E. After that is 2F, but it's all the way around the loop on the other side."

"I think we go to 2F," I said, double-checking my map.

"That's where we'll part ways then," Miriam announced. "2E for me! Of course, we all need go through the security checkpoint first."

"Oh God," Maya mumbled. "Not another line up!"

We'd forgotten about the security checks. It seemed so easy up to now. Might know there'd be a roadblock somewhere.

The train stopped and the doors opened, and everyone surged forward at once. Maya led the pack, groaning as she heaved her bag over the doorway opening. She gave the rebellious bag a jerk to keep it upright after realizing the problem wheel now seemed to be dragging instead of rolling. A quick glance assured me that at least it was still attached to the bag. I couldn't help but wonder if this was the same suitcase that had given her so much trouble on one of our previous adventures, documented in *I'd Rather Eat Pizza than See Pisa*. But then I shook my head to clear the cobwebs. That was a different trip . . . different travel companion.

In the distance I could see the gathering lineup at the security checkpoint. Miriam gave us a final waive before heading off to the left to a set of double doors with monogramed frosted windows leading to a private V.I.P. entrance. "Bon voyage, you two," she shouted, one hand on the door handle. "Have a great trip!"

"Wonder how she rates VIP status," Maya grumbled as we waived goodbye at Miriam then turned to trudge our way forward into the lineup

Twelve minutes later we exited the X-ray line, claimed our possessions from the conveyer belt, shoved our feet into our shoes, and then took off in search of our Venice flight.

"Don't let me forget to get some euros before we leave." I reminded Maya again as we walked among what seemed like a million other passengers. My feet felt like they weighed a ton and I was walking in slow motion. No doubt about it, jetlag was setting in.

"Forget about euros," Maya grumbled. "Find me an espresso bar. I'm sinking fast."

We rounded the corner and arrived at top end of a noisy concourse. From this distance it appeared to slope downhill for at least half a mile with glass walls lining the full distance on each side. Every gate seemed to be either deplaning newly arriving passengers or rushing to get stragglers onboard imminent departures. On the right was a small service center, staffed by three female employees wearing tailored navy-blue Air France uniforms, each of them dealing with a never-ending lineup of passengers with calm, professional efficiency. We took our place at the end of one of the lines, and in no time at all found ourselves at the front.

"*Oui?*" the agent asked. The minute she spotted our blue and gold US passports she switched to flawless English. "How may I help you ladies today?"

"We need to check in for standby for the Venice flight," Maya said handing over her cell phone, open to the photo showing yesterday's screen shot of her ticket receipt.

I was still digging through my shoulder bag for my old JFK boarding card, on which I'd scribbled the Air France ticket number. *"Voila!"* I announced the minute I located the document.

The agent flashed a half-smile before writing down both our ticket numbers then made her way over to the center of their work area where she entered our information into the solitary computer that the three were sharing. From somewhere beneath the counter, I heard two boarding cards printing. She returned to us with the precious documents, handed them over with one hand while pointing down the concourse with the other. "Your gate is at the very end. Number forty-seven. *Bonne chance."*

"My God, their software must be incredible," exclaimed Maya. "That was so fast!"

I agreed. Back home we'd still be pecking our way through a complicated template, overlaying dollar signs and x's while desperately trying to avoid all those colons and semi-colons—mistakes which initiated instant error messages, thus forcing the user to begin all over again at the beginning of the template.

"She said 'good luck?'" Maya repeated. "I thought you said this flight looked good for standby!"

"It did yesterday," I answered. "God knows what today looks like."

Maya looked at the Air France agent and shrugged a silent question. By this I mean she emphasized our unspoken question with the typical French shrug while holding both hands outward, face up. But if Maya hoped the agent would respond by returning to the computer to check flight availability, she was wrong because the agent had already called up the next in line.

"I should have asked her what the flight looks like before she went to the computer," I said. "My bad."

"Wonder if there's free Wi-Fi here?" Maya answered, falling in step beside me as we headed for the end of the concourse in search of gate forty-seven.

The concourse was the typical layout of even numbered gates on one side, odd on the other. The full length of the center section was filled with small booths, each selling assorted travel essentials, cosmetics, magazines, food, or even massages. There was something for everyone, it seemed.

I spotted a man inside one, straddled over a chair back, face down into what looked like a brown furry toilet seat cover. The young female sitting at his head looked bored while performing a robotic neck massage. Nearby clerks maintained intermittent conversations while ignoring the majority of passengers walking by. Mid-way down the concourse I spotted a manicure booth and looked at my nails. They could use some work. But I only had a fifty-euro note on me; that fifty was bound to be too large—or, considering the fact that we were in Paris, not nearly large enough. No matter, every seat inside the cramped booth was occupied. As I stood there trying to decide what to do, one of the manicurists looked up from the hand she was working on and asked me something.

I didn't understand her so shook my head and said, "*Merci, mai non,*" before walking away.

A snack bar came next. Maya ditched her suitcase beside me and worked her way forward to request two espressos to go, credit card at the ready.

She waived away the receipt and grabbed the two paper cups, just as she waived away my "Oh my God, *merci*" handing one of the cups over to me.

We continued our gate search with baggage handles in one hand and our steaming cups in the other. I stopped dead in my tracks after the first sip. Here I had visions of flavorful Parisian bistro *cafe au lait*, but instead this tasted more like days-old truck stop instant coffee.

Maya tasted hers and made a face. "*Merda*! This crap is terrible."

"I don't care," I said, raising my cup. "*Salute!* Here's to jetlag."

We downed the coffee like bad medicine and ditched the cups before continuing our stroll down the last half of the concourse. Suddenly Maya stopped and grabbed my arm. She gave me a wordless, wide-eyed happy look.

"What?" was all I could say, looking around. I had no clue what happy surprise she was alerting me of.

"Don't you hear it?" was all she said.

Again, I turned my head in all directions. "What? I don't hear anything."

"That's just it," Maya said. "No music! Isn't it wonderful?"

I paused to listen. Maya was right: this was not at all like the nonstop noisical shit we were subjected to back home; the never-ending loop of the same dozen golden oldies hour after hour for years on end. Oh, what blessed relief! The only sounds to be heard here were boarding calls, regularly interrupted by a two-toned chime indicating an overhead announcement yet to come.

"God, what a relief," I said, shuddering at the memory of our nonstop muzak at home. "I just don't understand why public buildings in America all insist on saturating their air space with constant electronic noise."

Maya nodded. "At top volume. No wonder we're all deaf by the time we hit thirty."

"Or 100% schizoid," I added. I didn't want to think about it.

Just then our attention was claimed by a family as they raced past. The man led the way, pushing an empty baby stroller at breakneck speed. The accompanying female followed hot on his heels, clutching a screaming baby, purse, diaper bag, and a wad of papers. Both held one hand aloft, waiving tickets overhead while shouting what could only have been the French version of "Wait! Don't go! Don't shut the door! We're here!"

I watched two gate agents scramble to clear the way in front of the doorway. At the same time a neighboring agent ran over to tag the stroller. All agents involved repeatedly checked their watches until the entire family had disappeared inside the jetway and the door slammed behind them.

"Just like home," I noted. "Well, sort of. Glad they made it."

Maya held a different opinion. "Bet they took a one-minute delay. Wonder if that means all three will get called in for a chat with their version of Monsieur le Dickhead."

I laughed at her words. "I'd have taken the delay, too."

"Not me," said Maya. "In fact, I'd have pushed early. No office lectures for me. Screw customer service."

"Go empty if you have to, as long as you go on-time, right?"

Maya didn't comment.

Next thing I knew we'd arrived at gate forty-seven. From our position on this side of the glass windows I could see a lineup of at least six smaller sized jets parked outside, three on each side of an extended walkway. A canvas covering had been erected over the full length to protect passengers from the elements.

Inside, a raised dais claimed center stage for the rotunda end of the concourse. The dais was surrounded by black velvet ropes attached to metal stanchions serving to separate (protect?) three agents in the center from a steady stream of passengers and their endless questions.

Two of the three agents sat behind a computer console; the third stood behind them. She appeared to be the one in charge the way she manned the microphone, making continuous announcements or calling out passenger names in order to hand over boarding cards. All three were dressed in the tailored navy three-piece Air France uniform.

The noise at this end of the concourse was, at times, deafening, what with the constant barrage of delay announcements, boarding calls, or flight updates.

"Air France *vol numéro . . . destinacion Roma, c'est on retard . . .*

"Air France vol *. . . destinacion Milan, c'est on retard . . .*"

"My god, all the Italy-bound flights are delayed," Maya whispered to me.

"Nooooo," was all I could say. I'd already figured that much out for myself.

I glanced out the window toward the distant taxiway. There was no aircraft movement to be seen in any direction. The distant grass was neatly mowed and golf course green. A stand of trees lined the far side, blocking any view of what lay beyond. It could have passed for any number of airports back home. Then a lightening flash caught my attention. I looked outside the window to see a wave of dark clouds rolling in over the trees. Within minutes all that could be seen was a waterfall of rain headed our way.

"Oh shit," I moaned, watching the incoming clouds. Maya remained oblivious. Instead, she stood up and approached the uniformed female holding the microphone.

"*Scusa, signora. . .* " she began, unhooking one of the rope stanchions in order to move closer to the center console.

"*O-U-I*" the woman answered, stretching out the word into one long syllable oozing with irritation at the interruption while raising her thumb from the microphone, pausing in mid-announcement to stare at Maya as she re-hooked the stanchion behind her.

"*Dove diavolo è il volo per Venezia?* Maya asked in native-sounding Italian.

"Eez late," the agent responded—in English, a barely veiled insult indicating Maya had been identified as yet another ignorant tourist and not an EU paisano. At the same time, the agent pointed toward one of the overhead monitors. All were lit up with red DLY codes.

"So much for friendly customer service," I muttered under my breath, watching.

But Maya held her ground. "*L'aero . . . dove si trova?*"

"Eez still in Italia. Zat is why eez late." The agent ended the conversation by rekeying her mic and returning to her announcements.

"Crap," was all Maya said, leading me toward two open chairs beside the windows.

I lingered behind, captivated by the agent's rapid-fire Italian. I couldn't make out a single word she said. To me, it sounded more like tonight's dinner menu than a boarding announcement: *Spaghetti con mozzarella, forse due linguini, ma non dimenticare le cannoli piu tardi aggi . . .*"

We waited roughly thirty minutes for the storm to pass. It disappeared as quickly as it had arrived. Suddenly I spotted an airplane turning off the taxiway, lumbering toward us before finally pulling into a parking space midway down the outside walkway. It was followed by a second, and then a third plane. Next thing I knew the boarding door flew open and dozens of passengers rushed out. The agent-in-charge, meanwhile, keyed her microphone and resumed making updates.

"Milano passengers Stomboli, Ceraudo, Figucchino, come to the desk. Milano flight now ready for boarding through doorway forty-three. Firenzie passengers will begin boarding in moments via door forty-three. Milano passengers seated in seats twenty through thirty, welcome. Roma flight will begin boarding next through doorway forty-six. Passenger Carbonella, please see me. Come now, quickly!"

"Why is she suddenly paging all these Italian passengers in English?" I asked Maya.

Maya turned her head to listen.

"Roma flight now boarding. Again, doorway forty-six for Roma. Passengers on standby for Firenze and for Roma, please come see me. Firenze passengers seated in rows ten through twenty, welcome. Milano passengers in rows one through ten, welcome. Please be sure of your gate! Final call for Roma passengers."

Maya made a face. "Because she's a snooty bitch, that's why. Did you know this airport is routinely named the most hated airport in the world? People like her are one of the reasons why."

A final round of instructions came with an increasingly loud decibel level, compounded by an echo now reverberating off the semi-circular configuration of glass windows.

"God, what a cluster," I moaned. "I should have brought my earplugs."

"*Passeggeri di Venezia, il vostro volo sará il prossimo.*"

"That bitch speaks native Italian," Maya hissed.

"Venezia passengers, your airplane has just arrived. Standby passengers, please come to see me."

"I'll go," Maya offered, standing up, eyes steeled on the agent. "*E non parlo inglese.*" She grabbed my seat request card and passport from my hand and headed off to face her compatriot.

I watched as the agent handed out at least a dozen boarding cards to everyone in the group except Maya, until, finally, she took our cards from Maya's hand. She took a moment out of the hectic activity to read them—puzzling to me since we'd obviously been cleared off the standby list. What was there to check? Then it dawned on me: she was studying our tickets to see who we worked for, what kind of discount we were using, and how much we'd paid.

Just as Maya returned sand picked up her tote, I remembered the ATM. "Oh, shit!" I wailed, scrambling to my feet. "I forgot all about getting euros."

"But we're about to board," Maya complained, clearly irritated.

"I don't care. Watch my bag," I said, taking off toward the desk, coming to a stop right in front of the agent-in-charge, waiving my arms overhead to catch her attention.

She chose to ignore me.

I ducked under the rope so I could get closer to her. I tried to catch the eye of one of the seated agents. "*Excusez-moi . . . où est le . . . le . . .* Shit!"

"*Où est le quoi?*" I heard them ask one another in confusion.

What was the French word for ATM? I tried saying it phonetically . . . "*le ah-te-em-ay?*"

At that, all three agents stopped what they were doing to stare at me with a look that clearly reflected they thought I was a total idiot.

At last, the multi-lingual head unkeyed her mic and leaned in toward her coworkers. However, their quick conference only confirmed that I desperately needed something.

"*Le quoi?*" she asked me again, forgetting to be rude for the moment.

"*Pour euros . . .* " I began, unable to think clearly. Thankfully, without attempting to translate, I made the universal gesture of rubbing thumb to fingers to indicate money.

"*Le cash machine?*" she asked.

"Oh merde yes!" I exclaimed. "Le cash machine!" I should have known that!

She exhaled loudly. I could tell she thought my anxiety about an ATM this close to boarding was a complete waste of her time. But she did manage to point a polished red index dagger up the concourse where we had originally entered. "Eez up there. At the top."

"*Merci,*" I said, turning and racing away, grateful it wasn't a middle finger.

I rushed past countless passengers, retracing my steps, looking back and forth to both sides of the concourse, but saw no ATM anywhere! Next thing I knew I'd arrived back at the concourse entrance service center again. "Oh, *merde, merde, merde.* Where the hell is it?"

Luckily there was no line at the service counter. "*Sil vous plait . . . ou est le cash machine?*"

Without a word, everyone behind the counter pointed to a spot behind me.

I turned around and looked . . . and there it was, smack in the center aisle where no one could miss it!

I managed to extract 200 euros in about ten seconds flat before hauling butt all the way back to gate forty-seven.

"About time," Maya hissed when I finally showed up, sweating and out-of-breath. "I wasn't going to wait any longer."

"Sorry," was all I could say, grabbing my wheelie, following her past the frowning agent standing at the doorway just as the door slammed shut.

～ **Chapter 4** ～

There's something comforting about arriving at a foreign destination when you've been there before. Maybe it's simply because the sights feel familiar, and that familiarity frees you from the stress and worry of figuring out where to go and how to get there while being dead tired from both the flying time and the resulting time change. I think that's why so many first-time visiting tourists opt for the easiest—yet more expensive—option and just flag a taxi the minute they step outside of a European airport.

Not me. I do diligent research ahead of time so I can get from the airport to the hotel without spending a fortune in the process. Since I'd been to Venice before, none of that applied this trip, so I just leaned back and watched the sights come into view as our jet lumbered its way down toward Marco Polo airport.

Dual lines of boat lane buoys came into view, extending all the way between the airport and the Venice Island as we raced by overhead. I glanced over to the other side of the cabin as we bumped our way down toward the ground. In the distance I could see the causeway that linked the island with the mainland skimming the water with a line of train tracks running parallel to it. I could even see ripples of whitecaps as we streaked over the shore until suddenly airport buildings came into focus.

The sound of clattering dishes could be heard just after our tires hit the ground, bounced, and settled down again. In the blink of an eye both engines screamed with reverse thrust accompanied by the stuttering application of brakes. The resulting slowdown was so strong that I involuntarily reached out to the seat back in front of me to halt my own forward momentum, dropping my passport in the process.

The atmosphere inside the cabin revved up as well. Passengers became fully alert. Some sat up straight and began adjusting their hair and/or clothes, while others doubled over in a final check for items on the floor or beneath neighboring seats. More than one gave frantic last looks toward the lavatories before noticing the lit seatbelt sign indicating: TOO LATE. A great majority appeared ready to pop their seat belts the minute we parked, so they could jump up and collect belongings from overhead bins. Honestly, you'd have thought the airline was offering a free global ticket to the first person off the plane.

I bent over to retrieve my passport and put on my shoes, marveling for what seemed like the thousandth time how this same scenario plays out at the end of every flight I take, no matter how long or how short.

Maya and I stood and waited for the initial racers to pass, then for the regular people in the lineup ahead to move. Yawning bodies trudged forward, passing weary yet smiling faces at the doorway, all bidding us a professional good riddance.

As an inter-EU flight, I still find myself surprised to disembark directly into a concourse full of gift stores—just as you would on a flight from, say, Houston to Chicago, rather than walking through a long, segregated hallway toward the secure area traditionally known as 'passport control.' Had Maya and I planned on connecting out of Venice, we would have only needed to find the gate and check-in. But who knows, maybe it just felt weird because of sleep deprivation.

I paused long enough to glance at my phone; it was a little before eleven o'clock in the morning, local time. By my calculations we'd be eating lunch on the island in a little over an hour. My inner clock, however, was screaming that it wasn't yet five o'clock in the morning at home, and that I should lie down and get some sleep. The trick, I knew, was to remain vertical and to keep moving.

Large airports have lots of options for connecting flights to other cities, namely multiple concourses. Small airports, on the other hand, are much easier to navigate because you just need to head straight to the exit and you're done. That's the way it is at Marco Polo, which makes it especially easy if you're not fluent in Italiano. Like most European airports, the majority of ticket sales for local ground transportation are automated. And, thankfully, for the most part, Italian kiosks are user friendly: find the US or the UK flag (for English), insert your credit card, and you're in business.

I've learned the hard way that the grand mal exceptions are the vaporetto ticket kiosks—Venice's waterbuses—located inside the baggage claim area. These machines were designed for locals only; they remain indecipherable for the rest of humanity. Period. I long ago conceded defeat and stopped trying to use them, which is why I don't even consider taking the boat from the airport straight to the island anymore. Maybe by now they've added a user-friendly machine at the dock, who knows?

I don't book hotels on the island anymore either. It's both cheaper and easier to stay on the mainland and simply take the bus from the airport straight to Piazzale Roma parking lot on the island. The bus allows one stop along the way, which allows just long enough time to check-in at the hotel as long as it's somewhat close to a bus stop. This city bus is a far easier way to navigate. Who wants to haul luggage over cobblestones, stairs, and uneven sidewalks while searching for your hotel anyway? I've seen instances where a single cruise-bound passenger hauling an oversized suitcase over the uneven pavement managed to cause roadblocks twenty to thirty people deep. That's no way to begin a vacation.

Let's face it, when dealing with jetlag at the beginning of a full day of activities it's all about ease of use. Get your tickets, get out of the airport, get to the hotel, drop your bags, then get on with the trip, that's my motto.

Passport control was nothing more than a hiccup in our progress toward the front of Marco Polo and the adventure beyond. Our wheelie bags were with us, so there was no need to hang around baggage claim in front of a not-yet moving carousel. Poor Maya, her bag still wasn't cooperating. One rear wheel had locked up entirely, causing it to make a high-pitched squealing sound as she half-dragged it over the polished marble floor.

Maya repeatedly glanced my way, but the look in her eye warned me to comment at my peril. I wisely kept my mouth shut.

I gave a cursory glance at the infamous row of vaporetto ticket machines as we exited the room. Small groups of travelers stood in front of them, staring up at the instructions. Several had turned on their phone's flashlight to aid vision, as though that would somehow provide the key to unlock their indecipherable instructions. I noted lots of head scratching and couldn't help but snicker. Even the locals couldn't figure out how to work those things.

Pulling my wheelie behind me, I led Maya straight through the glass exit doors into the front lobby. A pair of ATMs stood off to the right, beneath the stairwell. One was for a local bank—the sign above it read: Members Only; the other was for tourist use, notable by the foreign flags depicted alongside its push button menu. I pressed the UK flag and waited for the instructions to switch to English, then hauled out my debit card and instructed the machine to fork over €300.

As soon as the bills popped out, followed by the receipt, I stashed them deep in my purse and made way for Maya. "Your turn."

"Not for me," she said, taking a step back. "I only use my card, remember? No fees."

I cocked my head. "But what if you need cash?"

She gave me one of those exaggerated Italian shrugs, and snorted. "Everybody takes plastic here. Besides, you'll have enough cash for both of us."

"Well then, we need to head upstairs."

"Why?"

"The transportation desk is up there. That's where we buy our bus tickets."

The booth is located mid-way down the counter. As an added bonus, it was staffed with English speaking agents. Maya trailed behind without a word, focused instead on her suitcase with its three functioning wheels.

"*Due billetes a la Piazzale Roma*," I instructed, trying out my Italian.

"You may take one stop along the way, " the clerk answered in heavily accented English, a clear indication that I'd fare better if I stuck to my own language. "But that stop is only valid for thirty-five minutes. No more."

The tickets, she said, cost €8 each. I placed a ten note on the counter and waited while she pushed my ticket toward me, along with two €1 coins for change. Then I moved aside to make room for Maya.

Maya tossed her trusty card on the counter along with a native-sounding "*Buorngiorno*." A quick Italian conversation followed, of which I only understand portions. I was fluent in numbers up to ten, however, so had no difficulty understanding the clerk announce the ticket price of €10.

"Ten euros?" I asked. "Why ten? Mine was only eight."

"Because of card," the clerk answered, switching effortlessly back to English. "No cash discount."

Maya shrugged an indifferent response without looking at me while the clerk finished the transaction and handed over the ticket.

"Bus number five," the clerk said, pointing down toward the main floor exit doors.

Tickets in hand, Maya and I retraced our steps back down the escalator.

I stepped on the top step and positioned my wheelie on the next step as it appeared. Maya, on the other hand, clung to the moving railing as she struggled to dislodge her crooked wheel from the step's grooved metal surface. "Why the hell did we have to go upstairs just to turn around and go back down again?" she grumbled, giving her suitcase a jerk.

"We wouldn't have had to if we already had some Euros with us . . ."

"I don't carry cash, remember?"

I ignored her snotty tone, chalking it up to jetlag. Maya didn't say another word as she followed me outside, dragging her uncooperative bag behind her.

The minute the double glass exit doors opened we were hit with a blast of hot humid air. It smelled like a combination of wet vegetation and diesel exhaust. All the greenery in planter boxes that lined the walkway outside were dripping wet, either from a recent rainstorm or from an early morning hosing by airport landscapers. Needless to say, the dripping cement ledge alongside each planter, normally filled to capacity with seated travelers, were all empty.

We continued across the taxi lane, toward the outer lane flowing with a steady stream of busses. As soon as one departed, another pulled in curbside behind it. An oversized metal awning hung part way over the sidewalk to provide some kind of shelter against sun and rain. Overhead signs along the wall indicated stops for specific bus numbers, along with their corresponding destinations.

We scanned the signs, searching for our #5's designated stop. " Don't forget, we have to validate our tickets as soon as we get onboard."

"Yeah, yeah," Maya snapped. "I've been to Italy before, remember?"

I gave her a quick look. "Why are you sounding so angry?"

"TMI," Maya hissed through clenched teeth, wrenching her bag upright.

"Too much information? Oh, sorry." was all I could say.

Maya shot me a half smile before dropping her tote next to the suitcase. It landed on the wet cement with a thud. "I know, I know. It's just that sometimes you sound exactly like my mother."

"And how you just talked to me, is that the way you talk to your mother?"

"I guess it's to be expected," Maya continued, ignoring my question. "After all, you two are about the same age."

"Tell you what, from now on I'll assume you know what I know. How's that?"

"Even though I've never been to Venice before?"

I nodded. "Yep, I'll just assume you know what you're doing unless you specifically ask me something. Deal?"

Maya nodded. "I just hope these tickets give us enough stopover time so we'll be able to get checked-in and changed before they expire."

I agreed. "I can't wait to get downtown and get a cappuccino."

"Or a double espresso," Maya said, flagging a passing bus driver. "*Mi Scusi,*" she began. "Where does the #5 bus stop?"

Both his eyes crinkled at the outer edges as he smiled and pointed. "Up the street, next to the number 5 sign." He said it in Italian.

"*Prego,*" was all she said, picking up her tote and slamming it on top of her wheelie before setting off.

"How silly of us," I said to the old guy, adding that we were just a couple of dumb tourists.

He laughed again. "*Si Si. Bene.* Now you know how it works."

"You think we'll have to wait long before we can get into our room?" Maya asked as we walked down the narrow sidewalk. She struggled to keep her tote on top of the wheelie as they bounced in tandem over the uneven cement.

Once we arrived at our #5 stop, we both leaned against the wall to wait. Every bus that passed us, however, was an AVO with a

'Mestre' sign lit up over the front. Mestre train station was not what we wanted.

The air here stunk of diesel exhaust, but by now there was a heavy concentration of cigarette smoke added to the mix. I couldn't help but notice that the curb was littered with cigarette butts.

"I'd forgotten how many people still smoke in Italy," I commented.

Maya yawned and nodded.

Bus #5 showed up eventually, and in a matter of minutes we hauled our luggage onboard and stowed it in the racks. We then validated our tickets before claiming a pair of empty seats mid-way down the aisle. An American couple soon passed us. How did I know they were American? Aside from the fact they weren't speaking the King's English, both were chewing gum and sporting khaki walking shorts and identical leather sandals.

"I just don't understand why you insist on taking a bus to get to a hotel that's not five minutes away." the woman complained over her shoulder.

"It's because it's not five minutes away," her companion grumbled. "I refuse to fork over forty euro for a five minute taxi ride, that's why. If you want to blow all your euros on a ride here, I suggest you save them for one of those stupid gondolas." His voice held an unmistakable end-of-discussion tone to it.

Maya and I looked at each other. "How much is a gondola ride?" she whispered to me.

"A ton of euros, evidently," I said, shrugging. I'd never bothered to check before.

It felt like we had no sooner started moving when we pulled in to the curb in front of a glass-enclosed shelter. Across the street stood the Marriott Hotel entrance.

"Via Triestina," I announced, getting up, leading the way forward. The Americans tagged along behind us.

We arrived at the Marriott front desk ahead of the American couple in spite of the time it took Maya to wrestle her bag off the bus.

"*Buongiorno*," I began, handing over a printout of our reservation and my passport.

The clerk read the name on my confirmation printout and cleared his throat. "*Scusi*," he said before ducking into a back office. He returned moments later with a second man in tow, this one wearing a formal business suit, unlike the branded vest of the clerk.

This second man introduced himself as the manager. "It appears we have a small problem."

"How small?" asked Maya, her chin rising in tired irritation.

I bit my lip and waited for the bad news: it seemed the hotel had oversold their room allotment, and since our reservation was the lowest priced, we were being forced out. "But," cautioned the manager before either Maya or I could react, "we have made for you reasonable accommodations elsewhere. Just down the street, in fact, at another well-known American establishment: a Best Western. I'm sure you are familiar with the name."

We were, and nodded in unison. We really didn't mind as long as we could get checked in pronto, change our clothes, and get on with the adventure. But we were both, first and foremost, frontline airline employees, with years of experience under our belts in dealing with the nuanced negotiations of overbookings.

I smiled. "So what kind of compensation are you offering us in exchange for this downgrade?"

The manager stiffened slightly at having been caught off guard. "Downgrade?" he repeated.

I nodded. "Clearly. Marriott is a well-known five-star establishment. Those stars represent a consistently reliable level of quality. This level is one of the principal reasons we made this booking." I couldn't bring myself to look at Maya, for fear her face would betray the fact that our booking choice was based less on quality and more on location (directly across from the bus stop, so no getting lost after dark on late night returns from the island) not to mention its generous airline employee discount rate.

"Best Western is well-known, yes, but it's a lesser quality three-star hotel." I could only hope that I was close to the truth, or that he didn't know its current star rating any more than I did.

He frowned and fingered his chin thoughtfully. "We thought the proximity to this hotel would be advisable. Both located so close to a bus stop, no?"

I nodded. He had me there. "*Sì, sì,* but how do you suggest we now manage to find our way to this new hotel... this Best Western?"

The manager straightened to attention. He was on familiar territory now. "We have a van. It's just outside. Our driver will take you and your luggages immediately. I will personally call and advise them of your pending arrival." He turned and in a rush of Italian ordered the desk clerk to go find the driver. Pronto.

A loud sigh of exasperation escaped from the American woman standing behind us. "See? If we'd have taken a taxi, we would have arrived long before ... We'd already be in our room by now!"

"Shhh," was all her husband said in reply.

"That's very kind," I said, flashing another quick smile at the manager. "But back to the issue of our compensation. What can you offer us? Perhaps free rooms for future use?"

About the same time, Maya plunked down her iPad on the counter. "This is just bullshit," she muttered under her breath, yet loud enough to be heard by all the hotel staff. "I'm logging into Facebook."

The manager shot her a quick glance then returned his attention to me. "I'm sure we could agree to something along those lines, yes." I couldn't help but notice that as he spoke, he shifted position so that his back ended up facing Maya. It was undoubtedly a subtle attempt to block his face from any negative online postings.

"Since we've been here in *Venezia* before," I said, "it really wouldn't do to have a couple of free days at the same place, would it?"

His left eyebrow rose and he shook his head ever so slightly, no doubt wondering where I was going with this.

Maya, meanwhile, held up her iPad and aimed it toward the two of us. "Smile!" she commanded. "I'm going to post pictures of us not checking in."

"How about a couple of free nights in . . . say, any European city?" I suggested.

Again the manager drew himself upright. "Madame, certain other European cities are much more expensive than we are. It would not be . . . how you say . . . cost effective for me to authorize such a thing."

"You're right, I said, agreeing. "How about we limit it to just Italian cities?"

"How about Milano?" Maya piped up.

"Well . . . I suppose we could agree to something like that."

Just then the limo driver showed up. He came to a stop alongside Maya, prepared to grab her suitcase, but then paused to wait for us to conclude our business. Meanwhile, he leaned over to check out the photos on Maya's iPad.

"I'll wait outside," Maya whispered, turning her iPad off, before directing the driver to take both our suitcases, but hers first.

The front desk clerk, sensing a pending solution, stepped to one side and called the American couple in line behind us over to him.

"It's about time!" the woman exclaimed, prodding her husband past me.

"So how does this work?" I asked, returning my attention to the manager. "Three nights in a comparable Milano hotel, valid for say, two years? For each of us?"

"One double." he countered immediately. "You had only the one booking here, no?"

"Agreed. But for three nights, yes?"

"Your booking here was for just two nights. And deeply discounted."

"Yes, but for two five-star nights. Now downgraded to two three-star nights. Big difference."

Though he didn't answer, I could tell he was close to agreeing.

"Plus breakfast," I added, pushing my luck. At 6€/day value for each of us, that would complete the deal.

"With breakfast?" he questioned, raising my confirmation printout to examine it again. I recalled there was no free breakfast at this Marriott.

"*Sì sì,*" I insisted. "Croissants and hard-boiled eggs. Cheap food."

"Okay, okay," he finally agreed, letting out a sigh as he began scribbling notes on my printout.

"So how does this work? Do you give us some kind of printed voucher?"

"I will have a letter of authorization with complete details ready for you within the hour. You must not lose it, as it will be necessary to surrender it at future check-in to validate your booking expenses. You understand?"

"Completely," I said, nodding. "I'll pick it up tomorrow, if that's okay with you," I said, extending my hand. "We appreciate your help."

As soon as we shook hands, I turned and headed toward the limo, now sitting just outside the front door with its motor running.

From my previous visits, I knew exactly where the Best Western was located—less than a five-minute walk away, straight down the highway to where the road forked. Maya and I could have walked the short distance to get there, but it was nice not to have to, especially considering the current time limitation of our bus tickets. I watched to confirm the street names as we turned left off Via Triestina and onto Via Orlanda.

"There's another bus stop about a block further down Triestina," the driver said in English, pointing off somewhere to the right as we veered left.

"How much does this ride normally cost?" Maya asked. "Just curious."

"Fifteen euro per room, for two persons. Any more, costs more." he answered as we turned into the empty Best Western parking lot.

Maya took her wheelie and tote from the driver and kicked it into a pull-along position then headed inside. "I can't wait to dump this thing."

I handed the driver a 5€ tip, and then followed her inside.

A lone twenty-something male sat behind the wood paneled counter inside. "*Buorngiorno,*" he said with a broad smile, jumping to his feet the minute we walked in. His suit was shiny with age, and appeared to be nearly a size too small, most noticeably in the waist. His tie was long and out-of-style narrow, and he kept flattening it against his chest as he nervously tried out his English. His friendliness was contagious. "I only need to copy photos in zee passaporti," he said before zooming off to a room behind the counter. He returned moments later, with plastic room keys in one hand and passport copies in the other. "Room 203," he said, placing the plastic keys inside a single small white envelope with the hotel's name and address printed on the front. "Around the corner to zee lift, and then eez upstairs. Breakfast begin at 7. Goes until 10. After that . . . " He drew a line across his throat to finish the rest of the sentence rather than having to translate it.

The room wasn't five—or even four-star plush, but it was perfect for our three-star needs. "A bed and a toilet, what more do we need?" I asked, sounding optimistic.

"A room safe would have been a nice touch," Maya grumbled, checking to make sure there wasn't one hidden somewhere on the other side of the empty closet.

"For all your cash?" I teased, not expecting an answer.

We changed clothes in record time, alternating turns in the bathroom, before racing downstairs, across the street and half a block beyond in search of the bus stop. Two busses passed by as we walked, but each of them showed "Mestre" as its destination.

"This is such bullshit," Maya suddenly announced. Next thing I knew she'd raced out into the street, one arm waiving overhead. "Taxi!" she shouted, running as a vacant car hit the brakes and careened over to the curb.

She stood leaning in toward the driver's window in the middle of the street. Directly opposite stood the plexiglass bus stop.

I heard her shouts from half a block away. "Forty euros?" This was followed by the Italian version of "You've got to be kidding!" before the car squealed away.

"I take it you said no thanks," I mumbled when she arrived inside the three-sided enclosure where I stood waiting. Before she could answer, however, another bus pulled up. This time its overhead sign announced our destination: *Piazzale Roma.*"

We hopped onboard without forgetting to validate our precious tickets and dropped into the first vacant seats we found.

I sat glued to the window as we wound our way through residential areas interspersed with brightly lit neon hotel signs. I recognized some familiar-sounding names from my earlier hotel searches as we continued toward the island. Soon we approached the water's edge. In the distance I could see those same floating buoys that outlined the water lanes for the many water taxis I'd spotted from the airplane window just prior to landing. Next thing I knew we were on the causeway, and then arriving at the island's entrance.

As we turned into the parking lot at Piazzale Roma, I counted ten busses lined up at staggered angles, all with their doors open. The whole area was a beehive of activity. People streamed in and out from all directions, some exiting arriving busses while others walked toward us from the nearby modern-styled arched bridge which connected the parking lot and the island. Others stood by, waiting for their bus to empty before they could climb onboard and sit down. Off to the left I saw a three-story reddish-brown building, from which a cable car steadily transported people to a couple of cruise ships floating in the distance. Closer in, a group of bus drivers had gathered next to a canopied news stand at the parking lot edge for a quick smoke break.

Maya and I walked across the lot, toward the arched bridge and paused to look at the scene below.

"Wow!" was Maya's reaction. She stood transfixed, looking out over the water. "I'm finally here! In front of one of the Grand Canal's most iconic landmarks: Santa Maria Della Salute. It looks so majestic." She pointed to the white Catholic church prominently situated front and center on the Grand Canal. "Just look at that dome! Made entirely of individual panes of tinted glass! Just think of the craftsmanship it took to make that!" She raised her iPad and began snapping pictures of nearly everything in sight.

I, too, stood looking at the familiar sight. "Hello again, old friend," I whispered, staring at the church. "Saint Mary of Health cathedral, built to celebrate the end of the plague in the mid 1600's."

Maya paused taking photos and looked over at me. "The bubonic plague?"

I nodded. "It killed about half the Venetian population."

Though I'd been here many times before, the reddish-orange tiled roofs and the pastel building facades set against the blue of the sky looked more like a painting than an actual view of live scenery. Just watching the frenetic activity on the water below—activity that we were soon to be a part of, still gave me a thrill. It was good to be back.

The stairwell ahead gave us pause. It was speckled with moving bodies, a great many of them struggling up the narrow steps with a varied assortment of suitcase styles and sizes. Dozens more disappeared down the other side, toward the wide sidewalk that bordered the canal. I couldn't help but wonder how many of them were in for a difficult time ahead, navigating unmarked waterways while hauling luggage and holding maps, searching for a hotel hidden away in a city convoluted with steps, bridges, twisting alleyways, and indecipherable addresses. I was thankful Maya and I didn't have to go through that. I took a deep breath and smiled. The air smelled wet, like it smells after a rainstorm. Yet there wasn't a cloud in sight.

"The vaporettos run all day long," I said, pointing at the yellow water boats in the distance as we walked toward the canal's main port. One pulled in to the station, next to a large sign marked, '*Ferrovia.*' We stood there watching people rush off the boat, while others dodged around the slow movers to get onboard before the gate closed and the boat pulled out into the canal again.

Next, I indicated the large white building behind us, opposite the vaporetto stop. It was set back away from the canal, lined with steps all the way down from its entrance to the sidewalk fronting the canal's edge. People sat alone or in pairs or small groups beside their luggage all over those steps. Some studied maps, others just sat there smoking or chatting, while others just sat, savoring the scenery and the sunshine.

"That's Santa Lucia," I told Maya. "The train station. Named after the church that originally stood there, demolished to make way for the station. Thank God there's no strike today." I couldn't help but remember my previous trip with friend and co-worker, Levida, documented in *I'd Rather Eat Pizza Than See Pisa*. I breathed a sigh of relief at the memory. That trip the trains were on strike, Levida's bunions were acting up, and our hotel was an hour bus ride away. I didn't want to go through any of that again.

"Why don't I see any gondolas?" Maya asked.

"They're all on the backside of the island, closer to the Rialto and San Marco. Near the tourist hot spots and the expensive hotels. Everyone here has either just arrived or waiting to catch a train, so most aren't much interested in doing any tourist activities yet."

Maya nodded.

"So, what do you feel like doing first?" I asked.

"Coffee! I gotta have an espresso."

"Okay, but until then try to stay upright, and keep moving," I suggested. "Come on, follow me."

In less than thirty minutes we arrived downtown, at the Plaza Roma parking lot. We walked over the connecting bridge and headed toward the Santa Lucia station.

We walked past the station, gawking at the water boats, the people and the constant activity along the way. About a block later we found a small café with four small round tables sitting on the cement walkway out front. A waiter hustled to reposition chairs so that each table held two. One table was unoccupied, so I slid in. Maya followed.

I pulled out my map of the island and spread it out on the table. Maya leaned in for a closer look. "How long does it take to walk all the way around the island, so we can get a quick overview?"

I shrugged. "Depends."

"On what?"

"On the crowds, especially here," I said, pointing at the Rialto on the map. "Tourist central. Not to mention how many times we stop to shop."

"Ballpark figure," she said, pausing to order two espressos from a passing waiter.

"An hour. Maybe two." I looked at my watch and yawned. It was now one o'clock in the afternoon; six in the morning back home. "If the espresso gives us a good enough jolt, I bet we can last at least four more hours."

"Let's do that then, a complete walk around mainly to take in the sights. Then we'll return here and get an early dinner before we call it a night and head back to the hotel. I figure if I'm in bed by six, I'll be fit company tomorrow."

I agreed, nodding, watching as she flicked her credit card in a two-fingered salute toward our waiter as he delivered two tiny cups. I bit my lip when he held up two fingers and waived them back in forth in front of her like a metronome, accompanied by tisk—tisking tongue clicks. "Cash," was all he said. In English.

"No credit cards? What a bunch of . . . what the hell kind of tourist place is this that you don't take credit cards?"

While I dug deep and pulled out a 10€ note, the waiter explained in rapid-fire Italian that there was a 20€ purchase minimum for credit. He was gone in a flash, so I ended up setting the money under the ashtray. Then I turned back to the map.

"We are here," I said, pointing at the train station on the map. "I think we should just stay in this district for the time being. As it is, it'll take hours to wind our way through the maze of streets here. This is shopping central, other than in the more expensive Rialto area. There's bound to be all kinds of waterside restaurants not too far from here, for later."

"We just have to make sure we're not too tired to walk back to the bus stop," Maya joked. "I mean, it's not like we can just flag a taxi."

"Sounds good," I agreed. "We can window shop and get the lay of the land while we're scouting out restaurants. We'll buy our vaporetto tickets tomorrow."

We set out through the Cannareglo district, refortified with extra-strength espressos coursing through our jet-lagged veins. We knew from the map which direction to walk, but I knew from experience it was easy to get lost inside the labyrinth of small side streets. There were dozens of twisting alleyways, all loaded with touristy shops selling jewelry, leather goods, and Murano glass items.

Navigation was easy, for the most part, primarily because at evenly spaced intersections a square ceramic sign had been posted up high on the corner building, indicating Per Rialto, or P. San Marco, with an arrow beneath the lettering pointing the way. We stopped frequently to investigate possible purchases.

We made many stops and detours, noting nearby landmarks, knowing full well we might never find the same store again in this maze of streets. On the other hand, there seemed to be an unlimited number of stores to choose from.

Maya was the first to discover the solution to to finding our way back again to select stores inside the maze of streets: the voice memo app on our phones. "You just press the red button to record, then you can identify landmarks and store names as you go. Label the recording whatever you want. You can delete it later."

"Oh, cool," I responded, intent on trying it out as soon as we found a store worthy enough to return to.

Ultimately our feet began aching from the cobbled squares, the many cement steps and the uneven sidewalks. Pain radiated up my shins long before hunger set in. When we came to a wine store, we decided to buy a bottle to take back to the hotel with us. I made a voice note of the store's name and landmarks leading to its entrance.

"It has to be something that doesn't require a corkscrew," Maya admonished.

"How about Prosecco then? No corkscrew needed to pop the cork."

"Perfecto," said Maya.

The storekeeper set our bottle inside a long narrow bag with rope handles. The outside boasted a printed cross section of the streets so we could find the store again.

Around the next corner we came to a dead-end street bordering one of the local canals. It was lined with small restaurants, each with lit signs overhead, and sidewalk lanterns. The heaters in the base of those lanterns effectively served to ward off October evening chilliness.

"I'm about done for," I announced to Maya, savoring the aromas of Italian cooking drifting our way.

"Me too," she said, heading toward a small pizzeria close to the water's edge.

As we sank into the chairs, I checked my cell for the time: 5:00 p.

I was happy to let Maya do all the talking with the flirtatious waiter. She explained that we'd just arrived this morning, and how we were trying to last as long as we could, but now we were both experiencing jet lag and hunger, which was why we wanted to eat dinner so much earlier than is normal. She ended by telling him we wanted their house special, with lots of wine. "You do take credit cards, no?" she ended.

"Oh sì, sì," he said waiving a hand. "We take anything."

Our pizza contained a little of everything: spinach, white and yellow cheese, peppers, olives, proscuitto, pineapple, shrimp, as well as anchovies. Along with each refill of wine, the waiter delivered a small basket of bread slathered in olive oil. I lost count after three glasses of wine. Next, I heard Maya refuse another basket of bread, telling the waiter we were finished.

"I hope he doesn't charge us for every refill," she said after calling for the check.

I hiccupped. "Bigger tip if he doesn't." He must have heard me.

It was all we could do to retrace our steps back to the train station, and then cross the bridge to the parking lot. From there we stumbled our way to the ticket kiosk at the lot's edge to purchase one-way bus tickets to the hotel. Since we didn't know what district the hotel stop was located in, and the ticket seller didn't understand our hotel name, we simply ended up buying tickets to the airport.

We were both fighting sleep as well as feeling the effects of too much wine on full stomachs as we trudged through the parking lot searching for the bus marked 'Aeroporto.' Thankfully it was still there, in final preparations to leave when we boarded.

Maya explained in wine-laden detail to the driver that although our tickets said aeroporto, we needed to get off at the Marriott Hotel. "*Capisci, no?*" she asked.

The driver nodded absently. "Hotel. Sì, si."

Not satisfied with his vague answer, she began to explain it all over again, but I stopped her. "Shhhh, you'll just confuse him."

The driver stared back and forth at the two of us. "You no wanna go airport. You wanna go hotel. Get off one stop before airport. *Capisco.*"

We were both sound asleep by the time the bus pulled up in front of the Marriott. Neither of us heard the driver's shouts to us from the front of the bus that we'd arrived. Only after he unbuckled his seat belt, got up, and ambled back to where we were sitting did we realize the bus had stopped moving.

He poked each of us in the shoulder several times, all the while shouting: "*Svegliati! Svegliati!* We at da hotel."

It wasn't actually all that late, at least not by local standards, so Maya and I rallied, shook our heads to wake up and headed straight for the front desk of the Marriott. There, we smiled and apologized for bothering the sole clerk on duty, and asked for the letters the manager was to have left for us. These contained our all-important future compensation authorization, and we didn't want to forget about retrieving them before we got too busy prior to departing Venice.

The clerk disappeared into the back office for long minutes, while we fought sleep in a standing position and waited for him to return.

Finally, he returned with a legal-sized white envelope with both of our names on the outside. "Open it," instructed Maya. I opened it and read the letter inside with Maya looking on. The clerk, meanwhile, stood and waited, drumming his fingers on the counter in front of him.

"Sounds good," we both agreed, filing the letter in my purse. We turned and headed for the exit with a parting. "*Grazie. Buona notte.*"

I barely recall the long walk back to our own hotel.

∽ **Chapter 5** ∽

The worst thing about jet lag is that if you go to bed too early—meaning several hours earlier than normal—you naturally wake up that much earlier than normal the next morning. That's what happened to us. In all likelihood our erratic sleep cycle probably had more to do with unrestrained alcohol consumption the night before, combined with an early yet heavy dinner that caused us to fade so early. So, it wasn't entirely unexpected that we found ourselves wide awake well before the sun came up the next morning.

"Maya," I hissed, throwing a pillow at her from my bed. "Wake up!"

"Oh God," she wailed, reaching for the bedside clock. "What the hell time is it anyway?"

"Time to get a move on," I said, heading toward the bathroom. "Might as well get up and get underway."

Maya sat up and rubbed her eyes. She crawled out of bed and crossed over to the window, stretched and yawned as she pulled back the drape and peered down on the street below. Then she let out a groan. "Awww, the sun's not even up yet."

"I have an idea," I said, pausing before ducking behind the bathroom door. "Let's head down to the island and go see the action at the fish market by the Rialto. I read that all the restaurant chefs will be there, looking to buy their evening specials. They're supposedly famous for their singing."

"Who? the fishermen or the chefs?"

"Not sure," I said. "But it doesn't matter, does it? We can grab some breakfast downtown while we're at it. Italian style is usually just café and a croissant anyway, right?"

"I guess," Maya agreed, fumbling through her suitcase, pulling out her iPad charging chord. "I gotta get a caffeine kick before I can even think about heading out. There should be one of those self-service espresso machines in the lunch room downstairs."

"I'll go down and check it out as soon as I'm dressed," I answered, closing the bathroom door behind me. Minutes later I emerged, ready to face the day.

Maya's peal of laughter greeted me. Oh, don't say that," she wailed, facing her iPad screen.

I did a quick time calculation, concluding it was about midnight back home. Who on earth could she be video chatting with? I leaned over to peek at the face on the screen, but Maya turned it away before I could get a good look. Male was about the only thing I could confirm. Boyfriend? I didn't know there was one.

I vacated the room and headed downstairs, giving Maya total privacy while I set out in search of the self-service espresso machine.

Downstairs, off to the right of the vacant front desk, stood the empty dining room. I pushed my way through the swinging doors and entered near total darkness. It was eerily quiet inside, so much so that for a minute I contemplated turning around and going back upstairs empty handed. I should search for a light switch, I thought, but changed my mind as being a waste of time.

It didn't take long after that to discover the automated machine. It was sitting on the counter at the kitchen end of the room. The sink was filled with dirty dishes, no doubt left over from the night before, even though the dishwasher door had been opened in readiness. "Waiting for the day shift by the looks of it," I said to myself, removing two clean coffee cups from a fully stocked shelf above the counter. A nearby cart was loaded with breakfast plates, bowls, and silverware. Next, I turned my attention to the beverage machine, poking the button marked *espresso* several times. I nearly jumped out of my skin when high-pressure steam suddenly erupted from one of the spigots in front of me.

"Shit," I said, backing into the dish cart. I lurched away in time to shove my cup beneath the spigot then repeat the process for a second cup.

Balancing both steaming cups without spilling, I hurried through the darkness toward the door and retraced my steps back out into the lobby and up to our room.

I had to set the cups on the floor in order to free up a hand to dig the room key from my pocket. I could hear Maya's laughter through the door. "Oh, what I would have given to see that. Serves that asshole right."

"What asshole?" I asked, stepping inside. Maya, sitting cross-legged at the end of her bed, dressed in nothing but a towel, terminated her iPad conversation and ducked into the bathroom by the time the door clicked shut behind me.

"You want your coffee now or later?" I shouted in her direction. By way of reply, she cracked the door open and stuck out her hand.

"Careful," I warned, tiptoeing to the door and handing the cup over. "It's hot."

"That stuff tastes like crap," was Maya's only comment when she finally exited.

I took one look at her skin-tight black leggings and exposed midriff with its rolls of excess poundage and said, "You're wearing that?"

Maya looked down at herself with a questioning look. "Why? What's wrong with it?"

"Well, for starters it's pretty obvious you're not wearing any undies. Those tights go all the way up the crack of your . . ."

"This is what everyone's wearing over here, haven't you noticed? I'll fit right in. Honestly, sometimes you sound just like my mother."

Her tone caused me to shut my mouth and force a smile on my face. "Well then, by all means let's go join the locals."

Less than twenty minutes later we found ourselves alone in the empty lunch room downstairs. Maya charged forward in spite of the darkness. She walked straight to where I told her the espresso machine stood and proceeded to punch buttons, this time opting for a café au lait instead of another espresso.

The first hint of early morning light had just made its appearance, so the room didn't seem nearly as large, or as sinister as it had before. As I looked around at the textured wallpaper on the side wall, I couldn't help but admire the Murano glass wall sconces as well as a tulip-shaped glass chandelier hanging front and center just past the entrance door. Its glass had been tinted with various shades of pink, lavender, and green hues, thus enhancing the contrasting appearance of its flowers hiding among the many arching stems.

We grabbed a table toward the front to enjoy our cafés before heading outside. "It's so dark back there I couldn't bring myself to poke around any more just for milk," Maya said, raising her cup.

"No worries," I answered, clinking my cup to hers before tackling the potent brew.

"You'll never guess what happened at home—at the airport—last night," Maya began. "Some woman was sitting in the gate, totally ignoring her two little prepubescent monsters. Reports are they were jumping from chair to chair and generally making a real pain of themselves, while their mother totally ignored them the whole time. Several passengers asked the gate agent to do something about them . . . Oh Sābra, you'll never guess who the agent was!" Maya squealed, leaning forward to whisper the name of our station's notoriously disagreeable senior suck-up, locally nicknamed, 'Ms. Priss.'

"Supposedly she told the boys to go play somewhere else . . . like the gate next door. It was empty," Maya clarified. "Next thing anyone knew was that one of the kids missed his jump and tripped on the chair . . . something like that. The end result was the little bastard fell and broke his arm."

"Couldn't happen in a more deserving brown-noser's gate," I said between snorts of laughter.

"I know," agreed Maya, trying to keep her voice low. "I heard she radioed the tower for help, saying she couldn't deal with 'these brats' because it was time to board. On-time departure comes first, you know."

"She actually said that?"

"Yup. Too many ears or cell phones lurking nearby. That's the problem with working in a fishbowl."

"Let me guess, the mom heard her?"

Maya nodded. "Yep, and now the Mommy Dearest is threatening a lawsuit over our personnel's 'lack of caring.'"

"Where was our 'servant leader'?'" I asked, trying to keep my voice low in case the hotel's help showed up and chased us out.

"In his office. Probably on Facebook," Maya cracked. "Either that or forging comp-time entries in the book."

"I can guess the rest," I said. "Why wasn't the gate agent watching the little darlings? No doubt their mom demanded immediate compensation."

Maya nodded. "Of course. Pissed as hell that the agent wouldn't even stop boarding to talk to the paramedics. All Ms. Priss did was to radio for Noggins to get his ass out of his chair and come handle the chaos."

"You can't do much else when you're working a flight by yourself," I said. It was an everyday nightmare we both could relate to.

I laughed. "Poor old Noggins. He probably didn't have a clue what to do."

Maya slapped the table in a fit of giggles before covering her mouth to hold back more laughter. "But he's one of our leaders. And they know everything."

"Doesn't automatically mean he's competent. Besides, he's a lazy bully. He works harder getting out of work than he would if he just did the job."

"He had to fill out an injured/ill report," Maya managed to get out before dissolving into more muffled laughter.

"Wonder who he got to print it off for him," I wisecracked.

"The rumor is that now Noggins is pissed at Ms. Priss because she didn't stop boarding long enough to help the mother."

I nodded, wondering what kinds of managerial torments Ms. Priss was about to experience. What's a poor agent to do? Either we catch hell for dealing with a problem but take a delay in the process, or for putting customer service behind the company's on-time goals. Either way we can't win. It's always the gate agent's fault.

"God, I am so glad we're on vacation." I said, rising from the table.

We rinsed our cups and set them in the sink, and then headed outside to the bus stop, where not so much as a single person could be seen in either direction. Less than ten minutes later we were on the city bus enroute to the island.

The train station steps were vacant when we finally walked past. A few of the overnight vaporetto drivers were standing together by the ticket kiosk, smoking and cracking jokes by the sound of it. They stopped talking and gawked as Maya and I walked by, the only two tourists out and about at such an early hour. The only sound to be heard was the lapping of water against the dock.

I nodded toward the group. "They're probably wondering if we're pulling an all-nighter, or if we're crazy jet-lagged tourists getting a really early shopping start."

"Maybe they think we're hookers?" Maya whispered, covering her mouth with a hand to suppress her laughter.

"Certainly not this one," I announced, jabbing a thumb at my chest. "Too old."

We walked past the tiny pastry shop located next to the train station. Dim lights were on inside, revealing two women busy unloading trays of fresh croissants and crème-filled rolls into the window display cases. "Looks like they're preparing for tourist mania in a couple of hours." I could smell the yeasty bread from here, even though I knew it was impossible to buy anything this early.

The vaporetto stop was directly opposite the bakery. We made our way to the ticket booth and checked the price list. Individual rides cost €7 each. An unlimited 48-hour ticket, on the other hand, cost €30.

"I think we ought to buy the 48-hour ticket," I said to Maya. "That'll save us from digging for euros every time we turn around."

"Yeah," she agreed. "Easier in the long run."

We bought our tickets from the machine and made our way to line #2, for the fastest way to the Rialto. "We'll take the slow boat later, so you can enjoy the leisurely grand tour of the canal."

"How long is the slow trip?"

"About forty-five minutes, what with all the docking time involved" I answered. "I think it makes about a dozen stops along the way."

"So, what's the big deal about this market again?" Maya asked. "This fish market we're headed to all the way over by the Rialto? Just to see some fisherman—who've been out all night—all busy singing while they unload their catches-of-the day?"

I nodded. "That's what the guidebook said. 'Singing like Pavarotti' to be exact."

"Doesn't sound like one of the top ten things in Venice to me. What else did your guidebook recommend?"

"Oh, let's see," I said, trying to recall. "It talked about doing the prison tour. Said it gives you a real feel for the hopelessness of those who were locked up centuries ago, how they suffered under truly miserable conditions."

Maya made a face. "I said someplace fun to see."

I shrugged. "It's not fun, exactly. But it's living history. I think the tour is pretty long, so you get your money's worth. It combines the prison tour with an overview of Venetian eighteenth century government—a state run inquisition that punished people for crimes against morality. Plus, they talk about their most famous prisoner, Casanova, the only one who ever managed to escape . . . "

"Casanova?" Maya scoffed. "He was a real person? I always thought he was just some made up legend. Like Robin Hood or something."

I shook my head. "No, no, not at all. He was very real. And quite accomplished, as a matter of fact. What got him into trouble was seducing most of the Italian nobility's daughters while waging bets and winning money from the parents."

"So, what's so special about that?" Maya asked. "You get to see the inside of some cinderblock jail cells while hearing about some Casanova's sexual exploits?"

"He's special because he's the only one who ever managed to escape."

"Part of his mystique, I guess. Do we have to buy tickets in advance, or can we buy them just before the tour?"

"Even if we buy our tickets online ahead of time, we'll still have to stand in line to get in the main entrance."

Maya exhaled in irritation just as the vaporetto showed up and slowed in preparation for docking. "So, I guess that means we end up standing in line no matter what."

"Just figure we're regular tourists doomed to standing in line for every event, exactly like at Disney World. It'll be easier that way."

Maya looked over her shoulder at me and made a face as we walked up the gangway toward the rocking vaporetto.

We scanned our tickets to validate them as we walked onboard. Seating was optional, since there were less than ten people in line behind us. Maya and I stood alongside the railing where we could get a bird's eye view of the scenery. In minutes the engines revved up and the water beneath us began churning. Next thing I knew we'd pulled out into the canal.

Mansions floated by in a blur of peeling pastel red, orange, and yellow walls, nearly all in various states of disrepair. Several of the building's ground floors were below water level. The great majority appeared vacant, although plenty of boats of all shapes and sizes rocked with the waves while tied between upright wooden posts that separated each building's parking space, so I had to wonder if maybe they were inhabited after all.

Regular rows of balconies extended out over the water, some made of metal, now rusted red with age. Others were made of wood, with peeling paint left unattended too long. The balconies alternated with recessed arched windows, revealing three or four stories inside. The archways themselves appear to be less Roman in style and more ornate—Byzantine, if I remember my art history correctly. Many of these windows are fronted by decorative columns, each topped with crosses or some other church-styled insignia. Further down the canal, the base floor entrance of many buildings appeared to be level with the water. At others, there remained some hint of a wooden dock and platform in front of an entrance archway.

Restaurants and hotels lined the opposite side of the canal, with flags hanging over doorways, alongside a decorative name sign. The water, I noticed, couldn't be called blue, but it wasn't easily labeled brown or green either. Salty, I wondered? Probably. It came in with the tide from the Adriatic, after all.

"Are all these buildings dark because the tenants are still sleeping, or is it because they're vacant?" Maya asked.

"A little bit of both, I think. Probably because so many have been flooded," I added, pointing at one of the below-waterline basements. "I read somewhere that laws issued by the Italian Historical Preservation prohibits owners here from making any changes or renovations."

"Jeez," Maya interrupted. "Who would want to own one then? About the only thing left for owners is to rent them out for movies,"

I agreed. Not a bad idea, actually.

A barge filled with a rack of plastic-wrapped dry cleaning powered past us, undoubtedly bound for one of the more upscale hotels. I didn't know if we were still experiencing the effects of low tide, but tops of rocks periodically stuck out above the water line alongside several docking posts. Most were covered with green moss, doubtlessly countless years old. Terracotta pots lined several upper floor balconies, spilling red flowers toward the water below.

I spotted a honeycomb of thick rusted metal bars covering several upper windows. I couldn't help but wonder if those were actual 18th century bars, and if their purpose was to keep young women in, or to keep Venice's notorious seducer—Casanova—out?

Where were the electrical lines, I wondered? I saw the periodic TV antennae perched atop an orange tiled roof, but nothing indicating electricity. I scanned the building fronts again, this time searching for power cables or breaker boxes. None. Where would they be? Certainly not beneath the buildings where there was more water than ground. Or did that explain why so many of the buildings were dark? I resolved to investigate further.

Suddenly the water churned with mini whitecaps as traffic funneled in together from every direction. The water became bumpier the closer we got to the Rialto. Froth appeared between the whitecaps and lingered. Boats and barges of every type headed in toward the dock together, each loaded with stacks of boxes of assorted produce, meats, sea foods, and building supplies while an equal amount of now empty, lighter-weight traffic crested the incoming waves in a synchronized attempt to motor out.

There, dead ahead, stood the Rialto, with its white rounded archways leading up to a peak over a wide central arch that spanned the entire width of the canal. A decorative whitish banister lined the walkway on each side, vacant of tourists at this early hour.

At the base of the Rialto, a sea of empty gondola's bobbed and rocked and bumped each other, all triple parked between a pair of red and white striped wooden poles extending a couple of yards above the water while awaiting the day's influx of clients. The gondoliers, in their distinctive uniform of black slacks, navy and white striped polo shirt, white or navy hat, and the ever-present Ray-Bans, lined the sidewalk in front of a makeshift wooden plank café bar that had been erected this side of the bridge. Every one of them looked to be waiting to begin their shift, talking or smoking in groups, while keeping an expectant eye on arriving vaporetto's with their incoming loads of tourist dollars and euros.

As soon as we docked and walked down the floating gangway, Maya and I found ourselves in the midst of barely controlled chaos. Vendors ran past us, in front of us, and all around us as they unloaded or negotiated deliveries to the canopied booths that lined the sidewalk. Others pushed carts. The air was filled with loud, busy voices: some greeting old friends, others shouting instructions, and still others haggling over the price of the catch of the day, or hawking fresh vegetables and fruit. There appeared to be only a handful of tourists amid the crowd.

The outside edge of the canopy over all these stalls twinkled with lights. I looked up at them and tried to follow their chords to see where the power line originated. But I kept getting bumped and lost my place.

"So, where's Pavarotti?" Maya teased.

I just shrugged. We couldn't have heard any singing even if that report was true. The noise of so many revving boat engines was bad enough, but added to it the backdrop of shouts of a couple dozen gondoliers to prospective clients amid constant back-and-forth price haggling up and down the lineup of stalls, made it so that I could barely hear Maya who was right beside me.

I grabbed Maya's arm, leaned close and shouted to be heard while pointing to the gondolas. "Can you imagine spending your work day under the hot sun at the back end of one of those glorified canoes? Pushing around cheapo tourists all day long?"

Maya turned and looked at me. "If you made enough money doing it, you would."

"I doubt it," I countered. "Aside from tips, how much can you make week in and week out. Can't be that much."

"I read somewhere they typically make $150k a year."

I looked at Maya in surprise. "Wow!" was all I could say, before looking again at a nearby group of gondoliers. That put a whole new light on things.

Maya pulled an elastic hair band off her wrist and put her hair up into a ponytail in preparation for warm weather. "So, what do we want to do first? Shop or play tourist?"

"Let's alternate. Shop first. But not here. The closer we are to San Marco or the Rialto, the more expensive things are."

"Let's just window shop and price things out while we wander around, okay?"

"What are we shopping for, exactly?" I asked.

"I have my heart set on a nice Italian leather computer bag. Only problem is I didn't bring a tape measure, and I'm not exactly sure what length I need. Guess I'll wing it."

I stopped at a freshly stocked produce stall and bought us each a pear. Maya headed to the stall next door and purchased two croissants. We divided them up and proceeded to walk and eat while inspecting each booth along the way. "Too bad there's no roasted chestnuts yet," I told Maya. "They won't show up till the end of October."

We eventually arrived at the Rialto and climbed the steps leading up to the street and stores. It was still early enough that only a few tourists had arrived. In fact, many shops were just opening for business. Newly arriving customers were busy claiming seats at tables among the café shops that lined the sidewalk. A dozen or so gondoliers remained loitering at that same coffee shop with the makeshift wooden plank we'd seen from the vaporetto when we first arrived, drinking the last of their espressos before snagging an arriving client.

Maya looked at the group of men and flashed them a bright smile. "*Buongiorno.*"

They immediately stopped talking and looked us over.

"*Stai cercando un tour del canale?*" one of them asked.

"A canal tour?" Maya repeated, sounding unsure. "Can't I just do a tour by myself by riding the vaporetto?"

"*Un passaggio?* A ride," another member of the group spat, sounding critical. "That's no tour."

Maya laughed off his veiled insult. "No, no tour right now. Shopping first. Maybe later."

The youngest-looking of the group pushed aside his espresso cup and walked over to join Maya and I, although he focused all his attention on Maya. "Americano?"

"Sì," she answered. "Technically. But half Italiano also."

"Eez good," the gondolier said. "*Allora possiamo parlare italiano.*"

Maya chose to stick with English, probably to better manage his flirtatious behavior. "How much you charge?" she asked.

"Depends," he said with one of those exaggerated Italian shrugs. "Oh? On what?"

"How long your ride."

"Well, how long is a standard ride?"

"*Trenta minuto,* "he answered.

"Okay, so how much for this short thirty-minute ride?"

"Eighty euro."

"Wow! That much?" Maya looked at him wide eyed, and stopped in her tracks.

He almost bumped into her as he rushed to explain that the price was set by the government. "Eez to make good living, you understand? Not my price."

"How many hours do you work each day?" Maya asked.

He studied her face before answering, clearly wondering why she wanted to know. But then, sensing no threat, he said, "Cinque ore."

"That's a pretty good living, isn't it? So that's two rides an hour . . ." said Maya computing the math using her fingers, "at half-hour each . . . that means ten rides in a five-hour day . . . why that's eight-hundred euros!"

"Some days, more," the gondolier added, confused by doing math in English.

Maya pulled out her phone for additional math computations. "So, in an eight-hour day, you'd do about sixteen rides . . . that would net you over a thousand euros!"

"Per day!" I emphasized, accompanied by Maya's nodding.

I was fairly certain our poor gondolier was lost in translation by now, but he kept smiling and waiting. "Tip not required. Only if you want."

"Do you serenade us during this short eighty-euro ride?" Maya asked.

He shook his head. "*Non capisco.*"

"Sing? *Cantare*? Por noi?"

"Sure, if you want. Cost more."

"Let me guess, price also set by the state, no?"

He nodded, but less enthusiastically than before, and his smile faltered. "Still cheaper than at night."

"It's higher at night?" Maya asked, sounding surprised. "Higher still if it's a full moon, right?"

The gondolier frowned, but didn't answer. Poor guy, he didn't understand.

"How much more for night ride?" I asked, seeing that the full moon wisecrack had him stumped. Besides, by now I was curious.

"One hundred twenty euro."

"You take credit cards?" Maya asked.

I shot a quizzical look at Maya. Surely she wasn't contemplating taking a ride. If she was, I wasn't going with her. Not for eighty plus euros I wasn't.

Our poor gondolier focused on Maya and blew out his breath. "Only cash. You can pay at tourist office—or online. Or at hotel. That way use plastic."

"No lower price if I pay cash?" Maya asked, aiming a pointed look in my direction.

At this point the gondolier's attention waivered. Tired of keeping up with our English banter, he figured out we weren't buying so made his escape and veered off in the direction from which he came.

Maya typed on her phone one last time. "Take an eight-hour shift, and, say only eight rides at daytime rates would be €640 . . . 8 rides at night, €960 . . . " She looked up at me with a shocked look on her face. "If he did two rides an hour for six hours . . . that's twelve rides . . . Wow! Then he's making almost 1500 euros a day! That's over €7000 a week!" She continued typing. "Oh my God, that's almost €30,000 a month! That's friggin' incredible!"

"At that rate he could take the whole winter off. We're in the wrong business," I joked.

"Unfortunately, they're all men. At least for now."

We continued on our way, meandering through the streets, in and out of shops at random all while following the posted arrows leading us toward San Marco and the famous Piazza. These arrows, leading tourists to identifiable landmarks such as Ferrovia, Per Rialto, and San Marco, were painted on large ceramic tiles that had been imbedded into the stonework high up on buildings at strategic intersections throughout the maze of streets. You can easily get lost in this maze, although if you walk in any direction long enough, you'll eventually come to a canal and a nearby vaporetto dock. Tourists are bound to get lost, but the rule is to keep walking; eventually you'll spot another of these corner signs.

Maya and I window shopped, going in and out of more shops than we could count. We worked our way through Murano Glass jewelry shops, with kaleidoscope patterned glass pendants, glass beads, beaded bracelets, earrings, and other collectibles. We found one shop selling hand blown glass paperweights. "Who the hell uses paperweights anymore," said Maya, heading for the door.

The next shop sold leather computer bags. Maya looked over the quality and prices at each, holding up possibilities at her side to gauge the possible fit of her laptop.

"Don't buy one until you get the correct measurements," I advised.

"Yeah, I know. There's always tomorrow."

"Especially since we're somewhere between the Rialto and San Marco."

"Then why did that last corner sign say 'Ferrovia?'" Maya asked.

"It said what?" I asked. I hadn't been paying attention.

I doubled back to where the sign was. "The arrow below the lettering is pointing the way back to the main train station."

"Oh," was all Maya said, making note of this store's name, address, and the nearest landmark in a note page on her phone in order to find it again. Two streets later we verified that indeed we had turned the wrong direction somewhere along the way and were now, in fact, headed toward the train station.

"We need to turn around and go back the other way," I advised.

"Give it a minute or two," said Maya. "The shopping here is too good to pass up."

A few shops later we paused to admire displays of leather purses outside doorways. Racks of them, loaded with varied sizes and colors stood on both sides of at least three shop's entrance doors. Every shelf inside each store was stocked with others as well. None, I noticed, were selling recognizable designer brands. Instead, these were some kind of local brand, with a stamped imprint on the bottom corner of the soft leather. Prices ranged between 35-150 euros each for the most part.

I took pictures of several—in particular the €35 styles, and sent them off to several co-worker friends. "I usually buy something for their birthdays," I told Maya. "This will be perfect."

"How about me?" Maya teased. "Aren't I your friend?"

I smiled. "Sure, but these are girls that I've worked with for over fifteen years. One of them was going through a divorce at the beginning of deregulation, when all transfers were suspended. Imagine getting stuck working with your soon-to-be ex, with no end in sight, while all your co-workers were busy picking sides. Thankfully I was working for a different airline at the time, so I didn't witness all the petty harassment she had to put up with."

"I guess that means I'm not a member of your bestie club yet." Maya's tone sounded teasing, but I couldn't help but wonder if there wasn't a bit of sincerity behind her words.

"Not yet," was all I said. Sometimes the truth hurts.

The next souvenir shop we came to was run by a middle-aged female. Her elderly father shadowed the inflow of tourists, keeping a sharp eye out. Maya talked with the owner while I engaged '*il papà*' in conversation. "I've been meaning to ask someone who lives here, where do they put the electric cables?" I said it in slow, labored Italian, pointing to the light fixtures overhead as I spoke.

He nodded and moved in close, warming to the subject in two languages. "Electricity? *Elettrica?* You wanna know about . . . *linee elettriche?*"

"*Sì,*" I said, hoping like hell he understood what I was asking.

"In Venezia, all zee *line* must run under paving. Eez law. Zee water, zee gas, zee *elettriche* . . . " As he talked, he ticked items off on his fingers, being careful to use clear and slow Italian. He thoughtfully interjected the occasional English word for my benefit. "*Elettriche,* eet follow zee path of peoples, under zee walkway. You see? Zee *line* go from house to house, all careful to be hidden from view."

"Is that why we don't see any cables outside?"

"You're not supposed to," he said with a gleeful laugh. "Eets all positioned on opposite side of where tourists go." Then he winked. "Next time, you look. You'll see."

"How do they make repairs?" I couldn't help but ask.

"Easy. Access via pavement stones. Easily to see on most every street. For *elettriche,* sidewalk stones marked EN. For lights, stones marked PL. Water servicio eez for private and public both. Same pipes, too. Also use by *vigili del fuoco* . . . fire department. Capisci?"

"But how is the system is grounded?"

He nodded. "Grounded eez always required, no? *Elettricità* grounds where eet attaches to zee appliance."

I smiled and nodded. I thought I understood.

His daughter, standing over at the cash register, caught my eye. "Don't ask him about the island sinking. He'll never stop." Though she said it in English, it was obvious he understood enough to begin lecturing on a favorite topic.

"The water eez no rising," he began. "Zee city is sinking. Venezia, she was swamp in beginning. Zee ground contains more than ten *millione* tree trunks pounded into mud. All come from nearby alpine forests. Sunk so deep they become petrified. But weight from so much stone buildings press down on foundation, and next comes high tide. Eet rots wood wherever it can . . . "

"Because of global warming," Maya added from afar as she handed over her credit card.

"Baaah," the old man spat. "No such thing. Is nothing but big lie they tell to raise taxes. Sinking is because of plates. You capisci? Venezia sits on Adriatic Plate. Everyone with brain knows is true. Is moving under Apennines' plate." He made use of both hands to show one traveling beneath the other. "When edge of one piece goes under different piece. Also happens now because removing much water out of underground."

Maya signaled me to meet her at the doorway, effectively ending further talk. "Let's get out of here or he'll be educating you for the rest of the day."

"But first just me ask him about their sewage system." I said, hesitating to end the conversation with someone, especially a local, that was so knowledgeable.

The old man nodded knowingly while following us to the doorway. "Periodically zay suck out canals. Get rid of how you say, sludge? . . . da stuff that no goes out witha da tide."

"How often do they dredge the sewage . . . ?" I began, as Maya grabbed my arm.

He blew out his cheeks, preparing for a marathon explanation. "Tanks for da *merda* now in most *pubblica* buildings. Plus, zee city have blue *merda* boat with long tank. Eetsa come every week. Zee workers, they take hose inside and then suck all the things out. Most *touristas* they no pay attention, so never see. But you watch. They out about all zee time."

"Oh, just drop it," Maya said, tightening her grip and dragging me out the doorway.

⁓ **Chapter 6** ⁓

Twenty minutes after leaving the Rialto, Maya and I realized we were headed away from Piazza San Marco not toward it, so we turned around and reversed course. Unfortunately for us shopping was noticeably more expensive the closer we got to what is traditionally known as 'tourist central.' Even though it was October (off-season to us airline folks), there were still plenty of crowds out and about, bringing pedestrian traffic to a crawl. Most people, I couldn't help but notice, were content to stand on the sidewalk and stare into storefront windows rather than enter for any hands-on shopping. That meant Maya and I were constantly on the heels of the group in front of us. We'd no more than get past one, when we'd find ourselves behind a different group of ambling gawkers.

"Damn," Maya said, leading the way around yet another. "This is ridiculous."

I agreed. "Can you imagine what it's like during the height of the summer when most everyone is here on vacation?"

"It's gotta be awful." Maya agreed, complaining that her feet were already killing her. "How about we take a little siesta. Maybe get something to eat while we're at it?"

I followed as Maya led the way toward a modern-looking hotel. She zeroed in on the line-up of four tables sitting along the building's front wall and plunked down at the first one she came to, signaling for a waiter before I could stop her. Each table was covered with a heavy white linen tablecloth and had a decorative square white awning overhead, all with a clear view of the Rialto in the distance. In other words, the place reeked of high-end expensive. Too expensive for us, I felt sure.

"Maya," I cautioned the minute I caught up with her, "do you see anything here that suggests affordability?"

"Affordability?" Maya repeated. "Don't be such a cheapskate. I just want a nice sit-down rest, that's all." Then she turned to the waiter. "How much for a lemonade?"

"€10.50," he answered. "But €30 minimum to sit here."

I choked back my "Told ya," and made my way to the front desk inside to inquire about room prices for no reason other than to satisfy my curiosity. I returned minutes later holding a brochure filled with pictures of large, comfy rooms with a canal view. "Baglioni Hotel Luna," I read out loud to Maya. "Double rooms, ranging from nine-hundred to a thousand euros per night . . . "

Maya didn't comment. She just stood up, and with a long, drawn-out sigh, waved goodbye to the waiter, who didn't appear the least bit surprised at our abrupt departure.

"Two thousand euros a night for two beds," I continued, loud enough for Maya to hear. "Plus, enjoy a wonderful breakfast each morning for just sixty euros! The water taxi dock is conveniently located right out back," I finished reading before pocketing the brochure. Maya never responded. She didn't even look back at the hotel.

Thankfully, we only had to walk a couple more blocks before we arrived at the pigeon-filled Piazza. The Basilica, the square's focal point, with its gilded domes, white spires and roof-top statuary immediately caught our attention, but the gold inlay and half-moon mosaics are the real attraction. They practically glowed beneath the midday sun.

Saint Mark's fills the entire end of the Piazza, blocking sight of the canal on the other side. The famous bell tower—the Campanile—stands to its right. The sides of the Piazza were surrounded by a series of archways, some with curtains pulled down to block the heat of the midday sun. The walkway hidden inside offers access to a wealth of small shops and restaurants. In the courtyard outside, several rows of tables and chairs had been positioned in a lineup running nearly the length of the Piazza, although less than half were occupied when we arrived.

Did I mention the pigeons? Too many to count, they covered nearly every square inch of the decorative stone floor. Whenever anybody moved, so did the pigeons. But not too far away, and not for too long.

Maya made straight for the nearest table and sat down. While she waited for a waiter, she pulled out her iPad and began taking pictures. I pulled out a chair and sat down opposite her. "I don't care if it costs fifty euros," she said, "I'm getting something to drink."

"Okay, but don't let the waiter hear you," I said, nodding my head in the direction of an approaching male figure wearing a knee-length apron that boasted the name of a restaurant in a hard-to-read script across its front. I couldn't make out the name, only that each letter reflected the red, white and green of Italy's national flag.

"Too late," he said with a broad smile. "I already heard you." Then he asked where we were from, saying he had recently returned from spending a year working alongside family members in New York City. "I'm Luca."

"May I make a suggestion?" he offered. "If you move to one of the plain tables, it will be cheaper."

"Cheaper?" I repeated. "Why?"

"Plain?" Maya echoed at the same time. "You mean the ones without a tablecloth?"

"Sì. Sì," responded Luca in friendly fashion. "Tables with tablecloths are for meals. Plain tables are for drinks. It's a five-euro surcharge difference."

We thanked him and picked up our belongings in order to move to one of the cheaper tables.

"I fail to see the need to surcharge for a stupid tablecloth," Maya complained. "Customers are customers, after all."

"Higher bill if you order food," I answered with a shrug, surveying the arrangement of the tables. "More sun on the cheap seats, too."

A group dressed in identical black slacks and white shirts carrying musical instruments showed up and headed for the front corner of the piazza and began unpacking. Soon the sounds of string instruments being tuned floated across the air. I gave them a second glance, long enough to see a figure in blue coveralls haul a thick snake of electrical cords off to somewhere behind one of the archways. It wasn't long before the band began playing. Their music was old-style classical, and loud thanks to an oversized amplifier sitting in a prominent position beside their front row.

"So, what do you two ladies want to drink?" Luca asked, shouting to be heard over the noise.

"How much is a lemonade?" asked Maya.

"Thirteen euro."

"Christ, that much?"

"Plus a five euro surcharge."

"Another surcharge?" I asked. "What for?"

"For music. Everyone pays."

Maya and I took a minute to decide whether to shut up and and order, or just forget the whole idea and leave, when Luca spoke up. "Get a Bellini," he said. "Almost the same price, but better. It's mixed with peach puree, so not too strong. But strong enough to help you float through the rest of the afternoon. Best of all, no hangover. Plus, I can toss in half a baguette to go with it."

"Free?" Maya asked, clarifying. "No surcharge?"

Luca nodded. "Sì. Sì. No charge. It's only bread. Just don't feed it to the pigeons or you can be fined. Helps soak up the alcohol from the Prosecco."

We ordered two at a cost of fifteen euro each, not counting the five-euro musical surcharge. "Thirty bucks for a fruit punch," I said to Maya after the drinks arrived. "I hope you're happy." It was then I noticed Luca was still standing a short distance away, waiting. I pulled out a wad of euro notes from my purse and held it up for him.

"I am," was all Maya said, digging through her backpack for her wallet. As she handed Luca her only €5 euro coin, she asked him, "How long can we sit here?"

"As long as you want. But the seagulls will more than likely run you off. They're awful."

"Seagulls?" Maya and I said in unison.

"I thought they were pigeons," I said.

Luca laughed at us. "Pigeons are pretty, sort of an iridescent dark color. The brazen nuisance birds are the white ones with the orange beaks. They're expert food thieves. They're as fast and as bold as gypsies. Watch your stuff or they'll steal it right in front of you."

We only stayed about thirty minutes. We would have stayed longer but for the seagulls. Their greedy little collective eyes remained focused on our bread basket. They came closer to it with every passing minute. A few streaked in and landed on our table in a series of diving hit-and-run strikes. Maya and I spent as much time shooing them away as we did soaking up the scenery. Maybe more.

"No wonder there's no tablecloth," Maya complained. "No laundry expense, and easier to wipe off the bird shit."

When we finally got up, we wandered around behind the Basilica in the general direction of the palace and then beyond, toward the canal. We passed the Bridge of Sighs which connects the Palace to the Prison, the very same place I would soon be touring. I looked at it in anticipation. Next, we walked to the tourist office to buy our tickets, but the line looked to be at least an hour long."

"We should hop on the boat and go back to the train station," I suggested. "The city's main tourist ticket office is right next door. And it's fully staffed, so I'll bet there's not much of a line there. And even if there is a line, it shouldn't take long to get processed."

Maya agreed then pointed to a gelato shop among the buildings sitting back away from the canal. "Let's get a gelato first. Then we can take the slow boat back through the whole canal to the ticket office. What the hell, I'm in the mood to play tourist."

Who wants to slurp a triple-scoop cone while standing shoulder-to-shoulder alongside strangers on a thirty-minute vaporetto ride? Not us. Especially when a camera crew caught our attention. They were following a costumed group wearing 1700's style ballgowns, strolling alongside the canal. Periodically they'd all stop and pose, with the water, the boats, and the distant islands in the background. That's when the camera crew would jump into action. Maya and I never said a word. We didn't have to. We simply turned and fell in line with all the others following along behind the group. Whenever the models stopped to pose for pictures, we moved in closer for a better look at their Carnivale costumes.

The lead woman wore a pink gown with some kind of feather arrangement hanging from her waist. They looked like fluffy pink ostrich feathers, but with a large single white one hanging front and center. The gown's skirt must have had some kind of hoop beneath it, because it ballooned out on both sides making her look every bit as wide as she was tall. The bodice was very low-cut. Dangerously low-cut, if you get my meaning. Centered among all the cleavage was an enormous artificial rose in full bright pink bloom.

The bodice of this dress was attached to some type of long-sleeved waistcoat, made of what looked like crinkled aluminum foil. Silver and shiny, it ruffled its way down from her shoulders to her waist, then ballooned out in back as though covering a bustle, before flowing down across her hoops where it became a full-length skirt. Made of rows of aluminum foil squares all sewn together, the skirt was open in front, revealing layers of ruffled pink fabric. A pink bow had been attached mid-skirt on each side, thereby accentuating the silver outline of the back half of the skirt. The wig she wore was a matching shade of pink. It towered above her head by at least a foot and was decorated with pink flowers. To top it off, she held a parasol of matching silver foil.

In striking contrast was the white of her mask. I couldn't tell who was inside—male or female, as it covered the face completely, from hairline—or in this case wigline, straight down in front of her ears, until it finally curved below the jawline, completely covering her chin. Its only decoration was a handful of painted pink flowers high up on one of the cheeks. Its oriental-shaped eye holes had been heavily outlined in black. Their open centers exposed a pair of dark eyes inside. The lips, naturally, had been painted bright red.

"Did they really dress like this?" Maya whispered.

"Special occasions only, I'll bet," I answered. "I'm wondering how the hell can she use the bathroom in that thing? It's too big to fit inside a stall."

Maya giggled. "Maybe she pee's standing up."

This female lead was escorted by a male figure, wearing black slacks and a black overcoat that hung to his shoes and buttoned all the way up the front. The collar was one of those accordion-pleated Elizabethan style decorations that stuck out about four inches and completely encircled his neck. Again, his mask was solid white, although its nose was hooked like a beak and extended down almost to his chin. His head was covered by a wide-brimmed, tall, black hat with a white buckle prominently displayed front and center.

"That hat looks like a pilgrim's hat," Maya whispered with a snort.

"I doubt the pilgrims wore white gloves though," I whispered back.

"Who's he supposed to be, anyway?" whispered Maya.

"My guess is he's the plague doctor. During the Black Death the doctors used to stuff the beak of their masks with aromatic herbs and spices in order to offset the stink of rotting bodies."

Maya did a double-take at the doctor's costume, but said nothing.

Those of us surrounding the models were eventually asked to leave, no doubt because our constant chatter proved too distracting for a photo shoot. Not only that, but our group had morphed in size to become a real interruption to their forward progress for different background poses and for camera positioning.

Thirty minutes later we docked at Ferrovia, directly in front of Santa Lucia train station. Half a block away we came to the main tourist center. Thankfully, when we arrived there wasn't much of a lineup so we didn't have to wait long.

"When is the next Special Prison Tour?" I asked when our turn came.

The male clerk behind the counter checked his timetable. "It begins at 2P and lasts for about two hours. Cost is fifty-five euros."

"Fifty-five euros?" Maya exploded after hearing the price. "For a simple tour? No way am I paying that much!"

The clerk looked at Maya then back at me, and then at the growing line behind us, waiting for us to buy our tickets or get out of the way.

"No problem, you do what you want," I said, laying down my euros. "All I know is that I am doing this tour and I'm doing it today."

"Do you even need to do a formal tour?" Maya asked, glancing over at brochures displayed on a revolving stand. "Why can't we just go see the sights on our own and then read about them later in the guidebook?"

"For most places we could," I answered. "But I have my heart set on seeing the prison cells inside the Dodges Palace. Every time I've been here before, I've always run out of time to do the tour. Not this time. This time I want to see it and experience it firsthand. Plus, I want to hear from a professional guide the details of how Casanova managed to escape."

"Oh, well, fine then," Maya agreed, checking the time on her phone. "We have a couple of hours to kill before your stupid tour, so in the meantime let's go find someplace where we can sit down and relax, maybe get a bite to eat. While we're at it we can figure out where to meet up afterward."

"We should get something light" I said, after clarifying with the clerk the time and the designated meeting site. "Because I'm saving up for a calamari dinner tonight."

"I know what we should do then," said Maya brightening. "Let's just go find one of those little cicchetti bars nearby, preferably one with outdoor seating and no pigeons."

"Cicchetti?" I questioned, mispronouncing the word as '*Ko*� *chetti*.'

"*Chuh*�*keh*�*tee*," Maya repeated, sounding out the syllables. "Rhymes with spaghetti."

"Like tapas, right?"

She nodded. "Finger foods. Normally eaten with vino, although we should try a Spritz instead." My quizzical look signaled culinary ignorance, prompting Maya to educate. "Made with Prosecco and Aperol—a bitter alcohol. Mix them together and they turn a bright orange color." I must have looked doubtful because she laughed and added, "Relax, you'll love it."

"So, what kinds of Cicchetti can you get this time of day?" I knew most of the Italian tapa bars didn't open until about 6pm, coinciding with the traditional late Italian dinner hour. What we needed for now was somewhere to just sit and relax. A few siesta snacks would only add to the ambiance, not to mention tide us over until dinner.

"Bruschetta usually," Maya answered. "Maybe some goat cheese crostinis. Or Carpaccio."

"Carpaccio? What's that?"

"Like steak tartare. Seasoned with lemon, mayonnaise, and honey."

"Raw beef?" I repeated, making a face. "Pass."

Still, I was game to try Italian tapas so we headed outside in search of the Italian version of a tapa bar. We walked a couple of blocks away, to where the walkway divided. The left fork, we already knew, led to wall-to-wall tourist shops. The right fork, on the other hand, led to a local bridge and then into the less touristed, more residential San Polo district. According to my guidebook, here is where a handful of smaller food bars can be found, the sort of which specialize in Cicchetti's.

A full city block occupied the space between the division of the two streets, with the main attraction being three competing seafood restaurants. We stopped in front of the first one to check out their dinner menu, posted on a fold-over chalkboard outside its entrance. A waiter wearing a knee-length white apron over black slacks stood beside it, chatting with passing people and handing out small yellow tickets.

He greeted us with a smile and handed each of us one of those yellow tickets. I glanced down at it. "For your pleasure: one drink. Gratis." I turned the card over to see if anything was written on the backside—there wasn't, while Maya engaged him in conversation.

"What's this for?" Maya asked him.

"Come for dinner tonight, and with the ticket we give you free drink."

"A drink of what?" Maya asked, sounding suspicious.

"Your choice," he answered. "Vino. Beer. Prosecco, maybe."

"How big a glass?"

He walked over to a nearby table and held up a standard sized wine glass by its stem. "Like this."

Maya nodded, then asked: "How's the food here? I keep hearing that Venice has some of the worst food in all of Italy."

The waiter stiffened at the unintended insult, but then cocked his head. "Is true if you eat near San Marco. Close to Piazza is more expensive, too. Eat here. Is better. And good price."

Maya should have just thanked him and shut up, but she couldn't let the subject go. "Yeah, well, it's easy to serve bad food and get away with it when tourists outnumber the locals. Who do you complain to if it's bad?"

"So many tourists take majority of meals in drive-through, so can't tell good from bad."

They stared at each other for a long minute, neither willing to back down. Finally Maya blinked. "Scuzi, I'm not trying to sound like a snotty tourist. Just saying." Then she explained that we were looking for a nice little cicchetti bar for now, something not too touristy but close enough to walk to in order to take a small siesta. Did he have any suggestions?"

He did, and proceeded to not only describe the place, but gave her detailed instructions on how to get there. In return, she promised we'd show up later this evening for dinner.

"Sure. Okay," he said, sounding like *that's what they all say* while handing each of us another ticket as a parting bribe. "Bring both."

"Two free drinks?" Maya asked.

He just gave us a bored smile and nodded. I didn't think he thought we'd return, even with a second ticket.

We collected more coupons from the other two restaurants as we walked along the road leading to the bridge. But no one else made the impression that the first guy did.

"I don't remember the name of the place," Maya said, leading the way over the bridge, "but he said lots of locals eat here, and not many tourists. They don't advertise, either. It's all word-of-mouth.

"Sounds good. You think you can find it?"

Maya laughed. "We'll soon find out. He said it's less than five minutes away."

After we crossed the bridge, and after turning left at the first intersection, we entered a noticeably quieter environment. At the end of the block, we spotted the flickering light of an ancient neon sign on the roof of the last building on this side of the water: *Cicchetti.*

"There it is," Maya said, pointing to a short, square building, the flickering neon sign serving as its only advertisement. The building itself was the last one in a series that could have doubled for warehouses. Most looked deserted.

Although the sidewalk dead-ended at the canal, a wrought-iron railing had been erected beginning at the point where the sidewalk and canal met. From there it continued along the waterway, running only as far as the length of the side of the building. It was an ingenious use of space in order to squeeze in a patron's patio in what had once been nothing but a side alleyway. A single strand of green and blue lights had been strung up high over the railing for decoration.

A padded seat had been attached to the wrought-iron railing. A weathered wooden plank fronted the seat, serving as a makeshift picnic table as well as the establishment's only claim to outside seating. Two couples sat at the far end, chatting in low voices over a plate of cheese and bread.

"I hope you're okay with my not wanting to do the tour," Maya began as I slid in behind the plank. "I just don't want to waste half the afternoon hearing about the exploits of some Venetian lothario."

I laughed. "It's okay. The tour is actually more about the prison's history than about Casanova. But you do get to see parts of the palace that you don't with any other tour—the torture chamber, for example."

Maya made a face and turned to greet the lone waiter, a youngish male who kept repeating, "No speekada Eengleesh," while handing over a pre-printed WiFi card.

I followed Maya's rapid-fire Italian as best I could as she ordered a Spritz for each of us and an assortment of the house's cicchetti's. The waiter nodded and walked away.

"House wine or a spritz for €1 each; cicchetti's are €4 for an assorted plate. Compare that to the €5 glass of vino and €1 per tapa at one of those touristy places near the Piazza," she said, tossing her backpack onto the table top opposite me.

"Or a €15 San Marco Bellini," I couldn't help but add, entering the code into my cell. Instantly, I heard the sound indicating an incoming text messages.

Maya flicked back her hair and removed her iPad from her backpack, then began walking toward the fence at the edge of the canal.

"So how are you going to pass the time while I'm off touring history?" I asked.

"I'll do some exploring on my own for a while. Finish my shopping. Maybe go buy that computer bag I saw before. For sure I'm heading back to Ferrovia to find my way over to the Salute cathedral. It's got to be gorgeous inside, what with three layers of arched windows around the entire basilica." As she talked, she snapped pictures of our little siesta spot, including a couple of selfies of the pair of us.

I read my text messages and couldn't help but laugh. "Oh God, everyone's texting me about those purses. At least six people are asking me to bring one back for them."

"That's what happens when you broadcast good deals from abroad," Maya said, returning to the table and stowing her iPad in the backpack. "You going to buy extras?" she asked, pulling out one of the brochures she'd picked up at the tourist office. She set it on the table in front of her and studied it for a moment.

"Maybe. We'll see," I said, glancing at another incoming message.

Maya flipped the brochure over to scan details on the back side. "Or maybe I'll hop a train and run over to Verona. It says here it's only a little over an hour away. And only €11 each way by train."

I looked up in surprise. "Why would you leave Venice this afternoon?"

"To see Romeo and Juliet's balcony, silly, why else?"

"That's not real," I said, blowing a raspberry. "It's all made up to con money from tourists who want to imagine they've seen something real of Shakespeare. There was no balcony in the play, anyway. It was an open window."

Maya didn't comment.

"The tour guides even tell you the balcony wasn't part of the original building," I continued. "You'll pay about ten euros to go inside and see a replica of Juliet's bed. Big deal. But hey, to make the trip worthwhile, check out the statue of Juliet in the garden next to the house. They say if you rub her breast, it'll bring you luck in finding your one true love!"

"You figure it'll take me more than three hours to do a quick turnaround?"

I nodded. "Yep. And that's not counting streets filled with slow moving tourists. Tell you what: if you're bound to go see it, why don't you get up early and do it tomorrow? I'll sleep in. We can meet up afterward."

"Yeah, that's a thought."

"Only problem is, God forbid, what if something happens and you don't make it back? How would I even know where you were?"

"That's the beauty of WhatsApp," Maya said, pointing to her iPad. "It's free so I can call or text you. This will be my turn to explore history."

I laughed. "I'm exploring history, Maya. Romeo and Juliet's balcony isn't real so it isn't history. It's new-age tourism, that's all." Maya opened her mouth to defend herself the same time the waiter returned with our order, so we quit talking to focus on sliding our possessions to a vacant spot on the table. "I'm not trying to insult you," I clarified, reaching for the orange-colored Spritz, careful not to knock the orange slice off the rim of the glass. "It's just that people your age hardly know anything of history anymore."

"It's boring," Maya whined, grabbing a crostini with a slice of prosciutto on a bed of goat cheese.

"But it was those boring figures of history who helped usher in major changes during the Middle Ages." I took a sip of the Spritz, then held the glass up and examined its color. "This stuff is really good. What's in it again?"

"Prosecco and Aperol," Maya answered. "Kinda like Campari . . . gives the citrus a faint bitter flavor."

"It's delicious."

"It's Italian," Maya said with a shrug before reaching for another crostini. "So, when exactly were the Middle Ages?"

"Between the time of the Roman Empire and the Renaissance. If I remember correctly, the period lasted about a thousand years. Venice was a wealthy and powerful Republic for a large part of it."

"Oh? How did they manage that?"

"It was originally a trading center, controlled by a small group of merchants who defended the city against all invaders. Under their guidance, it became a major port for departing crusaders. The crusades, like piracy, was as much about plunder as it was about religion. It was even promoted by the Pope, who militarized the Catholic church in order to get in on the profits. Continuous warfare is always profitable for the ruling class, and the merchants of Venice soaked it up. In the end, though, it was Napoleon who destroyed it."

"It's always about money, isn't it?" Maya asked, eating her orange slice.

"It is if you study history-changing individuals. Take Charlemagne, for example . . . "

"Who?"

"Charlemagne. Warring German ruler. Endorsed by the Pope, who ended up crowning him the first Holy Roman Emperor. Probably for a share of future profits."

"Never heard of him."

"Charlemagne was the only king who ever managed to unify Europe in order to rule it. Supposedly he was the inspiration for both Napoleon and Hitler.

"Those two I've heard of."

"How about Richard the Lionheart," I said. "Ever heard of him? He led one of the more profitable crusades. Another was . . . "

"Captain Hook," Maya interrupted, laughing at her own joke.

I choked on a crostini. "Jesus Maya, be serious."

"Okay. Okay. How about your Casanova? Just what impact did he make?"

"He was a fascinating guy. A lawyer. A medic. A clergyman. A con man. Need I add, a politician? He instituted the National Lottery of France. Made a fortune from it, too, but then he lost it all gambling. He tried doing the same thing in Russia, but Catherine the Great told him to take a hike."

"So, how exactly did he alter history?"

"Well, he managed to infect hundreds of women with syphilis, from Venice to Paris, to London, to St. Petersburg and back to Venice again. All before penicillin was discovered. You have to wonder how many thousands died as a result of his amorous pursuits. We'll never know."

"Some legacy," Maya snorted.

I shrugged. "Like it or not, figures like him changed the course of history. Others, like Napoleon, with his endless wars and pillaging led to the downfall of civilizations. It's important to learn what happened so we don't repeat those same mistakes over again. On the other hand, Martin Luther . . . "

"MLK?" May repeated sounding puzzled. "He's not from the Middle Ages."

"Not that one. The original Martin Luther, head of the anti-Catholic movement in seventeenth century Europe. He helped end the Catholic church's power over Europe."

"How'd he do that" Maya asked, draining the last of her Spritz, and signaling for another.

"He exposed the corruption of the Church's leadership, and the fact that the Pope had been exploiting the church for political power."

Maya shrugged. "So now there's Protestants. Big Deal. How do you know so much about this stuff, anyway?"

"Too many fifty-five-euro tours," I joked just as another message sounded. I paused to read it. At the same time the waiter returned with another pair of Spritzes.

Maya looked up and watched me as I read the long message, waiting for me to comment.

"Noggins," was all I said, making a face. I finished the last of my first spritz and reached for the second.

"I thought you blocked him," Maya said.

"I did. He must have guessed because this message came through as an email."

"Read it," Maya commanded.

"Ok: 'Remember how I said you owe me for your time off? Time to pay up, Hunter. I hear you found a deal on leather purses over there. I need one for my wife. Black. And make sure it's real leather, not that cheapo Chinese pleather.'"

Maya reached over and grabbed my phone. Using both hands, she shot off a reply before I could react. Then she smiled and slid the phone back to me.

"What did you do?" I asked.

She gave me a meaningful smile. "I just said, 'sure, no problem. How much do you want to pay?'"

We both laughed and raised our glasses in a toast. "He won't answer that one," I said. "I'll bet money on it. Not if he thinks I expect him to pay me back."

"But it was an order, wasn't it?" Maya said, biting her lip. "He does that all the time. He will punish you if you don't comply, you know that don't you? He's done that to me more than once. You have to wonder how the hell he ever got into management anyway."

"That's the million-dollar question. I guess it's easier to promote 'em up rather than kick 'em out. After all, Omega Air never makes mistakes."

"Did I tell you? I put in for the shift bid committee," Maya announced, changing the subject.

"What for?" It was painful to watch naïve young agents spend hours slaving over innovative work schedules, only to watch management dust off the same old tired schedule—unchanged in the least—just in time for the new bid. "Waste of time."

"One of these days we'll make a difference, you'll see. I'm not the only one who's sick and tired of working thirty-five-hour weeks and being labeled part-time. Since when are thirty-five hours part time, anyway?"

I agreed. "It should be half what full-timers work. Especially when you're only awarded half the full-time vacation credit for those hours. That's robbery."

Maya nodded. "I'm suggesting that the company offer part-timers a selection of fifteen, twenty, or even thirty-hour lines."

"You'd be better off floating your idea to Noggins. Let him pass it upward through channels."

"Why? He'll just take credit for it."

"So? What do you care as long as you get what you want in the end? Who knows, he just might manage to make a dent. He is, after all, a bona fide member of leadership."

Maya nodded. "Yeah, I'll admit to that much. Maybe if he gets credit, they'll promote him out."

"Dream on," I wisecracked. "While you're at it, suggest that vacation time be awarded based on total hours worked. That one will have to work its way up to corporate, but believe me, you mention something noteworthy like that and Noggins will be all over it."

"Do you think it could get him promoted out of the station?" Maya asked, sounding hopeful.

I shook my head. "He won't go. Why go somewhere where you may actually have to do some work? No, he's got it made right where he's at."

Maya hesitated, but then changed her mind. "You don't think we're being too hard on the old goat, do you?"

I took a deep breath, trying to decide how much to say. "Remember when your mom was in the hospital last year, and you needed time off to be with her? Remember how Noggins made you use all your vacation time just to get off at all?"

"Oh yeah, I forgot. Every hour had to be accounted for. He wouldn't even let me use sick leave because he said sick leave was only for when I was sick. Ended up I had to take leave without pay—plus bring him back a stupid bottle of Uzo from Greece months later."

"And yet he averages a week a month off."

Maya cocked her head. "That much? Wow! I've always heard he abuses time off, but I always assumed those were just exaggerations from everybody he's pissed off." Then it dawned on her. "A week a month? You sure? That's twelve weeks a year! Nobody in this company gets that much vacation time, leadership or not."

I nodded. "Positive. Though it's not all vacation time. A comp day every pay period. Family emergency here and there. Half days galore. Vacation week every other month. Airline management are just like politicians: an elite club exempt from all normal business constraints. Who's going to stop them? In a real business setting people like him would have been fired a long time ago."

"Too bad someone doesn't investigate him."

I laughed. "They're all hiding out in their little offices, passing emails. Or attending meetings. As long as we get the flights out on time, who's to know that management is AWOL?"

"We know!" Maya stressed. "Look at how these rumors have followed Noggins from one department to another." Then another thought dawned on her. "How do you know his time-off abuse is true, anyway?"

"I've been tracking it for over a year now. It's just a little insurance policy for my own protection."

"Why on earth do need an insurance policy?" Maya asked.

I sighed. "It started right after Noggins transferred upstairs from the ramp. I was pulling a jetway off an airplane, guided by the ramp agent. The air conditioning hose was still attached . . . "

"Normal procedure," Maya added.

"I know. But the hose was too short for that jetway. When it broke free, it bent the door hinge on the belly of the aircraft, so it wouldn't re-latch. Noggins blamed me and wrote it up as 'agent caused aircraft damage.'"

"But it wasn't your fault! Not if the ramp agent waived you off," Maya exclaimed sounding incredulous.

"Exactly. I think because Noggins was new to customer service, he was hell-bent to make his mark as a manager to be feared, so he decided to make an example of someone. The damage was so minor—it took less than fifteen minutes to repair—that his case against me was overkill. Everyone knew it. Still, it was a fifteen-minute delay. Somebody had to get blamed for it, so he chose me rather than rightfully give it to the ramp—the ramp he'd recently vacated; the ramp where pro union votes originate."

"But it wasn't your fault!" Maya repeated. "You don't just transfer in and then try to hang a twenty plus year employee like you would a new-hire unless you've got a really good case."

"You'd think," I said, nodding my agreement, taking another sip of my drink. "He suspended me, pending investigation. I was cleared, naturally."

Maya smiled. "So now you've got the goods on him should he ever try to heavy-hand you like that again."

"Like I said, it's for my own protection. What else could I do?"

"So, what's the verdict? Maya asked. "Is he the big abuser they say he is?"

"See for yourself," I said, opening my phone to the note page reserved for Noggins time off and handing it over.

Maya scrolled through the entries, whistling softly as she scanned the pages. "Comp time? He has comp time? He never stays late!"

I just smiled.

When Maya handed my phone back, I noticed the time. "Oh God, I have to go," I said. "No way am I going to be late for a fifty-five-euro tour!"

Maya pushed the last cicchetti toward me. "Eat it. It absorbs the alcohol, remember? The last thing we need is you getting lost or locked up in the Doges prison."

⌒ **Chapter 7** ⌒

The Doge's Palace and Prisons Secret Tour must have remained a well-guarded secret because only five of us showed up for it at the appointed hour. There we stood, waiting for our guide near the Palace's main entrance: a Japanese couple, a Scottish couple, and me. The Japanese pair seemed to understand English--though neither attempted to speak it. Their heads frequently bobbed up and down over their phones as they continually referred to either a translation app or its talk-to-text display.

The Scottish couple, of whom only the Mrs. appeared to be enthusiastic about the upcoming tour, was at the opposite end of the spectrum. Her husband made it abundantly clear that he was doing this tour against his will. "Can't expect much enlightenment from a culture that endured while sitting atop Europe's most glorified sewer, now can we?" he announced in a thick brogue. Me? Well, I said as little as possible. After all, I was here to soak up some history.

Our guide, a tall, emaciated-looking female with dark hair piled in a tight knot high atop her head, in stark contrast to skin as white as those Venetian carnival masks you see everywhere, showed up at the appointed hour and not a minute earlier. In spite of the afternoon heat, she was wrapped in a well-worn sweater, which she picked at constantly when she wasn't pushing a pair of thick black-rimmed glasses up her nose with the back of her hand. Her accent was thick, making it difficult to understand her right from the beginning. I'm not even sure I got her name right when she introduced herself: Adalgisa.

We followed her into the Palace via a secondary entrance door, skipping the long line of frowning faces standing in front of the main entrance. The minute we stepped inside, the wealth on display took our breath away. The entire ceiling was covered in original paintings, each one set inside ornate gold frames. The middle ceiling section was arched upward—reminiscent of the Sistine Chapel—and showcased at least a dozen paintings, each bordered with gold filagree. All the great artists were represented in this entrance hall: Michelangelo, Tintoretto, Leonardo as well as other names I didn't recognize. The polished floor was made of an intricately designed multi-toned marble.

"Since Venice is located on the Adriatic, it was closer to the Byzantine realm of influence than anywhere else, so naturally the architectural style of the Palace is more Byzantine than Roman."

All five of us listened intently while adjusting to Adalgisa's tortured English pronunciations. Even the Japanese deserted their phone's translation app minutes into the tour, probably because the app failed the accent test, too.

"Ancient Venice was all about trade, politics, and justice," Adalgisa began, launching into what sounded suspiciously like a memorized speech as she led us up a steep, curving wooden staircase inlaid with a ribbon of gold. "The Republic of Venice was ruled as an aristocratic oligarchy consisting of some twenty to thirty families from Venice's urban nobility. It was this group who elected the Doge, and also participated in the daily governing of the state. They were predominantly merchants, with income from trading with the East and other entrepreneurial activities, from which they all became incredibly wealthy. The fundamental item of trade throughout the Republic's eleven-hundred-year history was even more vital than oil is for us today: salt."

The Scotsman chuckled. "And we all know how a tight-knit group of incredibly wealthy men maintain their positions of power, don't we? They set up their own salt dehydration facilities and then set out to dominate the market."

Adalgisa ignored his comment. "This Palace was not only where the Doge—the elected ruler—functioned, this is where the Republic's laws . . . "

"The Doge of Venice, oftentimes translated as 'Duke', was elected for life, can you imagine?" added the Scotsman to no one in particular, ignoring the dirty look coming from his wife.

Adalgisa began again. "This is where the Republic's laws and its justice were determined. During the Middle Ages, justice was swift, ranging from prison terms, to sudden disappearances, even death sentences."

The Scotsman, listening intently with both hands clasped behind his back, nodded in agreement. "Often with no trial. Sometimes without even being informed of the reason for the arrest."

All heads turned to look at him, even Adalgisa, who ended up nodding a reluctant agreement. "There was, however," she clarified, "a system in place for Venetians to anonymously denunciate individuals they believed to be violating the law: the letter box. One, which dates back to 1618, adorns this very building. It can be found outside the main wall. This historic letterbox, known as '*bocce di leone*' depicts a lion of sorts, with a letter slot for a mouth. The lion, representative of the winged lion of St. Mark, is the symbol of Venice. This shows how much the Doge valued the opinions of ordinary citizens, and how seriously he took their complaints."

The Scotsman couldn't hold back any longer. "Yet these letter box denunciations were never used by ordinary citizens . . . "

"Cornelius, please," his wife hissed. "Stop interrupting."

"They were available throughout the city for any Venetian," Adalgisa insisted with a slightly raised voice. "For complaints ranging from say, trade disputes, to marketplace fraud."

"In theory, yes, but since the typical citizen of the Middle Ages was completely illiterate, I'd say it's a safe bet that these written complaints principally served members of the ruling elite."

Adalgisa seemed lost for words, but only for a moment. "The letter boxes assisted the Doge in maintaining law and order because, by law, the only accepted denunciations were those made against public officials, not private individuals."

"So, what you're saying then is that private citizens were pretty much left to duke out their complaints among themselves," concluded the Cornelius, determined to have the last word.

Finally, the Japanese man spoke up. "Sounds like during that period in history Venetians had to be wary of everyone."

The Scotsman flashed him a smile. "Exactly right! Especially when you consider that all proceedings were done in secret, and that their death sentences were without appeal. Great way to maintain law and order, ay? Not to mention keep a tight grip on tribunal power at the same time."

Adalgisa didn't comment. She just turned around and led us into the Great Council Chamber. "Needless to say, this room was even more huge back in the day," she said, stealing a wary glance at the Scotsman.

I looked over at him with a questioning look. How could the room have been larger in earlier times? He met my gaze, rolled his eyes, and shrugged.

"This is where the Senate would deliberate and come to agreements regarding financial matters and sentencing for prisoners."

"Excuse me," interrupted the Scotsman. "Wouldn't the prisoners have been interrogated first?"

"Sì. Sì, they were," Adalgisa answered with the beginnings of a frown. "In the dreaded Chamber of Torment, which we will arrive at presently. He would wait there in complete darkness, to be questioned, the entire time hearing screams of other inmates—not real screams, but rather screams made by paid actors to raise the fear level."

"He?" repeated the Scotsman in mock surprise. "No women prisoners, I take it?"

Adalgisa paused for a moment before pointing to a huge painting at the far end of the chamber. "This painting is the largest canvas oil painting in history. Is by Tintoretto and represents heaven on earth. It is said its purpose was to overlook the Council to remind them to make appropriate decisions."

"Appropriate to the crime, or for the continued power of the ruling elites?" asked Cornelius, giving the painting a second glance.

From the council room we walked into one of the attached palace wings, and from there into the private quarters of the Dodge. "As you can see, the rooms where the Dodge resided were quite small. They were intentionally less than what was afforded in private life so as to humble him. This was to remind him that his first priority was to the Republic, not himself."

The Scotsman let out a laugh. "We could use some of that reminding at home, couldn't we?"

Adalgisa waited as Cornelius' wife shushed him again, then continued. "The incoming Doge, would bring his own furniture from his private residence. Upon his death, his furnishings would be removed by his family to allow the new Doge to bring in his personal furnishings."

I was listening, but more than ready to get to the prison portion of the tour.

The Japanese woman hesitated, but then half-raised her hand. Adalgisa cocked her head and waited for the question. "How about his family? They live here also?"

The Scotsman answered before Adalgisa could mentally prepare a translation. "The majority of Venetian Doges were either widowers or so near retirement age that there was no living family presence."

Adalgisa nodded. "Better for focus on running the Republic." Then she reverted back to her presentation. "The Council consisted of male members over age twenty-five, all from elite Venetian families regardless of their status, merits, or wealth . . . "

The Scotsman cleared his throat, causing Adalgisa to clench her jaw and pause. She gave him a long stare.

"They were all elites, and since all elites were wealthy, isn't it pointless to say 'regardless of wealth'?"

"Not if you consider that some were wealthier than others."

Cornelius shrugged. "Tomato, tomatoe."

"While not a democracy as it's known today, the Venetian system maintained very specific checks and balances, which did not allow for any one person to gain too much power, including the Doge himself. I remind you it was a system that lasted for more than one thousand years."

The Scotsman smiled. "Do tell us more about these checks and balances."

"The Doge's Palace was similar to your Downing Street, where the head of state lives. There were many people working with him—advisors and Senators, for example, thus ensuring that no one group could obtain total power."

"Always sounds good in theory," Cornelius agreed, nodding. "Though it never quite works out the way it should in practice, does it?"

"The degree of complexity of the Venetian government system was very high, yet very clear so as to prevent misunderstandings," explained Adalgisa. "Every part of the government was strictly controlled by multiple councils. Lawbreaking by political figures was punished severely to be an example to others."

"Which proved to be the beginning of the end, unfortunately," Cornelius said, interrupting. "Sure, the Doge had great power . . . at first. However, the entire system eventually devolved into one of constant and strict surveillance by every member of those governing councils, until ultimately everyone was surveilling everyone else. Classic case of too many cooks in the kitchen."

Adalgisa ignored Cornelius' wisecrack by turning and opening a small wooden door, unnoticed until now. Suddenly, gone were the golden decorations, the high ceilings and polished marble floors. Gone was the bright mid-day light as we stooped to pass through the low doorway in order to enter a silent and solemn world filled with dark, windowless hallways and low ceilings. In fact, even the air here smelled different. It smelled old. And stuffy. The temperature in this part of the building was noticeably cooler. Hard to believe that nothing but a thin wall of wood and stone separated us and this new all-encompassing ugliness from the previous world of unimagined opulence and grandeur.

"Upon sentencing, the condemned would be sent to prison," Adalgisa continued in a subdued voice. "There were originally two separate prisons inside the Doge's Palace: the Pozzi and the Piombi. We are now inside the Pozzi—called *Wells* in Italian, named for their location deep inside the Palace. This was one of the worst places to be locked up in. The stone walls had no windows and thus, no ventilation . . . made worse by the fact that it reeked of human excrement."

Even though there was no such current stench, all of us involuntarily sniffed the air, then laughed self-consciously at our own suggestibility.

Adalgisa continued. "The structure here is made of Istrian stone. During the Middle Ages this area was completely covered with wood boards, from the walls to the floor, often also the ceiling. The only furniture was a table, which doubled as a bed. Only prisoners found guilty of the most serious crimes were locked up here."

"Politically serious crimes," Cornelius agreed. "From where, I should think, no one ever got out alive."

The light was so dim that it was difficult to see clearly. The walls were made of heavy stone blocks, with the occasional hole chiseled through for ventilation. It smelled musty—almost moldy, no doubt from the constant moisture. The cobblestone path leading us around the corridor was made of wide and uneven reddish bricks. Our whispers bounced off the stone and back at us, making our voices sound distorted and creepy.

I stretched out my arms to guesstimate the width of the corridor and came to within inches of touching a wall on each side. The cave-like stone cells with their domed ceilings appeared more likely to have been built for a wine cellar than for human habitation. Thick metal bars had been set into the upper portion of abnormally short wooden doors all along the corridor. A heavy metal bolt extended across the width of each door.

As we stood there staring at the empty cell, the thought struck me that we hadn't seen or heard another person or tour group since entering the prison. Were we the only ones here? If any of us suffered from claustrophobia, now would be the time to start exhibiting symptoms. But everyone just stood there, staring into the empty caves, lost in thought.

Cornelius spoke up in a soft voice. "The floor of the Wells was so low that during periods of high tides they flooded, thus becoming actual wells. Many a prisoner drowned here, forgotten or unnoticed until long after the waters receded." The scene he described was made worse by the muffled echo of his words as they bounced back from the empty cavern.

Adalgisa stared at Cornelius for a moment, then resumed the tour. "There are two identical floors like this, each with nine cells. They were built in concentric circles, with a corridor surrounding them. Only the keepers circulated, primarily for surveillance and to administer food rations through those small windows you see cut in each cell's door."

"Those iron-barred windows," clarified Cornelius.

"This meant the prisoners had no contact with the outside world. No fresh air. No sunlight. So, they were unable to distinguish day from night."

Cornelius pointed to one of the cells. "The ceilings are so low I'd imagine the majority of prisoners were unable to assume an upright position."

"Eventually the Council recognized the need for more humane treatment of prisoners, and so authorized building a new prison," Adalgisa explained. "In fact, they named it 'New Prison.' It is connected to the judicial court via what is now known as the 'Bridge of Sighs.' This title was because of the prisoners' expression at seeing their families for the last time before being escorted away."

"How many prisoners did this new prison hold?" asked the Japanese man.

Adalgisa was at a loss to quote numbers, but managed to sneak a glance at Cornelius.

Cornelius cleared his throat. "The New Prison was able to accommodate about four hundred prisoners. Compare that to the eighteen in the Pozzi, plus the six in the Piombi. Big difference."

Adalgisa flashed Cornelius a grateful half-smile. "It solved the Republic's prison overcrowding problem."

Cornelius shook his head. "No Lassie, what it solved was the increasing stench drifting ever upward into the sensitive nostrils that occupied the Palace."

"But it did solve the problem of where to put the ever-increasing number of prisoners," insisted Adalgisa.

Cornelius shook his head again. "Nonsense. What it solved was where to put all the new prisoners due to the Republic's ever-increasing number of crimes that called for punishment by imprisonment."

Adalgisa refused to comment further. Instead, she turned and led us up a set of rickety wooden stairs. They creaked as we followed. The wall along the staircase here was made of those same stone blocks. You could see they'd once been covered with wood. Portions of several planks had long since rotted away, exposing the crumbling mortar beneath. At the top of the stairs, we came to two small rooms, one on each side of the small square landing.

The inside of these rooms was a statement of the elite's wealth and power. The walls of both rooms were covered with dark rich-looking Mahogany paneling and the floors were patterned with colored marble tiles.

Another short but steep staircase led us to a second paneled chamber: the Chamber of the Secret Chancellery. "As you can see, the walls here are lined with cabinets which once contained highly-classified documents detailing years of the magistrates work."

"Bureaucratic paper-pushers," Cornelius muttered from the back of the group. "Nothing ever changes."

"This is where the secret work of the Venetia empire took place," Adalgisa continued as we followed her through another heavy wooden doorway. "The chancellor ruled over this part of the palace, and as such he was in charge of prisoner confessions and sentences. From here the Council of Ten would determine sentencing in the Council Chamber."

"Assuming the prisoner survived the interrogation, that is," summed Cornelius.

Adalgisa nodded. "Yes. But in fairness to the accused, the Venetian court always went through various procedural steps to determine guilt of crimes."

"Of course they did," our Scottish friend agreed, sounding sarcastic. "For some well-connected prisoners, they probably did. But not for all. Take Casanova, for example. He wrote about it in his memoir: *Histoire de ma vie*. He was never notified of any charges; he was simply arrested and tossed into jail with a five-year sentence already sealed by the Chamber before they ever shut the door on his cell."

"Cornelius," his wife hissed. "Stop interfering! I, for one, want to hear what she has to say."

Cornelius clenched his jaw but said nothing.

Adalgisa took a deep breath then exhaled loudly. I felt sure she was hoping Cornelius would listen to his wife. "The last degree of justice was exercised by the Council of Ten. They deliberated in absolute secrecy."

Cornelius, shook off his wife's arm. "And what a degree of justice it was! During their trials no one could enter the Hall! No one! Not even the accused! The trial consisted of nothing more than reading a couple of statements regarding the defense and the accused, then the verdict was decided by a single vote requiring an 80% majority. A full workday, don't you agree? No doubt finished with plenty of time to spare for a Spritz or two and a leisurely lunch."

"Trial by Inquisition," summed the Japanese gentleman.

Adalgisa didn't comment as she led us deeper into the attic rooms. "The Inquisitorial Chamber was established to protect state secrets. It consisted of three Inquisitors who used spies to get the information they needed."

"As well as torture, let us not forget," reminded Cornelius.

"They used to meet right here in this room," Adalgisa said, barely managing to perform a half-twirl with outstretched arms inside the cramped quarters. Then, with a nod to Cornelius, she added, "Right above us is where Casanova's prison cell is located."

"First or second cell?" asked Cornelius in spite of another shush from his wife.

First or second cell? I asked myself, puzzled. What was that about?

"First," answered Adalgisa, leading us into a side room and launching into the rest of her speech. "Various forms of physical and mental torture were applied in this interrogation room."

"Ah, the dreaded torture chamber," muttered Cornelius.

A lone wooden stairway consisting of only three steps sat in the middle of the otherwise bare room. Above it hung a frayed, thick rope, which had been tethered somewhere up in the rafters. I looked up and barely managed to see the other end of the rope dangling over the top of a large metal wheel.

"Here is where criminals were pulled up with their arms tied behind their back—a very painful position to be questioned in. This torture would continue until the prisoner confessed to the crime."

"Wouldn't take long, I'd say," mused Cornelius, staring up at the rope.

"Another method was also used with rope," continued Adalgisa, ignoring Cornelius. "This time the prisoner's wrists were tied and he was then pulled up and suspended like that until a confession was obtained. When held for a long time like that, this position caused muscle damage and circulation problems."

"I'm no expert," suggested Cornelius, "but I should think any kind of torture applied long enough would lead to a confession . . . or death."

Adalgisa ignored him. Instead, she turned and opened a small wooden door leading to where a series of cells had been constructed on the far side of the room. The six cells stood side-by-side, and were built of heavy wood partitions to which sheets of iron had been attached. The temperature was noticeably hotter up here. "This is the Piombi. Its name refers to its position directly beneath the palace roof, which is covered with plates of lead. This site was reserved for prisoners of higher status as well for certain types of offenders . . . "

"Political prisoners, defrocked priests, and high-interest moneylenders," Cornelius informed us. "Most hailing from the elite class, unsurprisingly. Or those with connections to noble benefactors."

"Sì," agreed Adalgisa. "Casanova being the most famous prisoner ever locked up here. He was sentenced to five years after the Inquisitor's spies accused him of being a card sharp, a con man, a Freemason, an astrologer, and a blasphemer."

Cornelius warmed to the subject. "All no doubt true. Casanova was a cad in the truest sense of the word. But technically his arrest was for 'Public Outrages of the Holy Religion.' In all likelihood though, it was nothing more than retaliation for his attentions to one of the Inquisitor's mistresses."

"You mean Casanova seduced her?" asked the Japanese man.

"More than once, I should say," Cornelius answered with a hearty laugh.

Adalgisa cleared her throat to reclaim our attention. "He was placed in a room with clothing, a pallet bed, and an armchair . . . "

"With 'rats as big as rabbits' according to his memoir," added Cornelius.

Adalgisa ignored the comment and continued: "where he suffered greatly from the darkness, the summertime heat, and an affliction of fleas. Finally, on All Saint's Night, 31Oct 1756, with cunning and tenacity of spirit, he managed to break through the ceiling of his cell; he then pulled himself up through the hole and crossed to the outer roof like an acrobat, until he managed to reach a dormer window. After breaking the glass, he reentered the Palace. From there he went downstairs and out the front door."

Cornelius took a sharp breath. "No, no Lassie, it won't do at all to make his escape sound so simple. In actuality Casanova's escape was much more interesting. So interesting, in fact, that he penned a recounting of the deed, which turned out to be a Middle Ages best seller, one which placed him permanently on the pages of history. Why? Because he was the **only** inmate who ever escaped the escape-proof Doges prison. Shall I continue?" he asked, directing the question at Adalgisa.

She merely cocked her head and shrugged, which we all took as a go-ahead.

"Like most of the well-connected in Venetian society, Casanova had an outside benefactor, a Count Bragadin, who lobbied endlessly for Casanova to receive better food and better accommodations. In accordance, he was granted regular exercise walks along the prison garret. It was here that he stumbled upon a piece of black marble and an iron bar, which he then smuggled back to his room and hid inside his armchair. He spent countless weeks sharpening the bar into a spike. He then used this spike to gouge a hole through the wooden floor beneath his bed, knowing full well that his cell was directly above the Inquisitor's chamber. Then, just three days—three days, mind you!—before his intended escape—a day carefully planned to coincide with a festival when no officials would be in the chamber below—Count Bragadin's latest plea for better accommodations was honored, and Casanova was suddenly moved to a larger, brighter cell."

Adalgisa just stared at Cornelius, not saying a word. I felt sure that as a licensed guide she must have known the complete story of history's most famous escape, but for whatever reason she opted to give us the barest of facts. Maybe she opted for the short version because we were long overdue and she needed to end the tour. Cornelius, after all, had undoubtedly delayed us. At any rate, she kept quiet and joined the rest of us in listening to Cornelius.

"Eventually Casanova set upon another escape plan, this time with assistance from a prisoner in the adjacent cell: Father Balbi, a renegade priest. Casanova managed to keep the spike during his move to the second cell, as it was still hidden inside his armchair. In his published account of the escape, he maintained that he smuggled the spike to Father Balbi beneath a heaping mound of pasta, thanks to the unwitting assistance of an inept guard. It was the good Father who used the spike to make a hole in the ceiling of his own cell, and who then climbed across the rafters to Casanova's cell, where he set about making another hole. When Balbi finally broke through, he and Casanova together climbed their way upward onto the sloping roof of the Palace, where they painfully and slowly pried their way through a couple of lead plates."

"Did they drop down into the canal to escape?" asked the Japanese man.

"Certainly not. The drop was too great, the canal too shallow, and the water was a sewer. Casanova was far too smart to subject himself to hepatitis and God-knows-what-else by swimming his way to freedom. He and the good Father ended up prying open a grate covering a dormer window . . ."

Cornelius glanced at Adalgisa in acknowledgement of her earlier statement that they'd broken a glass window to gain reentry into the Palace. "With the aid of a ladder they found on the roof, as well as with a makeshift 'rope' fashioned from a bedsheet, they lowered themselves into a room some twenty feet below, where they changed clothes and took a well-deserved rest. Bright and early the next morning, they broke a lock on an exit door and casually entered one of the Palace corridors. From there they traveled downstairs where they convinced a guard they'd been inadvertently locked inside following an official function the night before. They walked outside to their first taste of freedom in more than a year at six the next morning. From there they escaped by gondola to the mainland. Ultimately Casanova made his way to Paris, where he remained in exile for the next eighteen years of his life."

"Whatever happened to Father Balbi?" I asked.

"Sadly, he disappeared into the annals of history," said Cornelius.

Adalgisa checked her watch. "Well, this two-hour tour has taken us nearly three hours. We must hurry to finish. With that, she turned and led us down two long flights of stairs. "This brings us to the Chamber of the Inquisitors. This much-feared group was established to protect Venetian state secrets."

"Not as zealous as the Spaniards, but all inquisitors earned their fear," added Cornelius.

Three hours? I asked myself. How was that possible? It didn't feel like the tour had gone on that long. Poor Maya, she must be wondering what happened to me. After all, we agreed to meet at the gelato stand around the corner from the palace more than an hour ago. I pulled out my phone to text her, but I couldn't get a signal. I had no choice but to rejoin the group for the conclusion of the tour.

I hurried down the stairs and caught up with the others in time to hear the Japanese woman ask what caused the Venetian Republic to end.

"The fall of the Republic was caused by a series of events that culminated on May twelfth . . . "

Cornelius interrupted immediately. "In a single word: Napoleon. It was, in truth, a long and complicated military double-cross, but the short version is that the young general had been sent on a mission to confront Austria by the newly formed French Republic during their revolutionary wars. He chose to travel through Venice, which was at that time, officially neutral. Why? Who can say? The Venetians reluctantly allowed him and his formidable army to enter their country. Then, in an act of unbridled aggression, Napoleon and his marauding mercenaries changed course and proceeded to thoroughly loot Venice. Furthermore, they stole, sank, or destroyed the entire Venetian Navy as well as its shipyard, a humiliating end to what had once been one of Europe's most powerful forces, thus bringing about the total annihilation of the longest-lived republic in history."

Adalgisa didn't comment, she just turned and opened a low door partially hidden behind her. One by one we ducked down and crossed over to the other side. And just like that we were back in the world of full-size oil paintings, ornate gold decorations, and marbled floors.

"I hope you are well satisfied with the fascinating knowledge you've gained today," Adalgisa said to the group in parting.

As soon as we said our goodbye's, I headed for the exit. I'm sure I wasn't alone in wondering if this was the same door that Casanova walked through so many hundreds of years ago. But when I heard Adalgisa call out to Cornelius, I turned around to see what she wanted.

"Who are you?" I heard her ask.

"Cornelius MacDonough, at your service," he answered cheerfully.

"What do you do? I mean how do you know . . . all this information?"

"History professor. Edinburg University. Doesn't do to just toss out bits and pieces and a few dates, Lassie. Not a bit. To make it memorable you've got to make it interesting." With that, he took his wife by the arm and steered her toward the exit.

‿ **Chapter 8** ‿

Maya and I had agreed to meet after my tour at the little gelato shop facing the canal behind the Palace, but she wasn't there by the time I finally arrived. On the other hand, since I was the one who was nearly an hour late, I would have been shocked to find her waiting. I decided to hang around until she showed up no matter how long it took, so I headed to the gelato shop and bought a double scoop and then scouted out a place to sit. I ended up on the front steps of the neighborhood church a couple of doors down. I only had to wait about twenty minutes.

"My God, what the hell happened to you?" Maya asked the minute she spotted me, covering the last couple of yards in an awkward gait what with two large shopping bags flapping against her side. Wispy tips of yellow feathers poked out over the top edge of one of the bags.

"Tour went late. I tried texting you, but I couldn't get a signal from inside the Palace."

"Sounds like that means you got your fifty-five euros worth."

"And more. How about you?" I asked, indicating the feathers poking out over the top of her bag. "What have you been up to?"

She plunked down on the church steps beside me, then carefully set the paper bags down on the ground between her feet. "I'll tell you all about it over dinner. But not now because I'm so full of gelato I'm ready to puke. Every trip back here to see if you'd shown up yet, I'd go buy another scoop or two."

I nodded. After all, it was my fault. "So, what's in the bag?" I asked, leaning over to take a peek.

Maya laughed in embarrassment. "I shouldn't have spent so much on a stupid mask, but I couldn't resist." As she talked, she pulled out a Carnival headpiece and mask combo topped with yellow feathers. In the middle of the mix was a handful of narrow brown speckled feathers. "Some kind of Italian pheasant, I think. Isn't it beautiful?"

"Beautiful might be a stretch," I answered. "But it's different, that's for sure."

The forehead covering consisted of stiff triangular pieces of brown and burgundy rhinestone encrusted fabric. Glued over that layer was a second intricately shaped piece of fabric with an enormous rhinestone affixed near the top. Spikes of golden beads on thin wires radiated out from it. Stiff golden shields covered the length of the mask down over the ears, ending in curved pieces that turned inward toward the mouth, reminiscent of Roman gladiator face shields. A second shield had been attached to the first, overlapping it, but then the top portion curved downward in order to cover the vulnerable neck. A turtleneck collar made of stiff fabric identical to the forehead piece encompassed the rest of the exposed neck area.

"How much did you have to pay for it?"

"You don't want to know," Maya said, laughing nervously.

"But I do."

"Way too much . . . "

I waited, curious.

"115 euros," she finally confessed.

"A hundred and fifteen euros!" I squealed. "And here you had a fit about spending fifty-five euros for a tour."

"I know. I know. I don't know what got into me. I shouldn't have bought it."

"Oh, don't sweat it, Maya. I once bought a Chinese peasant hat only to end up hanging the stupid thing on my kitchen wall. It's been up there collecting dust ever since. Total waste of money and energy. We all do it."

"But that's the thing, I usually don't."

"Live and learn," I said, shrugging, watching as Maya gently replaced the mask inside the paper shopping bag. "I have a friend who always used to preach: 'if you can't eat it or drink it, don't buy it.'"

"Words to live by," agreed Maya. "For next time."

"What's in your other bag?" I asked.

"I found that leather store again, so I went ahead and bought my laptop case. And two purses."

"Did you get a good deal?"

"I think so. They're good quality leather, and cheaper than what they cost back home."

I stared at Maya, waiting to hear prices, until she finally relented. "The computer bag was 90 euros. I got the purses for €35 each."

"Well, that wasn't awful." I said. And it wasn't.

"So, where do we want to go next?" Maya asked, happy to change the subject. "I hope you're not ready to eat yet though, because I still can't face any food."

"I thought we decided to do dinner at that restaurant over by the train station—the one where we got those free drink coupons. They don't serve until seven tonight."

"Oh yeah, that's right," Maya said. "How could I have forgotten about our free drinks? Free is always good."

Just then an idea struck: I pulled out my map and unfolded it out in front of us. "We're not that far from the Accademia bridge. How about making a quick run over there?"

"What for? What's to see there?"

"On my first trip here, I found a great little jewelry shop less than a block away from the bridge. It's on a short street that cuts straight across to the other side of the canal. And it's a non-touristy, very quiet area."

"Yeah?" asked Maya, giving the map a second glance. "What kinds of things do they sell?"

"The typical souvenir crap. Plus liquor. Pretty much the same stuff we've seen all over town, but we're so close. Besides, I haven't purchased much at all. This will give us a chance to see the last of the four bridges that span the whole canal. It's the only one we haven't seen yet."

I think Maya was so relieved to not be alone anymore that I could have suggested a bus ride to the airport and back and she would have agreed. So, without further discussion we stood up and made our way to the nearest vaporetto stop.

Less than twenty minutes later we pulled in at the ramp alongside the Accademia bridge. One block to the left and I found myself in familiar territory. "This street ends at the Zattere vaporetto stop," I said, spotting my little souvenir shop a short distance away. I didn't even look at the shop's name sign overhead; I only noticed the credit card stickers that covered the door window as we walked inside.

The front display case was filled with many of the same items we'd seen in the maze of tourist shops near the train station, although the prices here were much lower than anywhere else we'd been. The top of the counters were loaded with trays of jewelry: multi-colored paperweights (who uses those anymore?), round Murano glass wine bottle stoppers with stainless-steel ends, even cheap carnival masks. You name it, they had it.

I admit I went overboard on this last-chance shopping excursion, but I didn't care. I picked up a small basket from the stack next to the entrance and began adding items one-by-one: three wine bottle stoppers, five or six boxed Murano glass pendant & earring gift sets, plus four or five hand blown multi-colored glass hearts. There was a display stand on one of the cluttered counters that contained an assortment of Millefiori glass pendants, each a kaleidoscope of colors for the low price of six euros each.

"No chains attached," Maya whispered.

"Yeah, but six euros is six euros," I answered, adding five to my basket before Maya reacted.

"Holy crap! You keeping track of how much you're spending?"

I just shrugged. "I know, but these are great gifts. And you can only get them here. You want one? Pick one. My treat."

"So much for 'if you can't eat it or drink it, don't buy it,'" Maya whispered, checking out my basket again. Next thing I knew she headed over to the doorway and picked up a basket for herself, and was now following along behind me. With her large paper shopping bags dangling from one arm and the store basket from the other, I could hear her bumping her way down the narrow aisle behind me.

I tempered my impulse to grab one of everything after Maya reminded me of the cost, because even at the discounted prices found here, the price of all these souvenirs added up in a hurry. Finally, I called it quits and headed to the check-out counter.

"Do you discount if I pay cash?" I asked. I figured it couldn't hurt to try.

Maya rolled her eyes and hissed, "Oh God, not this again." She stood behind me, her credit card already out at the ready.

The clerk gave me one of those 'stupid tourist' smirks then shook her head. "No, because prices here are marked."

I had plenty of cash on hand, so figured I was in good shape no matter what the total came to. I pulled out my wallet and forked over two one-hundred-euro notes, and was in the process of pocketing the change when I happened to glance up above the rows of shelves. What I saw took my breath away. I just stood there staring with my mouth open. Hanging above the aisles all across the shop were least a dozen hand-blown Murano glass chandeliers in various sizes and colors. One in particular caught my attention.

Maya followed my gaze and groaned. "Are you crazy?"

"You know, I almost bought one of these on my first trip here. But I didn't. I regretted it for a long time afterward. I'd forgotten they even sold them here."

"Well then, I guess you'd better get one now or forever hold your peace," Maya said, sounding more resigned than supportive.

I wasn't sure if she meant it or not, but it didn't matter; I wanted one and it was now or never. "Exactly what I was thinking."

In a last-ditch effort to dissuade me from going ahead with the purchase, Maya asked, "What will your husband say about it?"

"Oh, he'll have a cow," I answered. "But he'll get over it."

The one I was interested in was an iridescent white color trimmed in a bright yellowish-gold. The color had been added as the molten glass was shaped, I knew from a previous Murano tour. It was delicate and detailed work, one which required years of training. On this particular model, the individual stems reached up high then arched downward until ending in two-toned tulip-shaped flowers. The stems were a pale milky-white color that had a dimpled pattern that had been configured into the glass as it cooled. The ruffled upper portion where the 'flower' attached to the stem looked like bands of gilded gold. At least four or five long-stemmed leaves had been added. Some of the leaves pointed up, others downward, and all were hand etched in that same yellowish-gold color. Ornate top and bottom end caps matched the color. In addition, I spotted at least three yellow daffodil flowers extended upward from somewhere near the center, all mounted on thin clear glass stems.

The smirk disappeared from the clerk's face the minute I pointed at the chandelier. "How much is that one?" I waited while she dragged a folded stepladder out from behind the counter and hauled it down the aisle. Once she opened it, she climbed up and verified with me exactly which chandelier I was inquiring about. "Four hundred eighty-two euros," she shouted, cocking her head to one side while waiting for me to comment. I felt sure she figured I was wasting her time.

"This is a three-light model, yes?" I asked, shielding my eyes from the store's overhead light glare while trying to count the total amount of lights.

"Sì," she said, letting go of the tag, preparing to climb down the ladder.

"Is that a five-light version, behind it?" I asked. It was identical except that even from this distance it obviously had more lights, more leaves, and more daffodils.

The clerk hesitated, then nodded.

"How much for that one?"

I heard her exhale. I knew she was getting irritated, but the promise of a sale won out and so she climbed down to move the ladder closer to my new selection, then climbed up to check the price. "Six hundred eighty-four euros."

"How much is shipping?" I asked.

"I don't know. I would have to compute it when I do the paperwork."

"Betcha it's every bit of a hundred bucks," Maya whispered over to me.

"What do you think?" I asked Maya. "I like the price of the smaller one better."

"I like them all," was Maya's immediate response. "Did you notice there are two designs? Some have the flowers pointing up, and others have them pointing down. "I think the ones pointing up throw off more light. But I guess it depends on where you're going to put it."

"In my entranceway," I mumbled, studying them both while the clerk remained on the ladder waiting for me to decide. I couldn't help but notice that the clerk didn't act like it was such a chore now like she did when I first inquired, which led me to suspect she must be getting a commission on the sale. In the end I chose the smaller of the two, with the lights facing down. While I searched for my credit card, a store helper began untangling chords to take my selection off the floor.

The clerk left the stepladder in the aisle, and returned to the check-out counter where she pulled out a heavy fold-over sales receipt book with shipping and customs information attached. She had to go to the back room twice to get the pattern name and model number off the sales tag in order to complete the order form. I handed over my U.S. driver's license for her to copy the delivery address. Finally, she turned the book around for me to print my telephone number and email address, and sign the form.

"I thought you didn't use plastic?" Maya whispered while I stood there with my credit card out waiting for the clerk to finish the paperwork.

"Whatever gave you that idea?"

"I don't know . . . you're always getting cash . . . all the bargaining . . . what you always say about cash is king."

"It is, that's why I always ask about a discount," I said. "Never know."

Maya suddenly thought of a question and turned to the clerk. "How about the wiring? Will this be wired for use in the USA?"

"Of course. These are customized in every detail. Is also well-packaged and insured. You should get it in about four weeks."

"Shipping costs €108," she finally announced. "You still want it?"

"It would be pretty awful if I said no now, wouldn't it?" I said to her, laughing. But she didn't understand me, so I shut up and handed over my card.

As soon as I received the shipping receipts, Maya and I headed outside, toward the Accademia bridge. "You want to walk or ride to the restaurant?"

"My feet say ride, but this is our last chance for shopping, so maybe we should walk. We have at least an hour to kill before the dinner hour starts."

"How about we ride part way then?" I suggested. "We need to get past the Rialto to get into the affordable shopping area. After that, off to the restaurant and dinner, then back to the hotel."

Maya agreed, so we hoisted our shopping bags and set off to the vaporetto landing. "Can you imagine how much we would have spent on vaporetto tickets if we hadn't bought the 48-hour pass?" Maya mused as we scanned our ticket and walked up the entrance ramp.

Have you ever noticed how it always seems to take less time going home that it did to get to wherever it was you were going to in the beginning? Our trip back toward the restaurant was the same. In what felt like mere minutes we arrived at the vaporetto stop just past the Rialto. Once we entered the familiar maze of shops, our walk morphed into a leisurely stroll of window shopping. The fact that we'd already been inside the majority of these stores at least once already removed any compulsion to go in again. The crowds were gone and the shops were nearly empty, since most of the tourists had already gone off in search of dinner.

Soon we came upon that same street with the racks of leather purses bordering open shop doors. Maya led me to the store where she bought her two purses . . . at least where she thought she bought them. "They all look alike."

I led the way inside with the intention to buy five or six to satisfy the requests of coworkers at home.

"Don't forget," reminded Maya, "Noggins wants you to get a black one for his wife."

I picked two off the rack outside. They were marked €38 each. I carried the bags over to the girl seated inside. "How much if I buy more than one?"

She stared at me for a long minute. "How many more?" she finally asked—in perfect English.

I shrugged. "I don't know . . . maybe six."

"€35 each." She continued to stare, waiting for my response.

I met her stare. "What if I buy ten?"

"Thirty euros each," she answered without pausing.

"How about if I buy twenty?" I was on a roll and couldn't stop.

"Twenty?" Maya exclaimed. "Are you nuts? What are you going to do with twenty purses?"

"€30 each." The clerk continued watching me, waiting for my reply.

"That's only an 8€ discount" I said to Maya, knowing full well the clerk understood. "That's hardly worth it." I did some quick math calculations: 27 euros x 20 bags = 540 euros. I had a little more than 400€ on me, if I remembered correctly.

"If I pay cash, that means no VAT tax for you," I prompted.

Now it was her turn to do the mental math. "Twenty-five euros each. Twenty for 500€. Cash."

I turned to Maya. "Do you have any cash on you at all?"

"What? Why would you ask me that? You know I don't carry cash."

I turned back to the clerk. "Where's the nearest cash machine?"

She pointed outside, to the right. "On the far side, against the wall."

Maya and I raced outside to the other side of the street, straight to the ATM. I inserted my debit card, but kept getting repeat reject messages, each one reminding me that I'd already enjoyed one withdrawal that day.

"Just use your credit card," Maya instructed.

"I would if I could, but I've never set up a pin for it. I doubt I can get a cash advance without one."

"As much as you've traveled, I can't believe you never . . . "

I cut her off midsentence. "I know. I know. Don't remind me. In the mean time I need a hundred euros, give or take, otherwise I'll have to go back and try to renegotiate a partial credit rate."

"Oh, hold on," Maya commanded, reaching into her purse for her credit card, then grabbed my arm and pulled me off to one side. "Here, let me give it a try."

"Seriously?" I asked. "If this works you can pick one out for yourself. Call it a reward."

"As long as you don't ask me to be your mule and help carry all this shit back to the hotel," she muttered, inserting her card. "You just better hope I can remember my pin." In short order €150 popped out and Maya handed it over. "I will take you up on your offer though. Make it a black bag, just like the one you're getting for Noggins."

We walked out of the purse store a short time later hauling two oversized black plastic bags containing a grand total of twenty-one purses, leaving me with the paltry sum of twenty-five euros. Even so, we laughed about our great shopping adventure all the way back to the restaurant.

At the restaurant, we took a minute to study the dinner specials posted on the menu board out front. They included pasta, fish, or lasagna for the price of twenty-two euros, along with a never-ending basket of garlic bread.

The aproned greeter took one look at all our shopping bags and led us to a table on the front veranda between the side wall and an empty table. We handed him our four drink coupons the minute we sat down. He acted like he wasn't going to accept all four until Maya talked him into bringing us a bottle of Prosecco in lieu of separate drinks. "Big tip," she said, smiling.

"Why are you promising him that?" I questioned, after he left. "You have zip for cash and I'm down to my last twenty-five euros. That pretty much leaves three euros for a tip."

"Relax," she insisted, pulling out her iPad. "We'll be gone before he'll have time to count it. Besides, you don't have to tip over here."

"Yeah, it'll probably be included in the final bill," I grumbled, searching through my purse for leftover coins. I came up with an additional fifteen euros was all.

The waiter returned in no time with two glasses and a perspiring bottle, along with a piece of paper containing the establishment's WIFI password. Next, he pulled out his notepad to take our orders. I ordered calamari and a salad. Maya chose the Italian version of meat-and-cheese-lovers lasagna.

"So, I'm still waiting to hear about how you came to buy that expensive carnival mask," I began the minute the waiter left. Prosecco in hand, it was time to recap.

"Don't ask me where that shop is cuz I'd never be able to find it again. All I know is it was deep inside that crazy maze of streets next to the Rialto. It was packed with every possible style—including those beaked doctor masks."

I shuddered. "Why would anyone buy one of those?"

"Probably no one does," Maya began, raising her glass to mine. "But they're authentic replicas of the ones used by doctors during the plague. The woman in the shop said they stuffed aromatic herbs inside the beak. She said it served as protection, since no one back then had any idea of how the plague spread. Did you know that Venice lost a third of their population to the plague?"

I nodded. "Not just Venice. Most of Europe did, too."

"That store had dozens of really fancy carnival dresses, too, just like the ones we saw over at San Marco. My God, would you believe some of them cost thousands of euros?"

"Who'd pay that much for a costume?" I laughed.

"Some do! There were two Brazilian couples in there, and they were both buying complete outfits. They dropped a small fortune on them."

While we waited for our food, I relayed the highlights of my prison tour. In the end, I think Maya was far happier from her carnival shopping expedition than she ever would have been with the prison tour.

"I never realized carnival was that big of a deal," she said, as her iPad chimed. "Do you know medieval Venice even passed a law authorizing three months of mask wearing? From Christmas to Lent." She leaned over her iPad and zeroed in on her messages.

"They needed a law for that?"

Maya nodded, preoccupied. "Probably because of the plague. And because 18th century morals were so bad, they needed official permission for any activities not specifically approved by the church. I'm talking extramarital affairs. Sure, these masks are mostly souvenirs now, but in the 1700's they were worn daily." She stopped talking long enough to focus on one of her messages.

Suddenly she put one hand over her mouth and looked up at me with wide eyes.

"What?" I asked, sensing trouble.

"Noggins," she said, laughing. "Guess some passenger showed up at the gate with two service dogs. The agent at the ticket counter said one of the dogs was muzzled when the woman checked in. She was in a wheelchair, and quoted disability rules forward and backward in order to get an okay for not one but two service animals. Well, the long and short of it was that by the time the woman got to the gate, both dogs were in her lap and the muzzle was gone."

"So?" I questioned, wondering where this was going.

"No muzzle," Maya repeated, as if no further explanation was necessary. But I frowned and shook my head. I still didn't get it.

"The gate agent got bit when she reached for the woman's boarding card! Reportedly, the little shit drew blood. What could the agent do but suspend boarding and call for a supervisor. Then the woman couldn't produce the animal's vaccination records. Said she put all that stuff in her checked bag."

"Oh wow," was all I could say. I'm glad I missed Noggins' wrathful fallout afterward.

"According to the computer, she had no checked bag! All her crap was allowed as carryon because she claimed they were all assistive medical devices."

"I swear these people must get some kind of professional coaching on these ADA rules. They know them better than we do."

Maya nodded with bright eyes and poured the last of the Prosecco. "But get this: Noggins wasn't in the building!"

"Don't tell me, another family emergency half-way through his shift?"

Maya glanced back at her messages. "A ramp supervisor finally came upstairs to talk to the woman. Meanwhile, the gate agent took off down the jetway and dispatched the airplane!" Maya dissolved into laughter as she finished the tale. "So she wouldn't take a delay!"

"Meaning she denied boarding to a disability passenger?" I asked in wonder at the thought of all the repercussions and investigations resulting from that hot potato.

Maya was still laughing. "Yep, all cuz of two snarling service animals."

"Noggins will skate, you watch," I ended. "He always does. No one's going to alert corporate of his shenanigans. And if they do, no one there will deal with one of their own."

"We'll see," was all Maya said as our food arrived.

Over dinner Maya talked about her walking excursion. "I was originally headed to the Salute cathedral," she began. "But I ended up detouring to go see Marco Polo's house."

"Venice's other famous native son," I added. "Good for you. What was it like?"

"It was a bitch finding his house. It took me over an hour! I went down alleys and across bridges. I had to stop and ask directions every couple of blocks. Then, once I did find the house, guess what? I couldn't go in!"

"Why not?"

"Because it's a private residence now! It's not even a museum. They just have a stupid plaque outside on the wall saying that this was the house where young Marco lived."

"Did the plaque tell you anything about him?" I asked.

"Not a thing. I stood outside and read about him in my guidebook," Maya said. "Quite a guy, let me tell you. Son of a wealthy merchant family. Did you know he set off on his epic journey when he was only seventeen? And he didn't return for twenty-four years! His poor family, they must have thought he was dead. But, once home, he got command of a Venetian galley . . . ended up getting captured by Genoa. They were at war with Venice then. He got captured. While he was in prison, he entertained other prisoners as well as the guards with stories of his travels throughout Asia."

"Which prison?" I asked wondering if it was one of the Doge's prisons. "Since Venice prisons didn't provide frills like pen and paper, it had to have been in Genoa."

Maya shrugged. "No idea. All I know is that he was there for three years. His cellmate wrote down all his stories and he had them published once he was set free. The book was a big hit at the time. In fact, they say his manuscript is originally what inspired Columbus to set sail for America."

While we were talking, a family arrived at a nearby table. I glanced their way and noticed two oversized yellow squirt-guns sitting out on a vacant table next to theirs. Maya followed my gaze and caught their attention. "What's with the water guns?" she asked.

I didn't understand much of the conversation that followed, but enough to know that Venetian hotels had recently declared war on the seagulls.

"Hotel gives us guns," the Mr. explained. "Gulls famous for flocking in San Marco. Known to grab pizza right outta hands. Pigeons, too. They land on expensive hotel balconies all around the square. Make-a da mess everywhere."

"Do they work?" asked Maya, pointing to the guns.

The whole family smiled and nodded. "Sì. Sì. The birds they recognize them now. so not so much necessary to use. Just keep them in sight on table."

"Well, no need to keep them on the table here," said the waiter standing nearby, waiting to take their order.

Finally, we called it a night and paid our bill. I used cash, and Maya used her card. I tossed the last of my euro coins on the table before we collected all our bags and headed out for the short walk back to Plaza Roma to catch the bus back to the hotel.

Once back in our hotel room we began the process of packing up. Since I didn't bring much in the first place, I didn't have much to pack. My main chore was inventorying the purses one last time, taking care to toss one over on Maya's bed.

Maya, meanwhile, had connected to the hotel's WiFi and was engrossed in a FaceTime video chat with her aunt at home. One by one she held up the two purses she'd bought as gifts, and finally her leather computer bag. She turned each item around and opened up their inside pockets for viewing while fielding constant questions and comments.

"How many?" I heard her aunt ask.

"Two."

"Why do we do this?" I interrupted, surveying the pile of souvenirs laying on the end of each our beds.

"Do what?" Maya asked, lowering the iPad.

"This..." I said, pointing at our pile of souvenirs. "I mean, look at all this stuff. All for gifts. Every trip, too. Why do we feel compelled to constantly buy gifts for everyone every time we go somewhere? You know what? For me, it ends here. Today. I'm not doing it anymore."

"Oh yes you will. I'd bet money on it."

Maya's aunt's voice cut through the air. "How many of those black ones did you get?"

"Two, I told you" Maya shouted in the direction of her iPad.

"You need three."

"One more?"

"Maybe two . . . just in case."

After Maya disconnected, she pulled a tape measure from her backpack and held it up to her new leather laptop case. "Crap!" she wailed, tossing the tape measure on the floor. "It's two inches too small! I'll have to exchange it tomorrow before we can catch a train to Bologna."

"No big deal, as long as you can find that same store again."

"I can now; I recorded the directions using that Voice Memo app. Walk and talk, so now it's a walk and listen. No big deal."

⌒ Chapter 9 ⌒

You'd think that on this, our last day in Venice, we would have been up bright and early. You'd think we would have been anxious to get started on part two of our little Italian excursion. You'd think. But you'd think wrong.

For whatever reason neither Maya nor I could get going that morning. We'd packed up our belongings the night before, so there wasn't much to do other than head out. I had plenty of room inside my wheelie for all my purchases, but poor Maya, she ended up having to move excess items into that "just in case" collapsible duffle, which was now already half full. So, along with having to half-pull, half-drag a two-tiered wheelie around thanks to a problematic wheel, she found it difficult to keep either of them upright because the bottom bag kept tilting sideways. I hesitated to suggest she repack them in order to balance out the load, however. I didn't want to hear one more time how I sounded 'just like her mother.'

"Why don't you just buy a new suitcase while you're exchanging that computer bag," I managed to suggest. "Maybe they'll have a cheap one."

Maya shot me a sideways frown. "I already have a cheap one. And look how far that's gotten me."

I shut up. Better say nothing than to add oil to her slow burn this early in the day.

In spite of our free hotel breakfast, this was the first morning that we'd actually taken the time to partake. Since it was long past sunrise on this visit, our entrance into the dining room was as though we'd never seen it before. Only a handful of people sat lingering over empty plates by the time we arrived. We claimed a table near the coffee machine and parked our bags. While Maya headed over to work the espresso machine, I strolled back to the entrance, to the large chandelier hanging there, in order to inspect it further in daylight.

It contained a mixture of pink flowers set against various shades and thicknesses of green stems. It was the traditional full-sized, five light model, with the lights facing upward. I stared at the circles of light reflected up on the ceiling and was thankful that the model I bought had its lights facing down.

"So, what's the plan?" asked Maya when she returned to our table carrying two steaming mugs of coffee. Balanced on top was a paper plate loaded with a pair of flaky croissants—days old by the looks of them.

"After we get downtown and get our bags locked up in storage, what are you going to do? Or did you want to come with me while I exchange the computer bag?"

"Not sure," I answered. "I'll probably just hang around outside the station and wait for you. I mean, how long do you figure you'll be gone?"

"That's just it, I don't know. You sure you don't mind waiting?"

"Nah, I'm old. The older I get, the easier it is to sit and wait. Besides, I have my kindle with me. I'll probably just sit on the steps outside of the train station and read. Or maybe I'll walk to the other side of the canal and take in the Salute Cathedral. Who knows."

"Too bad I didn't get to see it this trip," Maya said sounding wistful, her coffee cup suspended mid-way to her mouth. "I was going to, remember? Just like I was going to run over to Verona and see Romeo and Juliette's balcony."

"We could still do it," I suggested. "The trip's not over yet. We could forget about Bologna. Once our bags are out of the way, we'll be free to move around and do anything we want."

"I know. But we're running out of time. There's no way we can fit it all in today. I have to get this computer bag exchanged, and I have to get two more purses, remember? And that's before we even get started doing anything else."

"Can't you do both in the same neighborhood? Shouldn't take long. Better yet, just do the exchange now and buy your purses in Florence."

Maya took a couple of shallow breaths fighting against feeling overwhelmed. "No matter what we do, we'll have to store our bags. No way can I schlep these two around for long, not with that stupid wheel. If we go to Verona, we'd probably only have enough time to see the balcony. That means we'd have to take the train from there straight to Florence. And that means you'll miss out seeing your medieval surgery site in Bologna. I don't want to be responsible for that. How much time would we need to see both the balcony and do Bologna? I don't even know how long it takes to walk to either one of them from the station. It always takes longer than we plan. What are the train schedules like, anyway? Hell, I don't even know which way Florence is from here, do you? Or Verona? Or Bologna, for that matter." Poor Maya, she looked like she was going to cry.

I turned to my phone and pulled up a map I'd saved to photos during the trip planning. I enlarged the picture and studied it for a few minutes. "Verona is due east, which means we'd either have to store our bags at each stop along the way, or else double back here to get our bags before heading south to Florence. Bologna looks to be about half-way between here and Florence on a line going south-west."

"Meaning?" asked Maya, dabbing at her eyes.

"Meaning that realistically we only have enough time to do one side trip before heading to Florence, not both."

In the end we decided to stick to our original itinerary and forget about Verona. So, with a firm plan for the day in place, we headed to the front desk to turn in our keys before strolling outside into the bright sunshine pulling our bags behind us . . . well, I was pulling mine; Maya's wheel locked up in protest the minute it hit the rough pavement forcing her to half-drag it behind her.

We headed straight to Santa Lucia station, entering the cavernous building in search of the baggage storage office. The instructions I'd found online said 'ground floor, platform 1.' Sounded simple enough. But, in actuality, it wasn't until after we located Platform 1 and walked its full length that we even spotted the sign: *Deposito Bagagli*. It was posted so high up on the far wall that we almost missed it. A smaller sign next to the office's open half-door displayed storage prices: €6 for each bag, good for five hours. After that, the price increased hourly. Two couples stood off to the side of the doorway waiting to retrieve their items.

The minute Maya and I approached the window, we were greeted by what looked like an elderly pensioner wearing a pair of dark blue coveralls. "*Quanti*?" he asked, wiping his hands on his coveralls before reaching for a tag with a tail of string hanging from one end. Next, he pulled a pen out of the upper pocket of his bibs.

I glanced past him, at the cluttered room beyond. It looked identical to the behind-the-scenes chaos typical of any airline's baggage service office following a holiday or a weather day: rows of metal shelving filled to overflowing alongside alphabetized signs. Every shelf appeared filled with suitcases, baskets of small items, and large tubs containing multi-piece items. There was even a baby stroller parked at this end of one of the rows.

Two other men wearing identical blue coveralls scurried back and forth across the floor to squeeze in more items onto already packed shelves, or hauling items down and checking inventory tags against claim tickets before bringing them to owners waiting at the doorway.

"*Solo uno*," I answered, handing over my euro coins, while Maya not surprisingly plunked down her credit card.

"Honestly Maya, don't you even have six euros on you?" I asked.

She shook her head. "And It's not six. It's twelve. I've got two bags."

As soon as we received our claim tickets, the bottom half of the door opened to allow our bags inside. I couldn't help but watch the attendant's reaction after setting off with Maya's wheelie. He reached for the handle, but looked around in surprise at the rear wheel's instant squeal of protest. The bag didn't budge. The poor man, he walked around behind the bag and tried pushing it. It still didn't budge. So he finally bent over and hoisted the whole thing up in front of him and lugged it as far as the baby stroller, where it remained.

Maya never said a word as we turned away from the office and made our way back outside. "You're sure you don't mind waiting?" she asked one last time before departing.

"Nope. I'll be fine. You just stay safe out there," I teased.

As soon as Maya was out of sight, I made a beeline back inside to the ATM and make a €200 withdrawal. Instead of the usual payout of fives, tens, and 20s in colorful banknote bills, however, the money came out in a mixture of bills and coins. I didn't mind the unusual mix, as long as the total added up correctly. What I minded was getting a handful of those bronze 'throwaway' cents along with the €1 and €2 coins.

Those throwaway coins are more of a nuisance than anything else—comparable to receiving all your change in pennies back home. These coins come in 1, 2, and 5 cent denominations—amounts so small that no one wants them. In fact, I once witnessed a vendor cart operator toss a handful of them into the fountain behind him in a fit of anger rather than put them in his cashbox.

Assured that my change was correct, I folded the bills over and stashed them in the large pocket of my travel wallet. I dumped all those throwaway cents in a separate side zip pocket. Then the thought struck me that maybe I had enough to exchange them for a €1 coin.

I did a quick calculation to check, otherwise I'd end up looking for a fountain myself before this trip was over. Surprisingly I had enough, so I walked over to one of the manned ticket booths and inquired.

"Only if you use to buy a ticket," said the cashier.

I thanked him for nothing, then wandered out to the Trenitalia ticket machines to see what our travel options looked like for later. I checked the time. It was now 9:15, so I figured I should look for departures beginning around 11am.

I saw trains listed for Bologna departing at 11:26 and 11:40, as well as 11:45 am. Why so many at nearly the same time, I wondered? Further inspection revealed that the first train was a Frecciarosa (high-speed) of 1:33 duration. Tickets for that one cost €28. Wow! That was more than I expected. The second train was a *Regionale*, and thus slower, with a posted stopover in Mestre, the mainland station. Its travel time was 1:46 minutes. That wasn't all that much different from the non-stop high-speed train. Must be the thirteen-minute stop was just long enough for passengers to get onboard. The 11:45 departure was also a regional, but going through Padua instead of Mestre. The price for each of these two was a more affordable €12.35 each.

I made a mental note of a few other departures just in case the stars aligned and Maya returned earlier than expected. There was a 10:17, a 10:26, and a 10:29 departure. I didn't understand why there would be such a glut of trains all departing so close together, but rather than question it I decided to head to that little bakery just a block past the station. Maya and I had passed it countless times during our shopping forays and they always seemed to have a window filled with delicious-looking items. Better yet, there was a line-up of stools squeezed between the glass windows and the sidewalk, an ideal spot to munch and wait.

I arrived to see two hand-written signs taped to the windows on each side of the entrance door. Above the first set of stools the sign announced: **Croissant Eat Only.** On the other: **Cappuccino Only**. The women working behind the counter were all wearing official-looking white lab coats, reminiscent of those snotty perfume clerks at Sephora on the Champs-Éysées in Paris. These three were every bit as friendly.

The woman who waited on me refused to respond to my Italian, so I tried Spanish. It's close enough that a majority of the locals understand at least some of it. She just shrugged. I switched to English, but she made me repeat everything twice.

Finally, she asked what I wanted inside my croissant. She asked in Italian.

"Crema," I answered. Easily translated in any language.

She took off through a pair of double doors into the kitchen, and returned minutes later with all of a teaspoon of vanilla crème inserted through a miniscule surgical incision on the top of my not-so-fresh-looking croissant. I ordered a cappuccino to go with it. It came in a small white ceramic cup with a miniature spoon sitting on the accompanying saucer.

"Quanto?" I asked, reaching into my purse for my wallet. How much?

"Inside or out?" she responded. Again, in Italian.

I frowned, unsure of what she was asking. I didn't understand.

"Costs €2 extra for seat on sidewalk." This she said in heavily accented English.

"Por qua?" I asked.

She just shrugged, as though I didn't need to know. More likely she wasn't up to translate the reason why and so refused to try.

"Inside then," I said, eyeing a vacant space at one of the swivel stools lining the wall. There was even a thin ledge between the window and the stools where you could rest your cup while you were eating. All I knew was that I wasn't paying over $2 bucks to occupy a seat on the sidewalk for the length of time it takes to eat a croissant and drink a tiny cappuccino.

"Cinque euro," she said, drumming an index finger on the counter, indicating I should hurry up.

"Momento," I said, unzipping my travel wallet and pulling out three 2 euro coins. But as I before I'd managed to close my wallet, she'd plunked a handful of change on the countertop in front of me.

I was dumbfounded for a minute as to why she was giving me change before I'd even paid. But then I looked at the coins she'd laid out and it made perfect sense: she'd seen that I needed €1 worth of change and saw an opportunity to dump those nearly worthless throwaway coins on an unsuspecting tourist. It was an insult and I knew it. It was difficult enough to spend all those cents without getting more unnecessarily. No one wanted them. Neither did I.

"You shouldn't have bothered," I told her in English.

From the way she stiffened in reaction, I knew she understood. Nevertheless, she stood there giving me a level stare with angry eyes, waiting for me to pay.

I opened my wallet again and dropped my two one-euro coins back inside. Then I unzipped the side pocket where I'd been stashing all of those throwaway coins. Next, I began pulling them out one-by-one, stacking and counting—in English—beginning with the 1cent coins. I started a new pile every ten cents until all the 1 cent coins were gone. Then I switched to the 2 cent coins and began a new row. I continued until I'd laid out the last last of my 2 cent coins, ignoring the gathering lineup of spectators standing behind me. Eventually I laid out the last of my 5 cent coins, so I returned to the main compartment of my wallet and pulled out a solitary 50 cent coin, adding it next to all my wobbly piles. "Voilà!" I announced with a smile. "Cinque euros."

The clerk never said a word throughout the entire exchange, though her unhappy stare never left my face. "Bah," she finally spit out, as much as saying 'get lost.' She reached for the coins, meticulously picking up and counting each one. While she was busy counting, I picked up my croissant and cappuccino and headed for the lone remaining inside stool.

I left my cup, saucer and spoon on the ledge when I was finished, and doubled back to the train station where I took a seat on the steps out front. It was fun watching newly arriving tourists armed with high hopes, luggage and maps, all chattering about which direction to head first. Everyone, it seemed, was coming in rather than going out, understandable since it was still early in the day.

Small groups of people sat on the station steps alongside me in scattered groups. Those with snacks were busy shooing away growing flocks of pigeons. I looked across the canal at the landmark Salute Cathedral with its two domes, two bell towers, and octagon shaped white arches along its sides. Those sides were filled with statuary that I could see from here. Too bad Maya and I didn't have a chance to go inside it this trip. I checked my watch. It was already 10 o'clock. Did I have enough time to get over there? I guessed it wouldn't take more than an hour for a quick peek inside and be able to make it back to the station before Maya arrived. Why not?

I got up and headed toward the canal-side vaporetto schedule board to research the fastest way to get there. What I read made my heart sink. A €4 ferry traveled from here directly to the church, but it took 42 minutes to get there—and that wasn't counting the time I'd have to wait for the ferry to arrive. From the 'You-Are-Here' star on the map, it indicated that I could walk to Salute in 45 minutes. Either way, that didn't leave enough time. God forbid I wasn't here when Maya returned. I couldn't do that to her twice in as many days.

Back on the station steps, I looked out over the water at Salute again. It looked so close at hand that I found it hard to believe it would take a whole 45 minutes to walk there. But I believed the signs; they were designed for tourists, so they had to be accurate. I didn't want to just sit here doing nothing, either, so I decided to head out toward the maze of shopping streets and kill 30 minutes. Who knows, maybe I'd find something of interest while I was at it.

Fifteen minutes into my wandering, I spotted the boat. Actually, I heard it before I saw it. It was a bright blue color and sat low in the water. Its rear was red, with a red stripe along the body below the waterline. Two men stood up front, and a lone male manned the tiller in back. A silver tank occupied the entire center section, surrounded on each side by coiled hoses that appeared to be about 6" in diameter. I watched as it stopped just past a restaurant and a choreography of action among the three men took place.

The guy at the tiller applied the motor while using a steering oar to bring the boat right up next to the landing without stopping engines. The two at the front, meanwhile, each grabbed a different handle protruding from different sections of the coiled hose and dragged it off the boat, onto the sidewalk. The one at the front carried the hose inside the target building while the second jumped back onboard and fed out more hose until its forward progress stopped. Following a shout, the individual onboard scrambled to the top of the metal tank and started the siphon pump. Its noise was loud with rhythmic gurgling, but no one nearby seemed to notice. None of the ship's workers moved until the hose stopped twitching. Then as suddenly as it began, the process swung into reverse. As soon as the entire hose and both workers were back onboard, the boat motored away. Most tourists, I felt sure, never even noticed the *Pozzo Nero* sewage removal boat while sitting in their restaurant's scenic patio.

I began walking again, and soon came upon the shop where I bought all my purses. On the other side of the street, a short distance past the ATM, was a small grocery/sandwich shop. I checked my watch. I had plenty of time to enter and purchase a couple of bottles of water before it was time to return to the train station. On a whim I grabbed a couple of bags of salted nuts, too.

I ambled my way back to the station in the bright sunlight, enjoying my last few hours in Venice, when I spotted the sign: Hotel Ferrari. I remembered it's awful online picture. I hurried to cross the canal at the next bridge then doubled back to the hotel's entrance. Everything about it suggested old and cheap. Even the entrance carpet looked worn and threadbare. It was a perfect recommendation for Noggins, I told myself, grabbing one of their cards from the main desk before escaping outside to fresh air again.

Thankfully Maya was nowhere in sight when I made it back to Santa Lucia. In fact, it was another thirty minutes before she came rushing off the vaporetto. The minute I spotted her, I grabbed the plastic bag containing our lunch and stood up. I checked the time. It was already 11:15 am.

"My God," Maya began, joining alongside me in climbing the steps, "hardly any of the stores were open yet, so I had to wait. I mean, I found a few shops that were open, so I figured what the hell, and bought a couple more of those cheap beaded bracelets." She snorted. "I ended up all the way on the other side of the Rialto before I noticed the time. I had to hurry to find my leather shop again. That man, he was so nice, he swapped my bag without a single comment. Best of all, he didn't charge me any more."

"How about your Vaporetto ticket?" I asked. Since we'd originally purchased 48-hour tickets, ours were both expired by now. "Don't tell me you charged a one-way ticket?"

Maya's eyes widened. "Oh shit," was all she said through embarrassed laughter at the realization she'd ridden back here with no valid ticket in her possession.

"You're lucky they didn't catch you," I said. "Otherwise, they'd have fined you to hell and back."

"How big of a fine?" Maya asked as we approached the Trenitalia ticket machines inside the station entrance.

"Sixty euros, plus the price of a ticket. Or something like that."

Maya just shrugged, her attention focused on the list of Bologna trains and their prices.

We ended up buying cheap seats on the 11:45 departure. Thankfully, the Trenitalia ticket machines were models of efficiency requiring nothing more than punching a couple of buttons. One swipe of a credit-card later and out popped our tickets. No train number was on them. No assigned seating, either. In fact, the only thing I could read on my ticket was 'Self Service' and 'Via Padua.' The rest was a jumble of meaningless codes and numbers . . . much like airline tickets to novices, I suppose.

"I guess we'll have to check the entrance board to find our track number," I said, heading toward the tracks.

"Oh God, guess what we forgot?" I heard Maya wail from behind me.

I stopped and turned. "What?"

"Our bags," she said.

We both took off at a near-run to the end of track 1. Maya's bag, I couldn't help but notice, was still sitting alongside the baby stroller where the clerk had dumped it.

Once we had our luggage firmly in hand, we raced back to the front of the platform to find the information board and our assigned track number.

"Bologna Centrale, track 15," I announced, leading the way to the far side of the platform. We arrived just as the whistle blew. Maya scrambled onboard first while I hoisted her bag up so she could drag it over the edge and into the car. I tossed her tote up afterward, and then finally climbed up with my own wheelie behind me.

We marched straight inside to the cabin and sat down on the first seats we came to, delighted to see that no one else was onboard with us. We were still trying to catch our breath when the conductor entered.

"Oh crap," I heard Maya whisper. "We forgot to validate our tickets." She immediately jumped to her feet and began apologizing to him for our infraction, saying we'd been hurrying all morning long, and that it was all her fault . . ."

He closed his eyes and held up his hand for silence. He'd obviously heard every excuse in the book to escape the fine that accompanies this infraction, so her words now were just more of the same old excuse. When Maya stopped talking, he simply said, "*Treno sbagliato.*"

"Wrong train?" she repeated. "What do you mean wrong train?"

"*Sono le undici e quaranta. Hai prenotato peri le undici e quarantacinque.*"

"Eleven-forty or eleven forty-five, what's the difference?" Maya asked, gearing up for a verbal confrontation.

I didn't understand much of what followed, all I know is that he made it clear we couldn't stay on this train as he ushered us along with our baggage back to the doorway. Once there, he pointed at the next track over, telling us that was the track for our 11:45 departure. This train, the one we were on now, has no passengers, he explained. "Eez only going to Mestre for to begin journey to Bologna."

Maya would have stayed and argued the point, except for the fact that this conductor grabbed her wheelie by its handle and carried it down to ground level. But that didn't mean she didn't give him a verbal tongue-lashing throughout our disembarkation process. "I don't see what difference it makes. Five minutes, that's all! These are both *Regionales.* They cost the same. Ok, so one goes thru Mestre and the other goes through Padua, but we're not getting off at either stop. Wouldn't it be easier to just let us . . . ?" Meanwhile he turned his back on her to climb the steps, and disappeared inside.

She only shut up when the train began chugging down the track.

"How stinking rude was that?" Maya fumed, turning to me. Then her eyes opened wide and she laughed, pointing to the next track over. The 11:45 was just pulling in. The red lettering overhead left no doubt this was our train: Bologna Centrale

"Oh no, not again, Maya," I warned, handing her my ticket. "Quick, go find a validation machine before we end up getting fined."

⁓ Chapter 10 ⁓

The only thing I don't like about European train travel is the fact that half their seats face the wrong way—the wrong way for me, anyway. It might sound silly, but I have a motion problem that rears its ugly head whenever I ride facing backwards. It's not that I get sick right off the bat, just that I'm aware of growing discomfort the minute we start moving and so try to take steps to insure it doesn't escalate. That means I usually stare straight ahead, or at the horizon, and try not to turn my head.

So it was that when Maya and I boarded the Bologna train, I automatically gravitated to a seat facing forward near the back of the cabin—for easy access to the bathroom. Maya brought up the rear, tossing her backpack on the table between the two bench seats before attempting to wrestle her monstrous suitcase overhead.

I helped Maya lift her bag, in spite of her comments of: "It's okay; I can do it." Who was she fooling? She couldn't do it alone, and we both knew it.

As soon as our baggage was safely stowed overhead, we rushed to get seated in order to clear the aisle—a habit from years of airplane travel

"Did you remember to lock yours?" Maya asked. "We don't dare leave them at the station storage unless they're locked."

"We locked them up before we turned them in at the Venice baggage office, remember? They've been locked ever since."

"Oh jeez," Maya uttered after realizing that I was sitting beside her and that the seat facing us from the other side of the table was empty. "This just looks weird."

"I can't help it," I explained. "I can't bring myself to travel backwards for the next couple of hours."

Maya's eyes opened wide. "Or what? You telling me you'll toss your cookies?"

I shrugged. "I might, who knows? Point is, I don't want to take that chance."

Maya exhaled loudly, then stood up in order to scramble out of the seat, crawling over me in the process. She slid in on the other side of the table and leaned against the window with closed eyes to wait for our departure just as a hydraulic hissing alerted us to the opening of the rear cabin door.

Two youngish males, both speaking in rapid-fire Italian, scrambled onboard at the very last minute and made their way to an open set of seats at the front of the cabin. Without understanding all their words, it sounded like they were arguing about their tickets. They were still in the process of tossing backpacks up into the overhead rack when the train began moving.

I didn't even realize we were moving at first. Usually, you feel a bump as the car engages, then seconds later you feel the initial tug of forward momentum. Not this time. We just slid into forward and watched the scenery move as the train's speed increased.

A second hissing sound at the back of the car announced the conductor's entrance into the cabin. He began checking tickets of those seated in the last row of the cabin first. Most passengers, I noticed, had placed their tickets on the table for easy access while they were otherwise preoccupied with reading or texting. There was very little interaction between conductor and customer; he just scanned each ticket with his handheld machine, then put the ticket back on the table and moved on to the next passenger.

Maya held hers up when he arrived at our table. "See? We remembered this time!"

He never responded. Never even cracked a smile, in fact.

I rolled my eyes and groaned. "Oh jeez, Maya. He could care less."

"I was simply pointing out that we remembered to validate them this time," she said, shrugging.

I turned my attention to my phone, trying to get a Wi-Fi connection, but could not seem to connect. Figuring that it either wasn't offered on regional trains, or else it wasn't working, I set my phone aside and instead watched the conductor as he worked his way forward.

The first sound he made was when he asked the two late-arriving Italians for their tickets. That set off a barrage of fast-fire explanations from both men simultaneously. I understood little of the conversation, but I did understand that in their haste to make the train they'd forgotten to buy tickets. At least that's what one of them said. The other insisted he'd tried to purchase both their tickets but that none of the machines was working, a common excuse if the look on the conductor's face was any indication.

He was having none of it. "Hand over your identity documents," he said, pulling a two-way radio out of his hip holster, "or I will call for police to remove you the minute we reach Bologna."

Reluctantly, both complied. A long-winded conversation followed, with all three voices escalating each passing minute. Maya half-turned in her seat to watch the scene as it played out. She whispered occasional updates to me from behind a hand partially covering her mouth.

"He's giving them each a fine of €30. Plus, they still have to buy tickets . . ."

They didn't have tickets at all?" I whispered.

We paid €13.50 even though it was only for second class," Maya said, glancing down at her ticket. "Pretty cheap if you ask me." Then her head snapped up and swiveled to swatch the conductor. "Oh, wow! He's charging them €37.50 each, which is technically the first-class fare."

Another round of arguments ensued after the conductor advised the pair of their new €67.50 charge. They argued that if they were going to be assessed the first-class rate, then they should at least be allowed to move up to the first-class cabin. The conductor nixed that idea with a single emphatic, "No." After that, both men insisted they didn't have any means with which to pay.

The conductor's response to that was to-the-point. "Trenitalia will mail the bill to the address associated with your National Identity Cards. You get thirty days to pay or else a warrant goes out. Fines increase exponentially every day the payment is late."

"Can they do that?" I whispered to Maya.

Her eyes were as big and as round as saucers. "Sounds like they can pretty much do anything they want. We should have that kind of power as gate agents for misbehaving passengers. Fine 'em or kick 'em the hell off."

I bit my lip to hold back comments about what kinds of abuse that sort of authority would foster, but then changed my mind. "Can you imagine granting that kind of authority to someone like . . . like Noggins? Just think of the repercussions."

Maya's chin came up. "We're already dealing with that kind of unchecked authority, or have you forgotten? Our airport bullies can do whatever the hell they want. Question here is, is this conductor a lazy bully like Noggins, a corrupt thief, or a conscientious employee just doing his job?"

"Hard to say about this guy, but the mere fact he's the lone ticket enforcer onboard, I'd hazard a guess there's a lot of receipt malfunctions," I mumbled, turning my attention to the threesome up front again.

By now both Italians remembered they were wearing cash belts beneath their shirts, and inside that was . . . ta da! their credit cards. Neither said a word as they handed them over, watching silently as the conductor swiped each in quick succession into his hand-held machine.

"I saw that one coming," Maya said with a smug smile.

"At least they got receipts." I noted.

A young Italian couple sitting in the row opposite us began laughing after listening to our conversation. Maya shot them a sideways glance. "You laughing at us?"

"Sorry," the female half of the pair answered, twisting in her seat to face us. "We're not trying to be rude. Really, we're not. Your comment about remembering to validate your tickets was spot-on, because those fines are how Trenitalia makes money."

"Just like the how the airlines make money these days by charging for luggage," Maya added.

"Airlines now charge for bags?" her travel companion asked, sounding surprised at such an idea. "Which airlines?"

"All U.S. airlines," Maya and I answered in unison.

"Well, except for one." I clarified.

"They charge extra for good seats, too," Maya added.

The pair made a face and shook their heads. "We once forgot to validate our tickets. The conductor said he was going to charge us each a €30 fine, but first he insisted we get off and validate our tickets before the train's departure. That was an act of meanness. He could have just as easily validated them himself, especially since he was already planning to fine us. We stayed off rather than reboard and pay him. But when we got on the next train, that conductor yelled at us and threatened to fine us because our tickets were for the earlier train."

"Can they do that?" Maya asked.

Both of them nodded. "Technically on Regionals it doesn't matter which train you take," the female explained in good English. "But officials do things like this all the time. It's amazing what one lone conductor is free to do. All we can do is warn others that if you ever get fined, be sure to demand a receipt. Everyone knows if you pay cash, it will just find its way into the conductor's pocket."

"Sounds like an incentive to avoid Trenitalia," said Maya.

"That's the problem," the woman's companion noted. "You can't."

Before we knew it our train slowed down and pulled into Bologna Centrale. Maya and I pulled our wheelies down from the overhead rack and stood in line behind the others waiting to get off. The minute we stepped on the platform, we set off to search for the *Deposto Bagagli* office.

"There's the sign," Maya said, pointing toward a distant stairwell. It was nothing more than a pictogram of a suitcase mounted on the wall, with a red arrow pointing down the stairs.

Getting down those stairs was a real feat considering the state of Maya's locked suitcase wheel. Once on the lower level, we walked around the entire floor, but couldn't find any baggage storage office. On our second trip around, we spotted an identical pictogram, this time on the wall next to the steps leading back upstairs.

After we climbed back upstairs, we walked through the main gate and headed outside, thinking if the office wasn't inside, then surely it must be located outside. There, standing just to the right of the doorway we encountered an elderly man wearing those same official-looking blue coveralls that so many auxiliary Trenitalia employees always seem to be wearing.

"Where the hell is the bag deposit?" Maya asked him.

He gave a questioning look in answer.

"*Deposito bagagli?*" Maya repeated, this time in Italian.

He merely pointed back inside.

Instead of going inside and retracing our same steps again, we walked to the end of the building. There, we turned the corner and kept going until we came to an open door with an attendant on duty. Maya again repeated our question of the hour.

"Go back inside, and then go round back. It's on your left," he answered, in English.

So we turned around and retraced our steps back to the front of the building, and then walked inside and around back, as instructed. And there it was! A sign with a blue pictogram of a suitcase had been hung high up above a recessed doorway. Beneath the sign was an open half-door leading to the Bag Deposit office. A lone twenty-something female stood behind the service counter. Thankfully, no one nearby was waiting for luggage because both Maya and I knew it would take long minutes to get understandable directions once we were free of our bags.

I glanced into the depths of the office while Maya handled the bag check details. The shelves looked bare. No large items near or around the shelving units could be seen, either. "Doesn't look like they do a lot of business."

"Americanas!" the attendant gushed the minute she heard our English. "I have been! Once."

She seemed delighted to have a chance to practice her English with us, tagging our bags and then hauling them inside the office in mere minutes. "Where in America are you from?"

"Ohio," we told her, but received only a frown of incomprehension in return.

"It's in the middle of the country," I offered.

Maya nodded. "In what's sometimes called 'Flyover Country.'"

"Oh sure," the girl answered, frowning, clearly confused. "So, what else can I help you with today?"

"Can you give us directions to the anatomical museum?" I asked.

"Yeah sure," she answered. "I will try. But my English not so good."

She took a deep breath, then paused to mentally translate before speaking the next group of words. Maybe she was mentally conjugating verb tenses before speaking, who knew? In the end she did manage to give us understandable walking directions to the two towers.

She came out from behind her counter, turned and faced the front of the station, pointing at the exit. "You walk that way. Go to McDonalds on corner. Then you went . . . er, I mean go to right. Ten, maybe twenty minutes walking. You're there."

"And to the anatomic museum?" I asked again.

She tapped her foot in thought, but couldn't come up with the English words for how to find it. She laughed in embarrassment and ended up holding out her hands, palms upward in a sign of surrender.

"Can you tell us in Italian?" I suggested.

Not even Maya understood the fast jumble of words that followed. "All that and all she really said was to go find the tourist information office near the towers and hopefully they can take us."

"Crap," was my response. "How can one museum possibly be this difficult to find? Monique—you know, the easily distracted Monique from work. If she managed to find it, then it can't be all that difficult. Besides, it's supposedly world-famous!"

"Sounds like listening to Monique was your first mistake," Maya wisecracked, leading the way toward the station exit one more time.

Before we walked out the door however, we double checked the overhead departure board listings for Florence later that day. It was now 1:35 pm. I spotted regular departures every hour at twenty-seven minutes after the hour. Travel time, the board showed, was only 40 minutes.

"At least now we have a time we can plan around for later," I said to Maya, leading the way to the exit. "The last train leaves at 9:27 pm."

"Did you notice how much the tickets were?" quizzed Maya.

"Twenty to twenty-five bucks each."

From the front door we followed the sidewalk to the stoplight at the corner, then continued straight for a couple of blocks. At the golden arches, we turned right and continued walking, which, according to what we were told, should ultimately lead us into the historical section of Bologna.

The construction style of the buildings here was definitely from an older time. There was a covered walkway running the length of the block. Its ceiling, supported by high wooden archways that crossed overhead in regular intervals, connected to large square cement pillars bordering the street. Even the sidewalk appeared different from our more modern—and cheaper looking—poured concrete. Here, the walkway was a smooth, polished pattern of inlaid marble squares.

Those stone pillars bordering the walkway were a reddish-brown color. That color had been expertly matched, so that the wooden arches overhead appeared to be a continuation of the pillars. Between these overhead arches, the domed ceiling had been painted a yellowish color, giving the optical illusion of sunlight shining through from above. It was an enduring example of skilled Italian craftmanship.

The building styles changed every couple of blocks, each one looking more antiquated than the one before. We zigged at the next intersection, which led us into a block of painted concrete square buildings, each with ornate balconies protruding from upper floor windows. The most striking touch was the series of Roman-style stacked stone archways running along the entire length of the block. The street itself, sandwiched between buildings, was barely wide enough for two cars. A bus lane had been painted on the far side, effectively blocking that side of the street from traffic. Even so, a multitude of bicycles, Vespas, and small cars wove in and out at will. On our side of the street, the building front had been partitioned with oversized windows revealing a shopping mall inside.

"Oh God, look at that," squealed Maya, pointing at the Prada sign on the glass. "I wonder if the designer stuff is cheaper here than in Milan."

I reached for my guidebook and in short order discovered we'd arrived at the noted Galleria Cavour mall. "Want to go inside and price things out?" I suggested.

"What for? If we're not traveling to Milan, we'll have nothing to compare it to."

"There's the *Mezzo di Mercato* nearby. It says here" I noted, holding up my guidebook, "you can buy an Aperol spritz or an express pizza there for six euros."

Maya shook her head. "I don't have any cash on me, remember? We need to find a nice sit-down place that takes credit cards."

"Jeez, Maya. You gotta stop this no cash nonsense. It's just not practical."

"Well, for today at least, how about you cover all our cash expenses, and I'll settle up once we get back home?"

"You going to pay me back in cash?" I wisecracked. "Or write a check?"

"Neither. I'll Venmo you what I owe."

"I should charge you interest." Another half-joke.

"But you won't," Maya said, smiling. "Tell you what, I'll cover lunch today for this little service favor."

"Okay," I said, stuffing the guidebook back inside my tote bag. "Whatever."

We continued walking past the Galleria windows. All the major brands were advertised on those elongated glass windows: Armani, Bottegga Veneta, Dolce & Gabbana, Fendi, Ferragamo, Gucci, Marni, Prada, Valentino, and, of course, Versace. The mall continued for the length of the block. Plenty of couples and small groups stood outside, staring in. I couldn't help but wonder if they were afraid to go inside, for fear of finding something they liked and not being able to afford it. They gave new meaning to the term 'window shopping.'

In stark contrast, the building on the other side of the street contained no glass windows. Where there should have been windows, the openings had been boarded up. Even the upper story windows had been boarded shut. Black lettering had been spray painted over every conceivable portion of the plywood, but I couldn't make any of it out.

At the end of the block, the covered sidewalk abruptly ended, revealing a corner kiosk. A white canvas flap had been tossed back over the top, revealing a counter stacked with newspapers, magazines, and souvenirs. It reminded me of those tobacco/newspaper shops you see all over Europe, except that this one, in addition to selling the aforementioned products, boasted a display of leather goods hanging in haphazard rows all across the front and down both sides.

Maya gravitated to the stand. It didn't take long for her to pick out a reversable leather bag—black on the outside, cream colored on the inside, with handles long enough to wear as a shoulder bag. "*Quanto?*" she asked.

"What's the tag say?" the clerk seated inside responded.

"Smartass," Maya mumbled in answer, searching for the tag. "Ten euros!" She looked up at me in surprise. We both expected the price to be higher. "You got cash, right Sābra?"

"Was there ever any doubt?" I answered, reaching for my wallet. I dug out a twenty euro note. "Grab a second one while you're at it."

The closer we came to the historic center of town, the more the building styles changed. In just two short blocks, gone were the natural reddish-brown stone pillars, replaced instead with dark gray granite columns of medieval-looking square blocks. Each block appeared to be at least a couple of feet wide at the base, diminishing in size as the column gained height, until splitting at the peak into opposing Romanesque archways. The street side of the upper stories here had been painted a mustard-yellow color, except for the window trim and the balconies.

One block later, the buildings changed again, this time into painted brick walls two stories high. Each wall was fronted with grey marble archways, supported by matching marble columns, themselves consisting of two separate sections. A marble ring protruded from the columns where the two sections met. The lower level of the buildings here were set back from the street, with another of those covered walkways running the length of the block. Parallel to the street, supporting the building's upper story, ran a thin trim of gray marble, forming archways that came to rest atop a decorative cornice on each of the marble pillars.

Overhead wires hung everywhere; they ran from building to building, a great majority sagging in the middle. Others hung across the street, giving the entire area a cluttered appearance. In the distance I could make out the leaning red bricks of the twin towers.

Just before entering the historic center, we came to an intersection unlike any I've ever seen before. Instead of the usual four streets coming together at a stoplight, this one had three main streets as well as three others that angled in from nearby neighborhoods. These three streets, in stark contrast to normal street asphalt, were made of uneven cobblestones. They appeared to be medieval carriage lanes that predated the city's expansion. Along each of these cobbled tracks I could see small piazzas, each one flying the ever-present Italian flag. One contained a large marble fountain with a two-story high statue of Neptune at its center.

Once we entered this section of town, the roads zig-zagged off in different directions. None of the streets were laid out in straight lines. Several times Maya and I had to change direction in order to continue toward the city center towers. The majority of the doorways here were outlined with square stones, with doors made of think wooden planks with hammered brass hardware, reminiscent of castle doors. Even some of the roofs here were fronted with battlements with open spaces for defense similar to those found atop medieval castles.

Colored confetti made a sudden appearance along this portion of the sidewalk.

"Must have been some party," commented Maya.

The overall silence and thinning of pedestrians here lulled us into thinking that we must now be in the university section, and that either classes were in session, or students were sleeping off the recent celebration. Cigarette butts were everywhere. They littered the streets as well as the sidewalk. Alongside them were numerous wadded up sandwich wrappers.

"This sure doesn't look like any university I've ever seen before," I commented to Maya as we walked down the block, keeping one eye on the tower for reference and the other on lookout for a sign advertising the university's medieval anatomical museum.

"How many students have we even seen?"

"Maybe the students here don't look like what we think of as students."

"Do you see anyone carrying a book bag? Or even a backpack?"

"No, but I don't see many tourists, either," said Maya.

Suddenly we smelled a familiar scent and stopped dead in our tracks. "Is that what I think it is?" I asked, sniffing the air again to be sure.

"Oh yeah," Maya announced. "Well, that explains why we haven't seen any students. They're probably all in weed class!" She laughed at her own joke.

"Or sleeping off the effects," I added.

The last couple of blocks leading to '*Le due Torri*' suddenly morphed into tourist central. Street vendors were everywhere, selling dozens of trinkets, including keychains, ashtrays, and refrigerator magnets of the two towers. Restaurants lined the sidewalk all around this ancient part of town, with tables and chairs overflowing out into cordoned off streets amid rusted bicycle stands. The pavement here was constructed of large, square stones. All traffic disappeared at the outer road circling this tourist area. Inside, it was pedestrian only.

Many of the restaurants had short double-sided chalkboard menus standing out front. White scripted lettering advertised their daily lunch specials. Maya and I studied many of them as we circled the area.

"We should take the time to eat a full lunch while we're here," suggested Maya. "After all, Bologna is noted for its food."

I agreed, and began calling out restaurant specials as we walked. One establishment on the corner, a block away from the tower, was packed with waiters rushing in and out. Their sidewalk tables were completely full, however of the three tables sitting just past the curb, in front of a full bike rack, a newly vacated table was getting a clean red and white checked tablecloth. Maya and I looked at each other, then made a beeline to claim the table before anyone else could. After parking our belongings on the chairs, we went up to go study the chalkboard menu next to the restaurant's doorway.

Beneath a notice stating '*Servizi igienici reservati agli avventori*' (Toilets Reserved for Patrons), the advertised specials included bread, salad, and a glass of wine for the low price of €8.50 each. Beneath that was listed a choice of '*Pasta Fresca*', including *Ravioli ricotta espinaci*, *Spaghetti alla chitarra*, *Lasagna salsiccia e formaggio*, *Tortelli di patate*, or *Gnocchi*.

"Suddenly I'm starving," I said to Maya.

"While we're here, ask the waiter where your stupid museum is,"

Maya took off for the bathroom inside the building's kitchen, asking a passing waiter for their WIFI password along the way. I returned to guard our table, to wait for Maya to return. While I waited, I entered the restaurant's password in my cell and watched as nearly a dozen messages downloaded.

I deleted my way through the junk mail, until I arrived at a couple of short texts from coworkers. One simply said, 'Dayton Station Manager position on the bid. You interested?' I replied with a quick, 'No way!' and hit send. The next was a forwarded headline of one of the local newspaper's ongoing investigations: *'Omega Air's Worrisome Management Woes.'* I wondered what that was about, but shrugged and continued on to the next. Local reporters were always attacking Omega.

"Can you talk?" the text read. It was from one of the newer employees, nicknamed Sandusky. I didn't know her very well, because she was always taking LWOP (Leave Without Pay) to go home early, but I'd worked with her enough to know she was a conscientious employee and competent in spite of her lack of experience.

I typed a quick, 'On vac in Italy, what's up?' and sent it off.

She answered almost immediately. "Noggins said he wrote me a complimentary letter and put it in my file. Now he wants a private follow-up. I haven't done anything good or bad enough to warrant a letter. What do you think he wants?"

"Noggins wrote a letter?" I typed, knowing he wasn't noted for compliments. Or putting words to paper. "Doesn't pass the smell test."

"Is there any way to verify it's legit?"

"Next time he takes a half-day, get a different supervisor to escort you down to the file room. Easy to see if he did add a letter. Ask Dough Boy—the ticket counter elf. He's never strays far from his office."

"Mr. Daugherty?" she replied.

"Yep. Marvin. AKA Dough Boy. One look should explain it."

"Do you facetime?" she typed. "So much faster."

"I can," I replied. "But not for long."

Just then Maya returned and sat down. "Your turn."

Our waiter was right behind her, so we gave him our choices. Maya ordered the spaghetti, I took lasagna. As the waiter wrote down our orders, Maya gave him a steady smile. "How about if we each get a half-order of two different specials?"

He smiled back at her. "How about I bring you two extra plates? You divide how you want."

"Ok," she answered. "But can you at least help us convert two free glasses of wine into one bottle?"

Again, he smiled . "Okay, okay, I take care. Red or white?"

Maya looked at me. "White?"

I nodded just as my phone chimed with the inbound FaceTime call. "I can't talk long," I began as soon as I answered, "because I don't know how reliable this connection is."

"Have you ever heard of a supervisor asking you to come in at the end of your shift for a career review? Actually, he called it a deep-dive something-or-other."

I couldn't help but laugh. "As a matter of fact, I have. And they've always been known as managerial 'what-will-you-do-for-me-if-I-help-you-now sessions,' if you get my meaning. Whose career, anyway?"

Maya didn't bother to hide the fact that she was listening to my conversation, even when the waiter returned with a less-than-full bottle of wine and set it down in front of her.

"My career . . . at least that's what Noggins said."

"Ah," I answered, surprised only by the fact that my older-and-wiser opinion was being solicited. "Sounds to me like Noggins' joined Omega's lap dance club," I answered. "If you want my advice, tell him to take you off the work schedule and do his deep dive during your scheduled shift. He pulls people into the office any time, no matter how petty the complaint, so he can just as easily do the same to discuss your career. Try confirming the meeting in an email beforehand. See if he replies."

"Do you think it's on the level?" she asked.

I laughed. "No offense, but can you honestly call your less than part-time service a career? Look, all I can tell you," I said, trying to keep my voice low so as not to interrupt the waiter's ongoing wine deal discussion with Maya, "is go in with your eyes open. Try to have someone witness you entering his lair. They can wait outside, but at least that way you have proof you were there."

"When will you be back?" Sandusky asked, a pleading note creeping into her voice.

"Not in time to help you with this, Sweetie. Just pretend it's all legit. Polish up your resume and take it with you."

"My resume?" she asked. "What for?"

"Because he'll ask to see it if he's going to help your career, silly."

"It's nothing to brag about. I only did two semesters at the local junior college before I got hired with Omega."

"Well, that's two semesters more than a lot of other employees have. Trust me, Noggins could care less what's on your resume. If he even looks at it, it'll be out of pure nosiness."

"You sure? I had to take remedial English and math because of my high school grades. The rest was basic college freshman requirements."

"Just tell Noggins you majored in business. Believe me, he's not going to bother studying your resume. It's all for show."

"You really think so?" Sandusky asked, sounding unconvinced.

"Positive. Let Noggins do the talking. See what he wants. Tell him you have aspirations of becoming . . . oh, say, the next Dayton Station Manager. Just let your conscience be your guide."

"Station Manager?" Sandusky choked. "I'm no way near qualified for a position like that!"

"Don't be so sure," I responded. "Considering Omega's lap-dancing promotions the past several years, qualifications have nothing to do with it. Command headquarters make all the decisions so the station manager position is nothing but a figurehead, needed only to answer the phone and take orders. It's just someone to blame whenever something goes wrong. But it is a career boost if you're not looking for a lifetime of yes-sir's."

"And if your interview isn't on your knees," Maya piped up from across the table.

"Relax. Just play it by ear. Life is filled with choices. This is but one."

"Okay," was all I heard before the call ended.

Maya's eyes never left my face as she handed over a glass from a new, full bottle of local wine. She only looked away long enough to fill her own glass. "Who the hell was that?"

"Sandusky," I answered.

"Who?"

"You know, Samantha—the one with the screwed-up ID."

"Oh right," Maya nodded. "I know who you're talking about now."

"Noggins told her he wrote her a complimentary letter. Now he wants an after-hours meeting to discuss her career."

"What career?" Maya scoffed. "She's hardly ever there. And why does everyone insist on calling her Sandusky? I thought her name was Schlagen."

I laughed. "Technically it's Schlagenhaufen. Those morons in corporate couldn't figure out how to get all the letters in her name to fit on the ID, so instead of changing the font, they shortened her name and sent it to her as 'Sam Schlagen.' Took her months to get it fixed. She sent messages about it to Noggins, but he was no help. Neither was HR, locally or corporate. In the meantime, everyone started calling her Sami. She hated that. One thing led to another and before you knew it, Miss Sandusky stuck."

Maya made a face but kept her comments to herself.

"She really was Miss Sandusky 2017, did you know? Anyway . . . I took one look at her ID and told her to take a picture of it and post it on Facebook. It got the company's attention all right. She got a new ID within the week. I guess that's how I came to be her go-to problem solver."

"I thought it was a termination offense to post anything about Omega on Facebook," Maya noted.

I shrugged. "Anything derogatory or malicious, yes. But this was fact, not an accusation."

Maya drank more of her wine, then held up the bottle to refill our glasses. "You didn't just advise her to go for it with that creep, did you?"

She caught me mid-swallow, causing me to choke on my wine. "Of course not, " I answered, reaching for a napkin. "What gave you that idea?"

Maya took a deep breath. "Don't you think it's crappy advice to tell a newbie like her to let her conscience be her guide? She might not have a choice."

"You're wrong; everyone has a choice. You may not like the outcome, but no one can force you to do anything immoral, at least while you're at work. What do you think I should have said? 'Oh no! Don't do it!' Or maybe, 'Do whatever you think will help you get what you want.'" In the end, she'll do what she wants, not what I tell her she should or shouldn't do. Besides, she wouldn't be the first person at Omega to lap-dance her way into an undeserved promotion, would she? How she proceeds is her choice and nothing I say is going to change that."

"What would you do if you were in her place?" Maya asked, head cocked.

"You're comparing apples and oranges, Maya. I'm old; she's not. I'm married; she's not. At this stage of my life, what do I need a career for? She does. I'm in it solely for the travel perks and the income . . . and, hopefully, a not-too-distant retirement."

Maya didn't comment, but her frown didn't disappear either.

"Look," I continued. "I understand why some opt for shortcuts to promotions in spite of the price tag that comes with it. In this day and age, to be young and filled with career aspirations, it's near impossible to climb the ladder based on your merits when you're continually shut out by diversity appointments. I'm not saying it's right, just that I get why some do it. I'm just thankful I'm old enough that I don't have to deal with that kind of managerial assistance."

"But you have no idea if Sandusky needs it, either."

"Exactly," I said, getting up to head to the restaurant's facilities before our food arrived.

When I returned, Maya was facing her iPad in what appeared to be a fast-paced low-voice conversation. I couldn't help but wonder who she was talking to, so tiptoed up behind her and peeked over her shoulder. Guess who? Mr. Channel 5 guy! I waived at him. He stopped talking in mid-sentence before hesitantly waiving back.

Maya whipped around to face me, both cheeks on fire . . . then turned back to her screen. She began discussing our gorgeous weather and our plans for the rest of the day, signing off seconds before the waiter showed up with four plates.

Chapter 11

Before leaving the restaurant, we asked the waiter for directions to the university's anatomical museum. He played with his cell for long minutes before finally telling us to head straight to the *Due Sorelle*—the 'Two Sisters', the national nickname for Bologna's twin towers of Asinelli and Garisenda. "It's a bit past them, but stay on that same street, then look for Zamboni Street. The building you want is on the left, on the corner."

We thanked him and headed outside, searching the skyline for the towers. Up close, without the distraction of the other city buildings blocking our view, it hit me as strange that the taller of the two was the one still climbable. Maybe that's because the smaller (Garisenda) suffered a more pronounced lean, a lean now known to be caused by unstable subsoil. (The same problem affecting Pisa's tower, incidentally).

A secondary wooden castle-like fortress had been constructed around the base of Asinelli, while the Garisenda's lower level was encased in layers of heavy granite blocks. "It's technically called a *rocchetta*. That type of stronghold," Maya explained, giving the stones a steady stare.

"No wonder the damn thing leans," I commented. "Those stones must weigh a ton. And that's not counting the weight of all the bricks used in building the towers themselves."

The structure surrounding Asinelli's base had been themed to match the medieval-looking archways of neighboring buildings. A small historical display and souvenir shop occupied a corner of this castle surround, with one wall completely filled with dusty, framed photos of the ancient Bologna skyline and its multitude of privately-owned towers. One depicted an aerial footbridge connecting the two towers, with a caption beneath it advising that the bridge no longer existed having been destroyed in a fire.

According to an oversized *Historical Bologna* poster, the city once contained 180 such towers, all built by wealthy families not just as symbols of their wealth and power, but also to serve as lookouts supporting local defensive systems during Italy's internal war of pro- or anti- Holy Roman Emperor, and again during the allied bombings during World War II. Today, only twenty-two such towers remain.

"Hard to believe all these towers were a result of Medieval families competing to show off their wealth."

"Kind of like parking a brand-new Cadillac in your driveway today, right?"

Maya just shrugged, not liking my analogy.

Alongside the poster was a faded sketch depicting Bologna's twin towers and how they originally appeared to be the same height. A typed article beneath the sketch explained that Garisenda's foundation proved to be too weak to support its height, so it was never completed. In fact, the article continued, half of it was demolished in order to save the remaining portion. It still stands in the shadow of its much taller sister, Asinelli, the one originally intended to be the shorter sibling.

Another set of framed photos were side-by-side comparisons of the twin towers in New York alongside Bologna's famous twins. The caption beneath explained how architect Minoru Yamasaki is thought to have been inspired by the Italian towers when originally designing the World Trade Center. True or not, it was an interesting read.

"Just like pizza," Maya muttered. "Everything came from Italy."

Past the photos was a collage of posters and signs announcing student activities at the nearby university. Nothing, I noted, about the world-famous anatomical museum.

While I studied the posters, Maya struck up a conversation with an elderly man wearing a pair of dark blue coveralls. He was busy sweeping cigarette butts off the front sidewalk. Turned out, he was the gate-keeper in charge of allowing tourist groups inside. He struck me as a cheerful pensioner who enjoyed having a little part-time job on the side.

"How much are the tickets to climb the tower?" I heard Maya ask him.

"Five euro," he answered. "Forty-five minutes to go up and come down before the next group go up."

"Why only forty-five minutes?"

"Because stairs only wide enough for one person. Also, steps are old. We must limit total load they can bear every hour."

"How many steps to the top?"

"Four hundred ninety-eight," he answered cheerfully.

That news wiped the smile off my face. "Five hundred? Just to get to the top? That's a thousand steps total! I don't think I can do that many, Maya," I announced. "At least not inside of forty-five minutes."

"There are platforms every few floors. For to rest," the pensioner added, inadvertently revealing that he understood English better than he originally let on.

Maya turned to him again. "What happens if someone has a heart attack half-way up?"

He laughed. "They have to hurry down for to get medical attention,"

"Can we pay to just go up half-way?" I asked hopefully.

His eyebrows shot up and he shook his head as though the very idea was insane.

Maya looked at me. "It's only five euros. What do you think? Want to go for it? See how far we get?"

I shrugged. "I'll consider myself lucky if I manage a hundred steps. But I did see a couple of windows on the side wall when we first got here. As long as I can see something of Bologna's famous red roof skyline before I cave, I'll be happy."

Maya made a face, then asked: "Is your motion problem going to get to you during the climb?"

"To puke or not to puke, is that what you mean? I guess we'll find out."

With that, we pulled out our five-euro coins. The old guy laughed so hard he began wheezing. "You no buy tickets here. You buy tickets at city welcome center in Piazza Maggiore."

"Ahhh, crap," was Maya's instant response. "Why is everything always so damn difficult?"

"How far back is the piazza?" I asked the old guy.

He did a final sweep of his broom then placed both hands on its top as though preparing for a leisurely conversation. "Two, three blocks. Look for zee *statua di nettuno*."

"Every block we've passed today had a Neptune statue," Maya grumbled as we headed outside and back down the street.

Thankfully, the Piazza Maggiore wasn't far away. We only had to ask for directions once before finding the tiny tourist ticket office. We hurried to the window and forked over our coins, knowing that the clock was running out on our allotted time here and we were spending more than anticipated with this unplanned tower excursion.

Tickets in hand, we hurried toward the door. That's when I heard a voice yelling at us from behind. It came from the ticket window. I returned to see what the problem was.

"You forgot your change," he said, handing me two one-euro coins.

"I thought the fee was five-euros?" I asked, puzzled.

He flashed me a weary smile. "Only costs three-euros for elderly . . . people over sixty-five."

I didn't know whether to be flattered or insulted as I thanked him and pocketed my change. Maya, meanwhile, stood waiting at the doorway, grinning from ear to ear.

Less than twenty minutes later we found ourselves back at the tower entrance again. A group of rowdy high-school looking students, all laughing and jostling for position among themselves, were working their way to the front of the crowd on the heels of the broom-toting gatekeeper in order to be first through the starting gate. The minute he opened the door, everyone surged forward. Thankfully the old guy was experienced enough—and nimble enough—to sidestep the stampede. Maya and I were more than happy to bring up the rear.

I took a final glance upward at the outside wall before ducking into the low entrance cavern. Its lean was pronounced. Then the wall moved. Clouds raced overhead and began spinning. I shut my eyes, took a deep breath, and reached for Maya's backpack. I held on like a blind person following my guide dog.

It was dark inside in spite of the light tan color of the bricks. It was cold, too, with stone steps barely wide enough to accommodate a modern-day size-eight shoe. The passageway was so narrow there was just enough room for a single person, although a black wrought-iron hand-rail had been bolted to the outside wall for convenience.

"No way am I going up in there," I told Maya, peering into the blackness ahead.

"Why not?" she asked, her backpack scraping against the wall as she turned.

"Claustrophobia," was all I got out before panicky uncontrolled breathing took over.

"Oh, for God sakes, don't be such a wuss," Maya snapped. "We're not even in the tower yet! This is just part of the entranceway. It'll open up as soon as we make the turn and get inside."

I grabbed the handrail, closed my eyes, and hauled myself forward. One step, two steps . . . three. If there was a window this low in the wall, it must have been boarded up because it remained dark as midnight inside even after the first turn. Again, I focused on my breathing and clawed my way forward to catch up with Maya.

Suddenly we were inside the tower. A dim light from somewhere up high illuminated a small wooden platform which transitioned to the tower's staircase. I grabbed the wooden handrail and looked up into the beam of light streaming down from five-hundred steps above, and paused to watch dust particles floating down like miniature snowflakes. My focus shifted to the squares of staircases above. It was like looking into a kaleidoscope of varying shades of brown. When I blinked, the squares shifted. Instantly the room started spinning, so I plunked down on the step. I took a deep breath and bent over, holding my head in my hands, waiting for the spinning to stop.

"Damn you, Sābra," I heard Maya call down from a level above. "Where the hell are you?"

Reluctantly, I stood up. I grabbed the handrails on each side of the staircase and focused on the incline ahead. Six steps to go. At the top, I could see a wall of reddish bricks, and where the handrail made a sharp turn to the right at the corner. "I'm coming," I wailed into the darkness above. I took another deep breath, and pushed off with both arms. One step, two steps, three steps . . . until, finally, I reached the landing.

The staircases above still echoed with the distant voices of those same giddy teenagers who'd rushed the entrance, but the giggling and shouting grew fainter with each passing minute. I guessed they, too, were engrossed with conserving their oxygen as they climbed ever upward. Well, by God, if they could climb this stupid tower then so could I. Or at least I could try.

One step, two steps, three steps . . . four. When I reached the corner platform, I unclenched my hand in order to change my grasp to the handrail that bordered the next set of steps, then I set off again. One step, two steps, three steps . . . four. I continued in a steady rhythm until I caught up with Maya.

"About time," was all she said, turning on the narrow step and taking off again.

I sighed, but followed. "What was all that crap the old guy said about a resting spot every couple of landings?" I complained on next exhaled breath.

I lost count of how many more seven-step series we managed to climb. All I can recall now was the intense burning in my legs. And the sound of Maya's steady clop, clop, clop up the stairs without pausing to wait for me to catch up.

"Did you look down at the bottom?" I heard Maya ask from at least one level above.

"No." The thought to look anywhere other than at the wall at the top of the stairs hadn't occurred to me. I continued climbing half-way up the next series of steps, then tightened my grip on the handrail before leaning over to look down into the abyss.

My first thought was amazement that we'd managed to climb this far at all. I could see at least six separate square tiers of staircases below. Then again, the shifting shapes of that whirly kaleidoscope filled my head. I felt like I was looking cross-eyed, but couldn't manage to regain focus. Suddenly, the spinning dizziness overwhelmed me. I felt lightheaded. A hot flash rose up from my stomach to my throat. Oh shit . . . I twisted on the step in order to sit down and wait for the spinning to stop.

"You didn't look down, did you?" I heard Maya call down again. She must have been at least two tiers above me.

"Yes," I wailed, feeling sorry for myself. "I wish to hell we'd have never entered this vertical dungeon."

"What did you look down for?" Maya's voice floated down through the airspace.

"Because you told me to!" I shouted back. A flash of anger took hold, which, thankfully, replaced the dizziness. "If you didn't want me to look down, why in God's name did you keep asking me if I'd looked down?" Anger overcame the nausea.

"I asked if you did because I was going to warn you not to."

"Thanks a lot," was all I could say, hoisting myself up with both hands. I set off upward at a deliberate pace, intent only on kicking someone's ass once I caught up with her.

I reached Maya three seven-step tiers later. She was crumpled against the wall beneath a square window set into the bricks. Even in this dim light, I could see that her face had turned a sickly shade of pale.

"Are you okay?" I asked, less angry now than concerned.

"Remember how you joked about barfing up here?" she mumbled, making a face. "Well, I just did."

"No!" I gushed. "How? Where?"

"Over the goddamned railing," Maya moaned. "Where do you think?"

"Too much wine at lunch. I warned you."

"No you didn't."

She raised her phone and studied its display. "It's going on four o'clock already. Let's get the hell out of here. I'd love to get to the bottom before all those teeny-boppers come galloping down on top of us. Next thing you know we won't have time to find your anatomy museum, much less see anything inside."

"Okay, but as long as we've reached a window," I began, "I want a peek at the famous red-roof skyline Bologna's so famous for."

Maya reluctantly climbed to an upright position and held her hands together for me to use as a stepping-stool in order to reach the window ledge. I hoisted myself up and looked out into the distance.

The sight was beautiful, I'll say that much. Not as panoramic as it would have been from the very top of the tower, I'm sure. But I didn't care. I was content to have made it this far. As long as I didn't look down at the lean of the tower wall, I felt fine. I could see two other towers a short distance away, much lower than this one, with a cathedral between them. There was also a white bell tower on the far side of town . . .

"I can't hold you any longer," Maya gasped, losing her grip. With that, I scrambled down onto solid footing.

"You want to take a look?"

"No way," Maya said, wiping a hand across her forehead. I'm finished."

"We better hurry then," I said, hearing the first sounds of downhill clumping coming from above.

"How many steps do you think we managed?" I asked on the way down.

"Don't know, don't care," was all Maya said following hot on my heels.

Once down on *terra firma* again, Maya and I marched well past the doorway before pausing to turn for a final glance at the tower. We smiled at the sight of our friendly gate-keeper as he approached, except this time he didn't appear to be quite so friendly. He held a metal bucket in one hand and a mop in the other. Soap bubbles sloshed over the top of the bucket as he trudged past, muttering the Italian equivalent of, "Somma bitch. Somma bitch. Always gotta be one gets sick." Last thing I saw before we departed the scene was him hoisting the bucket up onto the cavern's entrance step.

Maya and I ducked inside the nearby souvenir shop where we each purchased a refrigerator magnet of the towers to commemorate our climb. We felt we'd earned it. After that we set off in search of Zamboni Street.

We walked for what seemed like forever before finally stopping at a corner bar to ask a patron inside for directions. He looked up the museum on his phone and verified that we were indeed headed in the right direction. So, we continued walking to the far end of the older university section of town. Confetti was all over the streets.

"It must have been some party," Maya mumbled.

A few blocks later we arrived at a boulevard with manicured lawns on each side of the pavement. Modern cement and glass buildings lined the left side of the street. At last, we found the building. A sign at the corner stated: *Luigi Cattaneo Anatomical Wax Museum.*

We walked up the elongated cement steps to a set of double glass doors. They were unlocked. We walked inside and looked around, but there wasn't a soul to be seen. We headed up a second set of stairs, arriving at another set of double glass doors. I tried the door, but these two were locked. A woman inside heard us and came out. She told us to wait, then disappeared back inside again. Minutes later she reappeared with an elderly silver-haired man in tow, who unlocked the doors. He never did introduce himself.

"Museo anatomico?" asked Maya.

"Sì. Sì," he answered. "Come in."

We followed him inside.

A short distance ahead, we arrived at a main hallway which spread out in both directions across this central access point. Glass display cases ran the entire length along each side. I could see doors spaced evenly along the length of the hallway, each one with a lettered sign protruding out overhead. Wide glass-topped display cases occupied the center area on each end of the hallway.

"You two medical students?" the gentleman asked in flawless English, leading us forward.

Maya and I both shook our heads.

At the center where the hallways intersected, we came face-to-face with three marble pillars: the first supported a super-sized wax replica of a human eyeball in colored detail; the second contained a giant ear complete with all its internal structures, again in color. The centerpiece of this wax threesome was a life-sized human head as perfectly formed as if Michelangelo himself had sculpted it . . . on one side, at least. On the other side, the outer layer had been stripped away to reveal intricate details of the structures beneath: the teeth, the bones, the pink tendons connecting the lower jaw to the cheek, ending with the starfish-shaped controlling musculature attached to the eyeball. Blue arteries and red veins—or was it was the other way round?—had been painted in painstaking detail on every portion.

"This isn't the right place," I whispered to Maya.

Maya shot me a wide-eyed look of exasperation.

The gentleman heard me. "What were you looking for?" he asked, sounding genuinely curious.

"The medieval anatomical museum," I replied. This place appeared to be an anatomical museum all right, but a more modern-looking clinical one, not the spruce lined amphitheater with showcased wooden statues of men without skin. "We wanted the one with a marble slab sitting front and center where medieval medical students could witness cadavers being autopsied."

The man nodded in understanding. "The Archiginnasio and Anatomical

Theatre," he stated. "That's what you're looking for. It's back near the towers, in the Piazza Maggiori. Lovely site. Full of history. A wonderful palace that absolutely deserves to be visited. But now that you're here, why don't you take the time to look around? This building is a showcase of medical history—that is, if you're interested in the history of medical science."

Maya and I both nodded. We weren't the least bit interested in the history of medical science, but what could we do? No one else was inside, and this man acted privileged to show off his museum to us. "What you have stumbled upon, ladies, is Bologna's Museo Anatomico Normale. It's filled with colored 3D wax models, in exacting detail, exposing various parts of the human body. The wax is colored not only for visual effect, but also to allow anatomy students to see firsthand the shades of malformed tissue and degeneration. The display cases in the hallway reflect diseases and the way they affect the shape and appearance of the human body. I trust you will find the models more interesting than disturbing. Above all, please keep in mind these models demonstrate real cases, real diseases."

Maya and I looked at each other with apprehension, wondering what we were getting ourselves into. Nevertheless, we continued walking behind the man, listening. I got held in fascinating captivity at the sight of the internal structure of a full-length leg. Alongside it, laid out in methodical order were enlarged, detailed sections of each piece of that leg, from the foot, to the ankle joint and then its toes—including toes with severe bunions—and the knee cap in various stages of flex, right up to the hip joint.

A sign above the door on the right read: *Opoectodymus.* "Cojoined twins," the man translated, opening the door and stepping inside. We dutifully followed, coming face-to-face with a suspended skeleton showcasing in bony detail an example of twins with two heads, two pair of arms, two rib cages, and two legs—not two legs each but rather a single pair of legs extending from a shared pelvis. It was gross to look at, yet captivating at the same time.

"I think I'm going to be sick again," Maya gasped, covering her mouth and racing for the doorway.

One entire wall of this room showcased shadow boxes containing wax cutaways detailing fetuses in the womb. In each, a thick, twisted, grayish-pink umbilical cord floated alongside a fetus, or wound its way around the neck. The next set of boxes showcased various stages of labor, with an arm or a leg protruding out from the birth canal opening. The next series showcased malformed infants, many with missing or deformed limbs. I couldn't look. I had to turn away at the sight of them.

"That's revolting," Maya commented shortly after reentering the room.

"Actual examples of childbirth complications," our guide said. "Eighteenth century sculptors working in tandem with anatomists were the first to use art to make teaching models like these. They colored the wax for effect, which greatly assisted students in a visual study of the human body. In actuality, they had no other choice," he explained, "because, with no means of preserving corpses at that time, there was no other way for students to learn."

"Is the umbilical cord really that color?" I asked. I'd never seen one up close before, not even when my son was born.

He nodded. "Everything you see here is true to form."

"And the cord is really that thick?" I asked, leaning in for a closer look. It appeared to be at least an inch thick, like some kind of twisted vine floating alongside these motionless bodies.

Again, the man nodded. "Prior to medical advances at the turn of the last century, fully 90% of stillbirths were a result of strangulation due to cord malposition. In fact, one of the uses of modern ultrasound technology is to verify umbilical position prior to labor."

"I think we've seen enough," Maya announced, grabbing my arm and giving it a meaningful tug.

"One last item you really must see before you leave," our guide said, leading us out the door and across the hallway. "You've no doubt heard of Smallpox disease, no?"

We both nodded, though not sure if we wanted to learn about it.

There, set against the wall, was a life-size head of a woman whose face was covered with smallpox blisters. Each pale tan blister was raised or wrinkled, in stark contrast with the tone and smoothness of what little normal skin surrounded them. "Smallpox was the first virus to be totally eradicated from the face of earth. Most people have heard of it, however very few have actually seen the effects of that horrible disease."

"Who would want to?" Maya let slip, making a face.

"Exactly! But this is how students learn to recognize disease. Only then can they effectively treat it." With that, he turned and led us back down the hallway to the three-pillar exhibit near the entranceway.

We thanked him for his time, telling him we found his personalized tour very interesting. I did, at least.

His final words were something to the effect that he only hoped this site would eventually become as popular as the medieval surgical center.

Maya never said a word as we exited the building. We were both silent as we crossed the street and walked to a bus stop on the boulevard. "There's a bus heading to the Piazza Maggiori in about fifteen minutes. You want to try to find your other museum?" Maya finally asked. In spite of the words, her voice sounded hopeful I'd say no.

"Screw it," I said. "I'm tired and topped up on anatomy education for the day. Let's just head to the station and catch the next train to Florence."

We ended up waiting at least fifteen minutes for a bus back to the station. We got off a block past the golden arches after we spotted a corner market. There, we picked up snacks and a liter bottle of water for the train ride ahead. After that we hurried to the station and to the baggage office to claim our bags. The same girl was still on duty inside.

"Oh, hi again," she said the minute she saw us. "Did you find what you were looking for?"

"Yes and no." Maya and I both answered, hoping we wouldn't have to translate any details about our day. Neither of us felt up to the task.

"Oh, too bad," the girl said before bringing our bags to the doorway. She sounded genuinely sad that our outing wasn't a blazing success. Then she flashed Maya a bright smile. "By the way, I fixed your wheel."

Maya, for once, was wide-eyed stunned. "Oh, wow! Grazie so much."

The girl laughed. "No problem. Gives me something to do. Besides, I like fixing things."

Maya and I discussed train options and prices at the ticket kiosk. She insisted she wanted a train with WiFi, which meant no *Regionales*. It had to be one of the Freccas, a little more expensive, but faster. We made our selection, grabbed our tickets, and headed outside to the platform to wait.

⁓ Chapter 12 ⁓

The Bologna station platform remained nearly empty until just before our train lumbered in. There couldn't have been more than a dozen people standing outside waiting other than Maya and myself. Then, all of a sudden, the platform was filled with people and baggage, all streaming toward the arriving lineup of cars the minute the doors opened, making it difficult for those in the process of descending the steps to get clear of the crowded doorway.

I always find it fascinating to watch peoples' behaviors during any kind of boarding/disembarking process. A great majority act like complete fools, as though they're the only ones that need to get onboard pronto. Why is it that modern society, no matter the country, when faced with the double pressures of crowds and time constraints, often take on the narcissistic attitude of 'Me first! Me too! What about me?" In the long run, if those waiting to board would simply stand back and allow the doorway to clear before moving forward, everyone would be able to get onboard that much faster. Unfortunately, it never happens.

Maya and I double-checked our tickets before merging in the back half of the crowd while beginning the hunt for our assigned car. For this trip we'd elected to purchase €26 upgraded tickets, complete with our all-important WiFi access along with assigned cars and assigned seats.

"Car 007," I shouted over to Maya as I walked down the lineup searching for the magic number.

She laughed. "Oh wow! I like the sound of that."

"Seats 6A and 6B," I added, saying a silent prayer the seats faced forward, as we inched our way toward our assigned car's stairway. I was curious to see what the inside of an upgraded car looked like, and how these seats differed from the cheap ones we usually bought.

Reclining seats, maybe? Seat-back TV's? But then I laughed and told myself on a two-hour train ride it really didn't matter.

Once inside our car, however, the sad fact hit home that this upgraded cabin looked no different from the lower priced *Regionale's* we usually booked. In fact, this car was identical in every way to the one we rode in to Bologna that very morning, except for the WiFi. A quick glance confirmed identical pairs of bench seats facing each other from opposite sides of a table. With ten such seating pairs on each side of the aisle, my calculations came up with a grand total of forty people per car. And this one looked to be filling up fast.

Chrome rails ran the length of the car above the seats on each side of the aisle, designed to contain baggage and assorted personal possessions. The front rail had been elevated slightly higher than the rest, thus serving as a barricade to prevent wayward items from spilling over onto unsuspecting heads below.

My cell phone rang the minute Maya and I climbed onboard. I answered, but the call was filled with static. "On the train," I hollered into it, while being jostled from behind. "Send a text and I'll get back with you later."

I stood behind a slim middle-aged blonde female a row back from my assigned seat. She wore an expensive looking button-up sweater—cashmere if I had to guess, and held a beige London Fog style raincoat over her left arm. She turned to look back at the lineup of bodies, all filled with exasperated expressions, standing in the aisle all the way back to the entranceway, no doubt wondering why in God's name it was taking so long to move less than an inch at a time. It turned out everyone was waiting for Maya to stow her bag.

She struggled to hoist it up over the chrome rail and onto the rack. But she couldn't even manage to lift it above her shoulders in spite of repeated attempts. The blonde ended up tossing her raincoat onto her seat then grabbed one end of Maya's wheelie and gave it a push. Afterward, she picked the coat up and then tucked it between her thigh and the outside wall as she sat in the seat facing Maya.

This helpful woman—very well preserved once I caught sight of her face—was wearing a classy beige slacks outfit. Everything about her smacked of expensive, probably because of her multiple gold bracelets and an oversized gold choker necklace with thick links hanging from her neck. Her hair was blonde—but not one of those do-it-yourself brassy blonde colors. Hers was definitely a professional job, a muted two-toned color that looked natural except for the faintest line of black that appeared among her loose waves whenever she looked down. She casually brushed her hair back with a hand before settling her head against the window. No wedding ring, I noticed.

One young-looking lout wearing a sport coat, blue jeans and a backpack grabbed my waist with both hands, then pushed and prodded in a near obscene manner until he managed to squeeze past me. "Why didn't you just tell me you were in a hurry," I snarled at his backside. "I would have climbed up on top of someone to get out of your way."

He never responded. Never even acknowledged he heard me, probably because he passed several others (in the same manner) by the time I finished my rant.

I turned my attention to the fact that our seats were (hallelujah!) facing the front. I announced the happy news to Maya as she sat down and slid over next to the window.

"Remains to be seen," Maya grumbled as I dropped down beside her. "Depends which way the train goes once we start moving." She unzipped her backpack and withdraw her iPad before stowing it between her feet below the table.

Next came a middle-aged nun wearing a full-length grey habit. Her headpiece sat slightly askew, exposing frizzled whitish-black tufts of hair along its front edge, no doubt from one-too-many embarkation encounters. Waiting in the aisle a short distance behind her stood a silver-haired gentleman wearing a dark pinstriped three-piece suit. His mustache matched the silver of his hair, and moved rhythmically as he chewed his gum while watching the nun. He appeared unconcerned by the dozen or so bodies waiting in line behind him. In fact, he continued chewing and watching as the nun made room to stow her carpetbag in the overhead rack by pushing and shoving other bags aside, before finally dropping with a loud sigh into the aisle seat opposite me.

I continued watching as this man casually tapped the nun on shoulder. When she looked up, he silently motioned with his thumb at the seat on the opposite side of the aisle. I braced for a verbal confrontation complete with obstinate waiving of boarding cards, raised voices, and a refusal to move. But she surprised me. She merely frowned her displeasure then hauled herself up to her feet and crossed over to the aisle seat.

With the merest hint of a smile to show for his efforts, the man sat down opposite me. He acted accustomed to giving orders, and having them obeyed. Unlike me, the nun didn't give him a second glance. She busied herself by adjusting her headpiece and systematically tucking in her wayward tufts of hair.

It was noisy inside the train with conversations and shuffling of feet. People's voices carried up and down the car. Hydraulic hissing could be heard from all the way back at the entrance. Shouts floated in from the station platform outside. When a cell phone rang, everyone paused long enough to check their own.

I pulled mine out and waited for it to display the WiFi source list, but couldn't focus on it what with the repeated bumps of passing passengers or their bags. Just as I located the *Trenitalia* link on the drop-down list, a backpack side-swiped my arm causing me to lose my place and nearly drop my phone. "Awww shit," I muttered, as I returned to the settings window and started over again.

"What's the password?" I whispered over to Maya.

She shrugged before looking up from her iPad. "Didn't know we needed one. I didn't"

I tried again to connect with Trenitalia's WiFi system. I nearly dropped my phone when the next passenger—a woman with hips that filled the aisleway—jammed against my elbow. Worse, I had to use the bathroom. But what with the steady line of inbound passengers, I knew I'd have to wait. My third attempt to connect worked, and suddenly a series of text messages began downloading, each accompanied by an incoming chime. The seemingly continuous chimes sounding off caught Maya's attention, if not everyone else's nearby.

"What's up?" Maya asked, leaning over to look at my screen.

"Sandusky," I answered, scanning the messages to get a quick overview of the latest office problems from home. "Turned out she no-showed that meeting with Noggins. He retaliated the very next day by reassigning her to baggage." I added, "Lucky for me if that means she'll be replacing me on that crap detail permanently."

"Hope it lasts," was Maya's only comment.

Another cell phone sounded off. This time the ringing belonged to the gentleman sitting opposite me. I wasn't trying to eavesdrop, but couldn't help but overhear bits and pieces, either: "Why is it that a certain papá only hears from his daughter when she needs something?" In spite of his words, he had a smile on his face revealing a lone gold rimmed front tooth. He kept his voice low as he continued the conversation. "Not tomorrow. I'm away on business this week." The only other thing I understood after that was something about his *collega* . . . his employee or partner, a guy named Luigi.

Eventually I lost interest and returned to my messages. "Uh oh," I said after reading the next.

"What?" asked Maya, looking up from her iPad.

"Sandusky claims Noggins told her not to punch in, to just report directly to baggage."

Maya took a quick breath. "You mean that bastard didn't make her walk all the way out to the concourse for one of his moronic briefings before giving her the reassignment and making her walk all the way out front again?"

"Evidently not," I said, scrolling through the message. "She said he told her he'd take care of signing her in. But then, according to her, he failed to remove her from the gate schedule, so she wasn't there to meet her assigned flight. Next thing she knew, station management charged her with no-showing her shift."

"Management?" Maya repeated. "Noggins is a manager! Why the hell can't he tell them what happened and clear things up?"

I continued on to the next message. "Noggins supposedly claimed that his job requires continuous personnel reassignments, that he can't be expected to remember every single one. He also claimed he never signs anyone into the time clock system."

Maya snorted. "He probably doesn't know how."

I agreed. "But if he did tell her he'd sign her in, then basically it's her word against his. Who do you think upper management is going to believe?"

"Jeez," Maya answered. "Tell her to contact HR. Have them check her sign-on into the computer system that day. Have someone in the parking office check her badge swipe in and out of the employee parking lot . . . "

"Whoa . . . whoa . . . I can't type that fast," I commanded, attempting to text a reply. In truth, I couldn't type at all what with the constant bumping of bodies passing in the aisleway. Yet I had to get some of our ideas written down before we started moving since I never knew in advance how the train's motion would affect me. Once motion sickness set in, everything else went out the door. I tried switching to verbal texting, but stopped after a couple of sentences.

"Oh crap," I groaned, showing the readout to Maya. It was nothing but nonsensical garbage.

"That's because your phone's set to Spanish," Maya chided after looking over at the display. "How the hell did that happen? Why don't you keep it set to English?"

I just shrugged. I had no idea.

"Oh, for God's sake, just use your voice memo app. Record the details then send them to her later. Walk and talk, remember?"

As soon as the voice memo app began recording, Maya and I threw out a half dozen ideas for Sandusky to pursue in order to mount a defense. Well, at least I did. Maya repeatedly yelled, "hire a lawyer," or "sue the bastard," whenever I paused to take a breath. All of it was neatly recorded, however.

"You think it's possible she really did no-show her shift?" Maya later asked.

I set my phone down on the table in order to slip off my sweatshirt while I pondered the question. "Why would she lie? Especially with Dickhead involved. This sounds exactly like something he would do."

"But what's his goal?" Maya asked, convinced it was less complicated than we were making it out to be.

"I don't know . . . maybe he's just trying to keep her so focused on her situation that she won't dare discuss his request for an after-hours meeting?"

"That doesn't make sense," Maya insisted, shaking her head. "Sounds to me like it was a simple mistake. He probably did reassign her, but ducked out early and so forgot to clock her in. Once payroll caught it, damn sure Noggins wouldn't confess that he was the one who made the mistake."

I had to agree with Maya's conclusion, and dictated as much into another recording and then turned the app off. By then the boarding line had thinned out to just a few late running stragglers. I turned to glance at the back of the car. Nearly every seat was occupied. "I'm going to head to the bathroom before we start moving," I told Maya, sliding out of my seat.

"Here, take this with you," she said, handing me one of our lunch napkins as she began withdrawing snacks from her backpack. "Never know."

I thanked her and made my way forward before anyone else showed up and blocked the aisle.

The sliding glass doors at the end of the car opened as I approached. but then stuck in a half-open position and stayed that way. A vertical chrome hand-hold bar had been positioned in the center of the landing between cars, so I reached for it and pulled myself clear of the stuck doors. They snapped shut behind me and I continued into the next car.

I could hear the sound of hydraulic hissing in the distance as another exterior door closed. The bathroom was just past the next doorway, and about the same size of an aircraft bathroom. I had no sooner locked the door and sat down when someone began pounding on it.

"Ocupado," I shouted over the sound of the continuous pounding.

When I finally opened the door, no one was waiting outside. "You might know," I grumbled, hurrying back to my car.

Another group was in the process of boarding when I entered the landing platform between cars. I fell in line behind them while they searched for their seats and began negotiations for changes, thus blocking the aisle while everyone shuffled seats and luggage.

I no sooner sat down when Maya spoke up. "Uh oh... "

"What?" I asked. "Now I gotta pee." Well, you'll have to wait until all those yahoos are seated. Might take a while because . . . "

"Quick," Maya interrupted, pushing me toward the aisle. "I can't wait. Let me out."

I set my phone down on the table and climbed out of my seat, watching as she disappeared down the aisle.

I could hear outer railway cars slamming shut all down the line, each one accompanied by a thud. Voices shouted the Italian version of 'all clear,' as we prepared to get underway. Next thing I knew we began rolling out of the station.

I glanced out the window to make sure we were moving, because our forward motion was smooth to the point of being almost imperceptible. Outside, the station platform lights had been switched on, and they receded into the distance as we rolled by. It was getting dark outside. I reached for my phone, still sitting on the table where I'd left it, to check the time. Nearly 6:30 pm. Suddenly the inside lights dimmed accentuating the countryside lights as we rolled past.

Maya returned as quickly as she originally disappeared. "Some dumb ass is getting his jolly's by knocking on the bathroom door the whole time I was in there," she grumbled, sliding over to her seat again. "They better hope I don't catch 'em."

I laid my phone down on the table again and inspected the snacks that Maya had laid out. Our half of the table now looked like a picnic setting, only with much less expensive choices, not to mention a shared liter bottle of water.

"Someone must be hungry," I commented, pushing the record button on the memo app as I settled in and prepared to continue the earlier discussion regarding Sandusky's dilemma.

"Starved," was all Maya managed to say, covering her mouth with a hand as she chewed. "Lost my lunch earlier, remember?"

That's when I noticed the blonde. She was staring into the window as though it were a mirror, totally engrossed in applying lipstick. I watched her for a minute before opening my cheese and cracker packet, but she never made eye contact, remaining focused on the job at hand instead.

Meanwhile, the tailored gentleman's phone rang again. This time his voice revealed a faint tone of exasperation when he answered. "Now what?" was all he said. Then I heard, "Discount, not free. That's why you have to use Bertani's. It'll have to make it up elsewhere, and there's not much time left of the season. Cash only, sì. You know how it works. And only with Luigi. Ciao, Bella." With that he snapped his non-smart phone shut. I looked to see if it was an Italian version of the Jitterbug, but it was too dark to tell.

I looked at my phone. I would have loved to double-check our walking directions from the Florence station to the hotel, but I was afraid to tempt fate by reading in the dim light. I tapped on my phone to check the time, surprised to see the Memo App was still recording. I turned it off, disgusted at myself for wasting so much battery life. I glanced over at Maya. She was happily munching through her food supply while flipping through 'Must See Florence Tourist Sites' on her iPad.

Next thing I knew the older guy was talking on his phone again. "Buongiorno Luigi," I heard him say. I didn't understand the rest. I was sidetracked instead at the sight of his hand reaching down beneath the table where it began stroking the blonde's thigh.

Ahhh, the Trenitalia version of the Mile High Club, I said to myself, leaning back, closing my eyes. Who would have thought?

A bit later I looked out the window. What I saw was the blonde's reflection as she used the window as a makeshift mirror to reapply her lipstick. I half expected her to raise her eyes to meet mine, but she remained steadfastly focused and paid me no attention at all.

"Va bene," I heard the man say into his phone. "Take care of it, okay?"

Was he booking a hotel room in Florence? Making dinner reservations for later tonight? I tried to see if he was wearing a ring. He was. Maybe he was calling his wife to tell her he was running late? But then who was this Luigi? I caught a glimpse of the nun's disapproving glare at him from across the aisle. I leaned my head back and closed my eyes again.

I didn't snooze for long in spite of the lulling rocking motion of our car over the rails. It might have been the scraping sound of our table being moved, or the whispered moaning that woke me. I still can't say. All I know is that I opened my eyes to see the classy blonde in a surprisingly unclassy position—half out of her seat, one leg intertwined with the silver haired guy's leg, murmuring seductive-sounding words in his ear. I glanced over at the nun. She was still scowling in their direction, not at all embarrassed to be watching their antics.

"Ohh Bartolo, ti ho aspettato tutta la settimana per essere di nuovo tra le tue braccia. Tis ono mancata?" She whispered it loud enough for me to hear, the whole time nuzzling his ear. I didn't understand all of it, but I did get the bit about how she'd waited a week to be in his arms again.

I reached out for my phone and touched the record button, still visible from the paused Voice Memos app. Then I slid it forward, toward the center of the table but off to one side a bit, next to my empty snack wrappers.

"Non vedo l'ora di spogliarti de tutti I vestiti" the woman whispered.

From the corner of my eye, I saw Maya sit bolt upright. She leaned against the window while dabbing at her eyes and biting back laughter.

"Tell you later," she mouthed, noticing that I was watching her.

I was scared to death to look at them, for fear I too would start laughing at the sight of two sixty-somethings behaving like teenagers. But I needn't have worried; they weren't aware of me at all. His eyes had a glassy stare, fixed somewhere high up over my left shoulder, a half-smile frozen on his face in spite of the fact that he never stopped chewing his gum. His mind was locked somewhere else, somewhere far, far away.

"*Tremito al pensiero di appoggiare lentamente la mia morbida lingua sul tuo fusto già eretto e duro come fosse di marmo.*" This time the whisper came out with a half groan. Worse, I didn't understand a word of it.

"See his face," I leaned over and whispered to Maya. "It's saying: 'I'm gonna get laid tonight!'"

"Shhh," Maya answered, turning a laugh into a cough. "They'll hear you."

"Believe me, neither of them is tuned into anyone else."

Maya leaned toward me and imitated the woman's soft whisper. "*Vorrei accarezzarti con le mie tette e strisciaroti su tutto il tuo corpo,*" means she wants to rub his body with her boobs."

"Here?" I asked with a grimace. "That's disgusting."

"Sounds better in Italian."

Next thing I knew, the blonde was rubbing his arm. Then his chest. I heard her lips smack his. He laughed. Then she laughed. He just sat there smiling, still chewing his gum. I looked away.

The train slowed as we approached the next station Bells chimed from somewhere up front. I checked the time. Too early by at least thirty minutes to be our arrival in Florence.

"I hope they're getting off," Maya whispered.

"What? And miss the show?" I shot back from behind my hand. "He's got such a woodie by now, I doubt he could make it to the exit if the car was on fire."

Maya's face flushed a bright red in spite of the dim light inside.

I glanced over at the nun again. She looked at me and pursed her lips before bowing her head. Maybe she was praying for the lovebirds. She held the pose. She held it so long, in fact, that the next time I looked at her, I stared at her chest to make sure she was still breathing.

It was dark outside when we crawled our way through the unnamed station then accelerated again. I picked up my phone and switched the voice memo off, then navigated to photos in order to search for the screen shot I'd taken while planning this trip, the one with walking directions from the Santa Maria Novella train station to our hotel near the cathedral. By the time I'd read through the instructions several times, my eyes wouldn't stay open, so I clicked my phone off and leaned my head back for the duration of the trip.

We could barely breathe as we walked to the front of the Florence SMN station pulling our wheelies behind us, because the air reeked of a combination of cigarette smoke and diesel exhaust. It was as noisy as any airport, too. Chimes constantly sounded off overhead, followed by a male voice making announcements against a background of whistles, steaming brakes and farting engines.

"Oh my God, this constant noise is as bad as that crap they play at home.

"Yes," I agreed. "But this is just noise. At home it's rhythmic crap … so bad you can't even call it muzak."

We found the station front's pharmacy exit, as noted in my recorded directions, and walked out onto the sidewalk. We pressed the crosswalk button and waited for the red light to stop oncoming traffic before walking over to the other side. The traffic at this hour—dinner time— was mostly taxis, all heading into the station.

"Now we just need to go straight for two blocks, until we come to the Piazza Unita," I said, recalling the saved directions from my phone.

As we walked, it was only natural for us to discuss the events of the train ride. "My God, I was never so embarrassed," Maya howled. "They were both way too old to behaving like that!"

"I'm convinced he's a lawyer. Or an accountant. She must be his mistress."

"Yeah, damn sure she wasn't his wife," Maya added. "Besides, she wasn't wearing a ring. Good thing they couldn't hear your comments,"

"Oh, I doubt they'd have understood me anyway."

Maya shook her head. "No, no, the woman spoke really good English."

"She did?" I asked, coming to a halt. "How do you know?"

"When we first got on, just after she helped me get my wheelie up into the rack, she told me 'There's room for your backpack up there as well.'"

"I didn't hear that."

"You were too far behind."

"Oh well," I said with a shrug, resuming walking again. "All I noticed was that she acted like some kind of Trenitalia escort service the minute the lights dimmed."

Once we arrived at Via San Antonio, we halted. "We're supposed to go left here, but which left?" Three leftward streets radiated out from the Piazza. I would have chosen the one with the most traffic. Maya, however, took the instructions literally and followed the far lefthand street.

"I recognize the street now," Maya shouted, picking up her pace.

Two blocks later, we arrived at the twinkling white light entrance of the Globus Hotel. "Don't forget, I warned you it's not fancy. I had a free night coming; that's the only reason I booked it."

The entrance foyer was small. In fact, the largest thing about it was the high desk, behind which a lone male stood, shrunk down into a loose grey sweater. He looked to be knocking at retirement's door. He acted tired; tired of working, tired of dealing with people; tired of life.

He checked us in, handed back our passports, and said "Happy hour in the back from 430 to 630p. Too late for tonight."

❧ Chapter 13 ❧

While the clerk checked us in, I ambled beyond the entrance foyer toward the back room with the intention of finding and checking out the breakfast area.

The room had been decorated in all white plastic tables and chairs, along with the usual buffet table set against the wall, running from the mid-point of the room to the far end. From the front of the room to the table, running half the length of the wall, was a bar. On the wall behind it hung a 'Happy Hour' sign that listed Chianti, Chardonnay, Pino Grigio, and Prosecco along with soft drinks. The sign also noted a €10 price tag for each drink beyond that first free glass.

I doubled back to the entrance just as Maya finished up with our check-in process. The clerk looked up with tired eyes and announced, "Complimentary upgrade to a bigger room," which came as an unexpected surprise. We were both pleased, and let him know it as we followed him down the hall to the elevator. He didn't go inside with us. He couldn't had he wanted to. There was barely enough room for two inside that small cubicle, let alone two people with bags.

"You go first," Maya said, stepping aside. "Send the elevator back down for me."

I did as instructed, more concerned by the fact there was either no upstairs hall light or else the bulb had burnt out. All I knew is that it was pitch dark in the hallway after the elevator had departed. I had no choice but to fumble around in the dark in search of the flashlight on my cell phone.

Using our cell lights to guide us down the dark hallway, Maya and I found our room and opened the door, switching the light on the minute we entered. The room was tiny, barely wide enough for two single beds. A small square end table had been squeezed in between the beds, a thoughtful gesture, but it had been turned sideways in order to fit, thus blocking one third of the bed. Two fan-fold luggage stands occupied the space between the outside bed and the far wall, leaving no space at all to walk around them.

Immediately to the right of the entrance door was a credenza. Its small counter sported a tray containing an electric tea pot, a small bowl filled with tea bags, instant coffee and sugar packets. A built-in open-faced wooden box containing two hangars on a pole served as the only closet on the inside wall.

"That better be the bathroom," Maya growled, indicating the closed door just past the 'closet.' She marched over and reached for the knob.

It was. But when she opened the door, it barely cleared the toilet inside. If that wasn't bad enough, a bidet had been squeezed in just past the sink. There was no counter space at all. A plastic container with two receptacles—cheap plastic vegetable bins—and been stacked on the floor beneath the sink. The top level contained two bath towels and two hand towels; the bottom bin contained assorted miniature bottles of shampoo, body wash, and a single oval of wrapped soap. In the opposite corner stood the glassed-in shower. A dingy off-white floor mat hung over its lime encrusted door.

"I'd sure hate to see the non-upgraded room," I joked as I dumped my bathroom case in the bowl of the bidet.

"Upgrade my ass," Maya grumbled. "We should go downstairs and demand to see one of the regular rooms. Just out of curiosity."

"Dare you," I answered, knowing she wouldn't. "What are we complaining about, Maya? Except for the €6 tax, the room was free. It's got two beds, the door locks, and it's got heat." It had too much heat, actually. It was roasting inside.

I searched for the thermostat and readjusted it to its lowest setting while Maya lugged her suitcase over to one of the stands and gave it a heave-ho. After that, we set out to get something to eat.

"There's a little pizzaria about two blocks away," Maya said, leading the way downstairs. "They have individual pizzas, and for a small fee you can add whatever toppings you want." Before leaving the hotel, however, we detoured to the front desk to register a complaint about the missing light bulb upstairs.

On the way to the restaurant, we passed a row of tented souvenir stalls, some still open. We were too hungry to stop and shop though, deciding instead to save that exercise for the next day. Maya was right about the restaurant being small. It was a tiny hole-in-the-wall site, with only three or four tables in the center section and another two booths against the back wall.

After learning that extra toppings cost only a couple of euros each, we splurged and ordered nearly everything listed on the menu. Maya ordered two bottles of Prosecco at the same time, one for now and one to go. "Might as well take one back to the hotel with us for later."

Over dinner we discussed our Bologna stopover, ultimately judging it a success in spite of the aborted tower climb, and completely missing out on the medieval anatomical museum. Our conversation dwindled down to making a couple of itinerary plans for the next day. I had my heart set on seeing both of Michelangelo's Pietà statues this trip—one here in Florence and the other in Rome; Maya intended to explore the gourmet foods of Florence's famous City Market.

During our walk back to the hotel, we passed that same row of tents that lined the street near the cathedral that we saw when we first arrived. We didn't have the desire to shop, but we did slow walk past them in order to get an overview of their items. Each displayed a different assortment. One sold nothing but cooking supplies: Italian chef hats, aprons, and potholders, even marble mortar and pestle sets. Others displayed only leather goods, from wallets to belts and bags. It was getting too dark to search out good buys, plus we were tired from the long day, so we left the shopping area and made our way back to the hotel.

Once in our room again, we summed up the events of the day. While I grabbed two Styrofoam cups off the credenza, Maya ducked into the bathroom and returned with a hand towel and placed it over the Prosecco bottle top before working the cork loose.

After the loud pop, she proceeded to fill each glass to the brim. I, meanwhile, played with my phone and managed to find the voice memo recordings, surprised to see at least six separate recordings in the list.

I clicked on the first one and waited. Our room was filled with indecipherable chattering for the most part, amid the usual cacophony of background noises. Suddenly, Maya and my discussion about Sandusky rang out. We both sat up and listened until our voices disappeared.

"Did you ever get back to her?" Maya asked.

I nodded. "Yep. Sent her the voice memo the minute we finished. This very one, in fact."

"Oh God," Maya said after a sharp intake of breath. "This one didn't contain that bit about whether or not we thought she was lying, did it?" I didn't think so, but played the recording a second time to make sure. If it was in there, it didn't come across clear enough to be understood.

"I suppose it's too late for her to apologize to Noggins and ask to reschedule the meeting?" Maya asked, taking a sip from her cup.

"What good would that do? Looks like he's already set her up."

"Tell her she should just go hire a flipping lawyer."

"Let's see what comes of the advice we sent her first."

Curiosity caused me to click on the second recording. A phone ringing was the first sound we heard, then a male voice asking, "Now what?" Following this came the begrudging authorization of "one and only one more discount." We listened as the male voice explained that the discount could only be obtained at Bertani's, cash only, and only with some guy named Luigi.

"I remember hearing him say all this on the train." I told Maya. I hit stop and looked over at her. "What's Bertani's?"

She shrugged. "No clue. But it sounds like it must be a store."

I took a sip from my glass then hit play again. "I'll have to make it up elsewhere. You know how it works . . . Ciao Bella." A long stretch of static followed, followed by more background noises. Next came Maya's complaint that we forgot to buy drinking glasses along with our snacks in Bologna, forcing us to share the liter bottle of water. I was about to hit the stop button again when another phone ring blasted through the air. The same guy was talking, but this time in a soft voice and in rapid-fire Italian. I couldn't follow any of it, so reached out to turn it off.

"Don't shut it off," Maya instructed, climbing off her bed to come over and sit on mine. She cocked her head and leaned close to my phone, listening intently. As soon as the conversation ended, she tapped the play button to hear it again. The recording was partially drowned out with background noise, but Maya replayed it enough times to understand the majority.

"Wow!" she finally said when it ended. "Did you get that?"

"Some of it," I admitted, "but not enough to make any sense."

Maya lifted the Prosecco bottle from the night stand and refilled each of our glasses. "Our gum-chewing lover-boy from the train is Bartolo. He authorized some guy called Luigi to give a 40% discount to either his daughter or her friend—I'm still not sure which—when she shows up. Luigi said he hoped it wasn't for anything too expensive, reminding Bartolo that he still hasn't finished paying off his last big purchase for 'Madame Secretary.'"

"That's gotta be the blonde who was with with him on the train," I said, nodding.

"Yeah. And it sounds like this Luigi guy doesn't like her very much."

My eyes opened wide. "Do you think they're mafia?"

Maya shook her head. "I doubt it. I mean nothing was said about getting revenge or bodies, or payback—nothing like that. This just sounded like two guys cutting a deal, that's all. Bartolo, I'm pretty sure is the boss. He instructed Luigi to mark everything in the inside displays up by 20%, then told him to post a 10% sale sign on those same items. Not sure why, but get this: Bartolo specifically told him not to change the prices on anything in the front window. He repeated twice how they needed those items to lure in as many tourists as possible in the few remaining weeks of the season."

"It sounds like they're doing some kind of inside job until they can make up the loss on other inventory. That's not illegal if he's an owner, is it?"

"It is if there's a co-owner who's not in on the deal. And, by demanding payment in cash, technically they're cheating the Italian government of tax revenue."

I snorted. I was well versed in paying cash to avoid paying the VAT.

Maya nodded absently and took another drink. "I think maybe it's embezzlement if he's not the owner." She reached over to the phone and slid her finger down to the next recording and hit play. Seductive whispering was already underway the minute the recording started.

"*Non vedo l'ora di spogliarti de tutti I vestiti*" . . . was all I heard before Maya hit the stop button. "What do you think she's saying?" she asked with a smirk.

"That bit about '*ora di spogliarti* '. . . is it about a spaghetti dinner?" I laughed the minute I said it because it was ridiculous for her to be discussing dinner in such a seductive whisper. "*Vestiti* . . . that means clothes, right?" I took a gulp from my cup.

Maya tried not to laugh. "Yep, that part's right. But, you idiot," she wailed, dissolving into giggles, "she's telling him she can't wait to rip off his clothes."

I backed up the recording to hear it again then took another sip of Prosecco. "They should teach this stuff in classes. How else are we supposed to learn it?"

Maya waited for the replay to finish before going down the list to the next recording to hit play. After a staticky pause, the whispering began again. "*Tremito al pensiero di appoggiare lentamente la mia morbida lingua sul tuo fusto già eretto e duro come fosse di marmo.*" Maya hit stop, then looked at me, barely managing to keep a straight face. "Did you get it?"

"Nope, not a word." I took another sip then burst out laughing. "Well, *lentamente* I understood. It means *slowly*, right?"

Maya nodded. "Break it down in bits."

"Okay. *Morbida* means dead, doesn't it? *Eretto's* gotta be erection. So, we're talking about a slow dead erection?" I knew I was wrong, but laughed anyway, spilling the last of my Prosecco in the process.

"Think about it," Maya sputtered, taking my glass from me and setting it on the night stand. "*Tremito al pensiero* . . . I tremble at the thought."

"Oh yeah, okay. I get that now."

"*Di appoggiare lentamente.*?"

"Do something slowly?" I offered, followed by more laughter from both of us.

"To lean slowly," Maya translated, stressing the *lean* while tapping the back button. But before hitting play, she took a deep breath and returned to the translation. "*La mia morbida lingua* . . . What's *la mia*?"

"Mine!" I shouted, raising my glassless hand. That one I knew.

"And *morbida*?" Maya asked next.

"Morbid?" I guessed, doubling over with Prosecco-induced laughter. "Gruesome? Gross?"

"No. No. No," Maya wailed. "My bad—It should be together with lingua: *La mia morbida lingua . . .* "

I gave her a puzzled look. I didn't understand.

"In this case, *morbida* means *soft*."

Suddenly I understood. "I got it!" I shouted, retrieving my glass as the full meaning sunk in: "I tremble at the thought to lean slowly with my morbidly soft tongue . . . "

Maya rolled her eyes. By the time we made it all the way through the translation, we were both howling like teenagers. And our bottle was empty.

"*Tuo fusto* means 'your stem'. *Eretto e duro* means 'erect and hard', and, for the pièce de resistance, *fosse di marmo* means 'made of marble.'"

"His marble stem?" I questioned through a long, drawn-out yawn.

Maya nodded and corrected, "His erect, marble stem."

I fluffed my pillow and tucked it beneath my head as I stretched out on the bed. "Stems always bring to mind wine glasses . . . or roses, maybe, " I mumbled, fading fast. "I'm thinking she meant something more like . . . his marble pillar of love."

The last thing I remember was hearing Maya stress how useful this had been as a vocabulary exercise—for my much-needed practice, followed by a snort. "But you're right about one thing, she meant 'his marble pillar of love' all right."

Not surprisingly I awoke the next morning with a killer headache, unlike Maya who jumped out of bed at first light and headed straight to the shower in anticipation of a fun-filled day ahead. I gingerly crawled out of bed, got dressed, then tiptoed downstairs to the coffee bar. Thankfully, the dining room was nearly empty when I showed up. Chitchat was not on my agenda.

Two espressos and a croissant later, my head had cleared enough that I could move it without needles stabbing the back of my eyes.

"I figured this is where you'd be," Maya announced setting her iPad down on the table before pulling out a vacant chair. She took off for the espresso machine while I squinted and watched her, amazed that she exhibited zero after-effects of our two-bottle indulgence the night before.

When she returned, she got straight to business. "Did you know that there are *three* copies of Michelangelo's David here in Florence?

I shook my head. "Not two?" was all I could say without causing my head to pound.

Maya handed me a pill. "Tylenol. 500 mg. Take it, it'll help." Then she opened her iPad, propped it up, and turned it so I could see a bronze David standing out in a country setting. "It's on the outskirts of the city. I'm thinking about taking a taxi out there to go see it. Want to come along?"

I downed the pill with the last of my espresso and slowly shook my head. "Waste of money."

Maya laughed. "You know, Sābra, you should really learn to stop drinking before you reach your limit. I always do."

"Next time," was all I managed to say.

"Otherwise, you would have lasted a bit longer last night and head the really good stuff."

My head perked up at that bit of news. "There was more?"

Maya nodded with a barely contained grin. "A couple more. Both involving different parts of her body, both in that multo-erotic whispering voice. One of the phrases was even new to me."

"Which one?"

Maya laughed and dug into a plateful of scrambled eggs. " I can't tell you now. That would spoil all the fun of letting you figure it out for yourself. It's a language lesson, remember?"

"I need another coffee," I said, pushing back from the table.

"Get some food, too," Maya ordered. "You'll feel better faster."

I took her advice, and so after getting another coffee I grabbed a fried egg and stabbed a slice of ham to go with it. Maya was right, by the time I finished eating I did feel much better. It wouldn't have mattered either way; I was not going to waste our only day in Florence on self-pity. I decided to ignore my lingering symptoms and keep on trekking until they were gone.

"We need to get packed up before we head out, unless you want to double back here before noon and check out then," Maya said. "We can store our bags at the front desk and pick them up just before we head to the train station later."

"What time's our train? I asked.

Maya opened her iPad and tapped her way through her bookmarks. "There are two departing a little after five tonight. One is a high-speed that gets us there about seven. Only thing is it costs almost forty euros."

"What's the other?" I asked.

"A *Regionale* that takes three hours, but only costs twenty-one euros."

"Does it really matter if it takes us an hour or three hours to get to Rome? It's going to be too late to do much once we arrive anyway, other than find the hotel and get something to eat."

Maya nodded. "I agree. So, let's plan on heading back here to get the bags by four."

With that decided we finished breakfast then headed upstairs to pack up before hauling our locked wheelies downstairs to park them in a corner behind the front desk.

It was sixty degrees outside and not a cloud in sight, in other words a gorgeous October day filled with fresh air, blue skies, and plenty of shopping. Just walking outside rejuvenated me. And walk we did, toward the black and white marble cathedral with its distinctive red dome, through a maze of streets filled with what seemed like a mile of tented stalls. A majority of those stalls were overflowing with leather items. It was, as Maya put it, leather mecca: gloves, purses, jackets, book bags, computer bags, wallets, belts . . . You name it, it was there. We walked all the way around the Duomo searching for the best buys. I kept one eye out for Michelangelo's workshop the whole time.

"You sure it isn't the *Museo dell'Opera* you're thinking of?" Maya asked, referring yet again to her saved notes from all those Florence tour searches. "That's the only Michelangelo site listed here."

"I've seen that one before, it's right here on the square. I could have sworn there was a second site. His workshop." was all I could say. "But I could be wrong. After all, it's been years since I was here last."

According to Maya's bookmarked note, Michelangelo's workshop is the site where the original David was carved, but now contains the famous Pietà statue. "It's building number 34," Maya summed up, dismissing further research by stowing her iPad to concentrate on the tent full of leather goods instead.

"Cuanto?" she asked the man behind the makeshift counter, holding up a square brown leather tote with a combo leather and brass curved handle on top. "Owwww, I like this one, too," she gushed, reaching for a small oblong square black purse, decorated with a large brass buckle. It had a thin leather strap hanging from it.

The clerk watched and waited, and finally announced, "*Quaranta euros ognuno.*"

I glanced over at her selections, then made a beeline to her side. "Maya, those are Fendi's."

"I know. Forty each isn't bad, you think?"

"That's a lot for knock-offs, but . . . "

Maya looked at me, surprised. "Knock-offs?"

I nodded. "You didn't think you'd find a real Fendi here for forty euros, did you?"

"No, but I wasn't looking for name brands either."

"How are you going to get them through customs on our return!"

"What do you mean? They're not going to do anything. Usually, they don't even check me. Hell, all they have to do is look at my passport to see that I'm well-traveled. I've got stickers all over the back cover."

"How well-traveled you are has nothing to do with them calling you over for a secondary inspection, Maya. Those agents are just like us; they can spot suspicious behavior and people hiding things before anyone says a word."

Maya nodded. "That does sound like us. But I'm not hiding anything. I'll simply declare X number of purses. Those we bought in Venice were some local off-brand anyway. If they ask about a couple of Fendi's in the mix, I'll just say I thought I got a great buy."

"They'll never believe that! As well-traveled as you are, they'll think you're a raving idiot if you didn't realize you knowingly bought a knock-off."

"What are they going to do to me? Lock me up? I doubt it."

"How about they take away your trusted traveler status? They could fine you. Or, they could confiscate the Fendi's. Worse, if they enter your name in their computer, you'd be guaranteed to get inspected after every international trip. "

"I'll take my chances," Many answered, turning away from me and back to the clerk. "How much if I buy two?"

He gave her a bored look. "Ottanta."

"Eighty? No discount?"

"Buy three. I give for €105."

Maya let out a sharp breath. "You call that a dea?! Come on . . . Give me a break. Can't you drop even €5? How about three for an even hundred?"

The clerk threw up his arms. "Bah," he swore. "Okay, okay, but you pay cash."

Maya reflexed as though she'd been slapped. "Cash?"

"*Sì, sì, contanti*" the clerk said, rubbing his thumb and the rest of his fingers together in a meaning that couldn't have been more clear.

Maya turned to me. Before she could say a word, however, I nixed the idea. "You're on your own for this one, kiddo. I haven't even thought about hitting an ATM yet today."

Maya turned back to the clerk. "Where's the nearest ATM?"

He exploded in a fit of temper. I didn't understand all of it, but enough to know that he was angry she wasted his time by negotiating in bad faith—"with empty pockets.' How was he to know if she was just playing games. Maybe he'd never see her again? He had a living to make.

"No, no, no," Maya kept repeating, trying to assure him she was on the level. "Just tell me where the stupid ATM is and I'll be back in *tre minuti. Per favore*!"

The clerk pointed somewhere behind him, toward the maze of streets behind Duomo square. Maya took off running, shouting to me to stay put, that she'd be right back.

I stayed behind as some sort of collateral. Why not? It was a great buy. But I did shout out, "Get extra euros just in case," at her receding backside.

Once Maya returned and handed over her 100 euro note, she and the clerk parted on good terms as though nothing had happened. We continued walking around the square with no particular destination in mind, just content to be out in the fresh air and sunshine.

I spotted the truffle oil shop first. The minute I pointed it out to Maya, she headed toward its entrance. "Which do you like best?" she asked over her shoulder, "the white or the black?"

"I'm not sure. They all look the same to me," was my simple answer. "I didn't even know mushrooms came in two colors."

"They're not exactly mushrooms per se," Maya announced. "Not at a couple hundred dollars an ounce!"

"How much," I asked, stopping dead in my tracks.

This tourist store didn't have any of those oh-so-expensive truffles on hand, as it turned out. Instead, they offered a selection of truffle-infused olive oils, and none of them cheap, it seemed to me. One was a 6" high skinny bottle of white for €27. The same bottle cost €21 for the black. But the oil in each looked yellow.

"What's the difference?" I whispered to Maya.

"One must be better than the other."

"You do cook, don't you," I asked, beginning to doubt she knew what she was talking about.

"I don't. But that's not to say I can't." She reached for her credit card, but I grabbed her arm and held her back. "Wait till we get to the City Market to buy. It's bound to be cheaper there than here in tourist central.

We no sooner resumed window shopping our way down the street when we spotted building number 34. Finally, there it was in plain sight: two clear glass entrance doors squeezed in between ancient stones making a semi-circular doorway: *Museo dell'Opera del Duomo*. The name had been etched into the clear glass doors, giving it an artistic touch, but with no contrasting color, it was easily missed. A sign on the granite wall outside the glass stated that the €15 entrance fee included entrance into the Duomo as well.

"Is this the place you were thinking of?" asked Maya.

I nodded, feeling foolish. How could I have thought there'd be two separate sites dedicated to Michelangelo on the Duomo square?

"You still want to go inside?" Maya asked, gazing streetside, watching the nearby café employees setting up chairs around their patio tables.

I hesitated. "I hate to spend €15 to see something I've already seen before. I mean, this place must not have made that much of an impression the first time if I thought there was a second venue."

"What's the deal with the statue you want to see in here again?" Maya asked.

"The deal is that there are two Pietà sculptures, one here and the one in the Vatican, but they're different, not copies. They were carved during two different periods of Michelangelo's works. I always get them confused."

"So? It's not like this is something you have to see, is it?"

I shrugged. "Michelangelo, in my opinion, was the greatest artist the world's ever seen, so it's only fitting that I get the facts of his different Pietà's straight in my head. This is my last chance to do it."

"Well then, just go in and see what you want to see. You don't have to take all day."

"What are you going to do in the meantime?"

"Don't worry about me. I'm going to stake out a spot in that café out front. I'll get something to drink so I can access their internet and then do some FaceTime with my aunt."

"You sure you don't want to see this Pietà with me?"

"Naw, no museums for me this trip. I'll wait and see the one in St. Peter's for free."

"You get entrance to the Duomo along with the ticket."

"Not planning on climbing any more steps this trip, either" Maya said laughing before heading for a patio table out in the sunshine.

In spite about what she said about Face Timing her aunt, I'm sure what she really wanted was to have some private time to catch up with Mr. Channel 5 guy. I couldn't help but wonder what, if anything, was going on with the two of them as I coughed up the fifteen euros and walked inside the museum.

⌐ **Chapter 14** ⌐

The idea that Italy preserved Michelangelo's original workshop as an authentic representation of where their favorite son spent so many years of his life has been stuck in my head for years. To that end, I envisioned a real sculptor's workshop; rough scaffolding or a ladder propped up against a work in-progress, with hammer and chisels laying nearby among scattered mounds of marble chips. Research disclosed that the original site had been long ago converted into a museum, and after the neighboring building was annexed, it triggered an extensive remodel. I've intended to visit the Museo dell' Opera del Duomo every time I cross the pond, but somehow I've never gotten around to see it since the remodel. Until today, that is.

All I can say now is this was no ordinary workshop turned museum I walked into that October morning. This building was a museum, yes. But what a museum it was; truly gorgeous inside, filled with some of the Italian renaissance's best works of art, set in the best possible light, in positions or honor and prestige the way their artist creators intended. My main goal was to see Michelangelo's Pietà, but I wasn't in a huge hurry to get right to it and then get out, either. I figured I'd just take in whatever sights interested me along the way, and then, after soaking up the wonders of sculpture, I'd exit and get on with the rest of the day. An hour or so inside, that's all I wanted, I told myself as I walked toward the first exhibit just past the entrance foyer.

A tour group led the way into the "Salone del Paradiso," in the distance ahead, their leader's voice announced. I filed in behind them, hoping for a free lecture.

In a way it reminded me of my college days, where a certain art class met once weekly inside a nearby museum. A feeling of nostalgia flooded over me, inducing me to work my way closer to the center of the group to better hear the guide.

"The space between the baptistry and its church is commonly referred to as Paradiso, since it evokes the joy of those just receiving baptism and are now crossing the space to participate in the Eucharist for the first time."

This Salon was a scaled-down reproduction of Florence's famous cathedral façade, adorned on three levels with columns and recessed naves filled with statuary consigned and created to complete the original in their originally intended placement. It was like a church within a museum. Or a museum within a museum. Either way, it was incredible.

"At the time of the Renaissance, churches with abundant sculptures represented a sign of wealth and God's blessings," the guide continued. "Florence's growing importance at that time was demonstrated by its ability to keep pace with other monumental churches being built throughout Europe."

I stuck with the group as we walked around the room admiring details of the statues and the architecture. From here the group leader wound her way toward the next wing, pausing at the Gates of Paradise along the way.

"These weigh 4500 kilograms, or in U.S. weights, 4 ½ tons," she announced, pausing so everyone had time to admire the two 17-foot-tall structures. "These gates, made by Ghiberti, are among the finest bronze sculptures ever made. Each scene in the panels represents a different Old Testament story. These are the very doors that decorated the Baptistery entrance across the street for more than 500 years. And there they remained, subject to atmospheric and automotive degradation, not to mention bubblegum at the hands of tourists, until the mid 1980s when they were removed into a more protected environment. The ones now standing outside the Baptistery are the replicas."

I dutifully admired the bronze gates along with everyone else.

"Brunelleschi designed the cathedral's iconic dome, which is a masterpiece of art as well as the enduring symbol of Florence. But Michelangelo, following the enormous success of his David, was the man chosen to make the largest impact on Renaissance Florence when he was contracted to sculpt a statue of each of the twelve apostles for the Cathedral. Not only that, but his Pietà—all three, in fact—remain major attractions for Italy. One in particular, belongs to this museum."

Now we were getting to the main interest, noticeable by the hushed reverence that preceded our entrance into the next room. I joined in as the entire group surged forward and then fanned out encircling the statue.

"The most famous Pietà, of course, is the one currently located in Saint Peter's Basilica in the Vatican. If you get the chance, go there and compare it to this one, since the two represent very different periods of Michelangelo's life and style. The St. Peter's Pietà was completed when he was just aged twenty-four. His youth motivated him to break tradition from all previous Pietà statues, which were made of wood and depicted small figures of Christ. Michelangelo made them bigger, for a more lasting impression. He emphasized the youth of the Virgin to demonstrate that God is the source of all beauty, and since she was the one closest to God, she was filled with both youth and beauty. Interestingly, it is the only one of Michelangelo's works he ever signed. When you go to Roma, look closely at Mary's sash and you will see it."

I made a mental note to do just that once Maya and I got to the Rome portion of our trip.

"This Pietà," the guide continued, pointing at the grouping elevated in front of us, "is often referred to as 'The Florentine Pietà' simply because it is housed here in Florence. But it is more commonly known as The Bandini Pietà, the ultimate owner of the statue. It's also known as 'The Deposition', or 'The Lamentation over the Dead Christ,' because it depicts Christ shortly after he was taken down from the cross, supported by The Virgin Mary, Mary Magdalene and Nicodemus. It is said that the cowled figure of Nicodemus is a self-portrait of Michelangelo himself. Notice that Mary is not touching her son: this is because she is now reunited with the Father."

I didn't understand this bit of Catholic lore, but moved in for a closer look anyway. I was tempted to ask which figure represented the Virgin and which was Mary Magdalene; also, why was one figure so much smaller than the other? But I didn't have the courage to interrupt the ongoing lecture.

"It is believed that Michelangelo intended this for his own tomb, because it was never a commissioned piece. We do know that he worked on it tirelessly almost every night over a period of eight years while in his late 70s, using just a single candle for illumination. The question of why Michelangelo, in a fit of frustration, attempted to destroy the work before completing it has been debated for centuries. Was it because the stone contained veins of emery and was therefore so hard that his chisel struck sparks with every stroke? Or was it because his self-criticism was so severe that nothing he did ever satisfied him? A third theory is that Michelangelo, for whatever reason, was so unhappy with the result that he began to change it into something entirely different. Unfortunately, we will never know the answer to this riddle. If you look closely, you can see where the left arm was repaired by Bandini's apprentice, Tiberio Calcagni. The left leg, unfortunately, was never recovered."

I walked around the statue several times, along with the rest of the group. The back side saas untouched. It looked like any other hunk of stone. I couldn't envision the possibility of larger-then-life figures inside it, as Michelangelo and so many other artists have done. My second trip around, I focused on the rock itself, to see what kinds of imperfections existed or if they were even noticeable, and how they might react to repeated chiseling. But I couldn't distinguish anything unusual among the varied shades of this stone in its natural state.

"The third Pietà, known as the Rondanini Pietà, is located in Milano's Castello Sforzesco. It is named for the site where it stood for many years, the courtyard of Palazzio Rondanini in Roma. It was Michelangelo's final version, and depicts the mourning Virgin Mary struggling to hold the upright body of Christ close to her. Some question whether it was ever finished, since Michelangelo worked on it until the last days of his life."

As the guide finished talking, she led the group into the next room. I headed in the opposite direction, toward the front doors and into the café out front. Maya stood up the minute she spotted me and began gathering up her possessions, ready to head out.

"So how was it?" she asked, gulping the remainder of her drink.

"It was good; I'm glad I went in. So, where to from here?"

She paused long enough to open her iPad and show me the map she'd downloaded, pointing out the route we needed to take. "We just go around the cathedral until we come to Via de Martelli. There, we go right and walk to Via de' Gori. Turn left and continue walking straight down the Via for about ten minutes. It takes us right to the City Market. Should be easy to see once we get close, because the building looks like an old train station with a red metal roof and lots of iron filigree decorating the outside. Plus, we should see lots of locals pulling those wheelie shopping bags toward the market once we get close."

As we walked, I recapped details of my quick tour, including what we needed to look for in St. Peters. About the time I finished, we arrived in the neighborhood near the market. The scent of cooking food reached us well before we sighted the distinctive building with its ground floor of cement archways beneath a glassed-in upper level. Delivery trucks zoomed back and forth to and from crowded loading zones.

Just outside the building's main entrance, we came to a series of stands containing fall flowers, late season fruit, and assorted small bags of nuts. The merchandise here for the most part was not processed or pre-packaged; it looked instead like it had arrived straight from the farm. Inside the building, on the other hand, was an open-air market with ceilings two stories high.

The center section was filled with table-top stands. Some contained cheeses, others fresh fish laid out on beds of crushed ice. Exhibits of fruits and vegetables were everywhere. Along the walls on both sides, were mini-markets, with shiny white glassed-in cases displaying bowls of prepared foods that could be purchased by weight. A selection of salami, hams, and prosciutto hung from strings or mesh bags from the ceiling behind several of those display cases. Another displayed strings of garlic, onions, dried peppers, and an international selection of gourmet paprikas.

Along the pathway leading to the rear of the market tables had been set up and were filled with samples, each one sporting a container of toothpicks. Invariably, a baguette of sliced bread had been set out alongside the samples. Maya and I tasted a little of everything as we worked our way down the floor, which ended in front of a huge wine store. No samples had been set out there, unfortunately, although you could purchase a half-glass of select selections. Row after row of wine bottles lined the entire back wall.

Maya bought two half-glasses and downed them in record time, encouraging me to do the same. The thought of alcohol so soon after my morning-after head made me pause. "Maybe later," was all I could say.

"Hair of the dog," Maya said, setting her empty glass down before moving on to the next exhibit.

Once we rounded the far corner and began working our way forward again, we came to a shop selling assorted varieties of truffle-infused oils. Their display table contained a line of bread slices laid out in front of a half-dozen saucers, each containing a small sample from their inventory. Behind each sample stood the corresponding bottle of oil, complete with sale price. Cubes of cheese on small plates had been laid out as well, placed throughout the table, each sporting a toothpick. A large bowl occupied the table's center spot, serving as a repository for all those discarded toothpicks.

As I sampled the different oils, I glanced up at the green-tinted windows on the second floor. By the looks of it, there were rows of sit-down eateries as well as stand-up snack counters all along the one side. They were all crowded, and all noisy.

"Oh look!" Maya squealed, pointing at one of the bottles mid-way down the display table. "Those the same ones we found next to the cathedral. And they were €21 and €27."

I leaned in for a closer look. Sure enough, these were €11 and €15. "What did I tell you?"

Maya picked up a toothpick and stabbed a square of cheese, and sloshed it around in the white truffle infused oil. "Honey truffle," she sang out, smacking her lips after tasting it, commanding me to try it.

"Delicious," I agreed, checking its corresponding bottle. We both sucked in a gasp at the price: €49 for 200 ml.

"Wow! Fifty bucks for less than 10 oz!" Maya exclaimed.

I reached for the triangular-shaped bottle and looked for the amount of white truffle bits in the bottom. There weren't many. "Looks more like diced garlic," I whispered to Maya, turning my attention to the label. "Says here it contains olive oil and white truffle flavor."

Just then a store clerk approached. She took the bottle from me and returned it to its place on the table. Then she smiled. "First you taste the honey, then the cheese, then, finally, the lingering savor of zee white truffle," she explained in heavily accented English.

"Why does the white bottle's label only list truffle flavor?" asked Maya, pointing to the bottle. "Does that mean no white truffle pieces inside?"

The clerk laughed. "Oh no, no, no. Eez just the way we label here. You will never see many pieces of white truffle in oil, because they typically sell for thousands of euros per pound. Italian white truffles are the priciest of all. They are so scarce."

"Wow," was all Maya said, tasting yet another sample. "Who sells them around here?"

Again, the clerk laughed. "Buying truffles is no easy task, since they are so rare and so perishable. You would have better luck foraging for them yourself. The regular foragers have undoubtedly already contracted their finds to upscale restaurants throughout the region."

"Do you cook?" she asked Maya.

"Yes, I'm Italian." She made it sound like no further explanation was necessary.

The clerk turned to me, waiting for my answer.

"Not me. I just eat Italian."

The woman turned back to Maya and lowered her voice, cook-to-cook: "Black truffles are generally less expensive, so they're more attainable for the average home cook. Though they're less aromatic, their flavor stands up better to heat so they're better suited for sauces—risottos, and the like. A tiny bit of superior truffle oil is a simple way to add an expensive flair to your food." Then she looked both ways and leaned in close. "I tell you a secret: Porcini mushrooms diced up very small is a noteworthy alternative."

We ended up buying a bottle of each of the two flavors—though only Maya bought one of the €49 bottles.

"You sure you're Italian?" I joked after we walked out of the market.

"All that tasting has given me an appetite," Maya announced. "Let's walk to the Piazza dell Repubblica and find a small ristorante in the heart of the historic center."

"We could eat upstairs here."

Maya nixed the idea, saying it sounded too hectic. "I don't know about you, but I'd rather sit out in the fresh air, relaxing in the sun at a table on cobblestones."

I had to admit, she had a point.

Our walk to this historic section of town took just under fifteen minutes. Maya led the way around the piazza in search of the perfect table; it had to be in sunshine yet near enough to its restaurant entrance for, she claimed, faster service in addition to free bathroom privileges.

The marquee out front listed only one item for its lunchtime special: *Tortelli di mugellani con ragù of cinghiale*, at a cost of €12 euros each. The added *'con vino della casa,'* I knew meant a full carafe came with the meal.

"It's probably watered down," Maya whispered as she pulled out a chair.

"You better translate," I insisted, still studying the marquee. "I confess I'm not a courageous diner at the best of times."

"Stuffed pasta—usually it's a mixture of cheesy potatoes with parsley, seasoned with nutmeg, in a stew of wild boar. It's always good. Relax, you'll love it."

I checked the time as we set our belongings in an empty chair and settled in. "It's twelve-thirty now. We have to keep an eye on how long we stay here, otherwise we'll end up having to hurry to get back to the hotel. God forbid we run out of time and end up missing the train. I don't want to arrive in Rome in the middle of the night and still have to search for someplace to eat."

"All the more reason to load up on lunch now," Maya agreed. "You want me to set an alarm?"

I ignored the sarcasm. "Tell me instead what itinerary possibilities you managed to find for later."

"What would you say to investigating Europe's oldest apothecary store?

I shook my head. "Doesn't sound exciting. Too touristy, more than likely. What do they sell?"

"Homemade soaps. Cough drops."

"Pass. What else you got?"

"Galileo's finger."

"Say what?" It sounded revolting.

Even Maya laughed at the sound of it. "I don't even know if they know it's really his finger, but it's supposed to be. Petrified, of course. It's at some Galileo Museum."

The waiter showed up with two full carafes of the house wine, one white and one red, asking: "*Quale vuoi?*" When we pointed at the white, he set it down in the middle of the table and took off. He returned minutes later with glasses and plates topped with silverware wrapped inside a napkin. "*Lo speciale de oggi, no?*" he quizzed. As we nodded in the affirmative, he raced off and disappeared inside the kitchen.

I waited till the waiter left to say more about Galileo's finger. "You weren't serious, were you?"

"it's no joke, but I knew you wouldn't go for it. That's why I saved the best for last."

"Which is?"

Maya preferred to keep me hanging. "It's a surprise! I swear, you'll like it, though. All I can tell you now is that it has something to do with Michelangelo. You'll see."

"Hey," Maya suddenly remembered. "Did you ever hear back from Sandusky?"

"Not so far," I said, pulling out my phone and checking my messages.

There was one text, which had arrived early this morning. It simply said, "I just couldn't bring myself to do it."

I text a reply: "Do what?" I was pretty fuzzy regarding where our last conversation had left off, so wasn't exactly sure how or where to begin now.

All talk ceased the minute our food arrived. It was plentiful, and it was delicious. Maya and I looked around as we ate, happy to soak up the atmosphere of this historical setting. As our plates emptied, the waiter returned asking about dessert.

Maya waived him off with a "No *grazie*," then poured the last of the wine in each our glasses. The minute he left, she said: "How about we look for a gelato stand near the Ponte Vecchio?"

Sounded good to me. I was warm, full, and content. I didn't care what we did next.

When my phone sounded off with an incoming text, I jumped. "I just couldn't bring myself to go in his office for a private meeting," I read.

"I know, I know," I sympathized. "Afraid of what he might have done?"

"Oh no, not at all. Afraid of what I might have said. I'm sure I would have tipped my hand that I was recording him. Or trying to trap him. As it is, I'm scared to death he'll find out I searched through my personnel file to verify if he put that letter in it."

"Why? You have every right to see your file."

"Without his permission? He'd turn it into a federal offense."

Maya leaned in close to keep up with the ongoing messages.

"What did you find out?"

"No such letter. He was lying."

"Ask her if she ever asked him about it. Have her tell him she never got a copy. I could be wrong, but I'm pretty sure management is supposed to copy us in on all personnel type correspondence."

I began typing the message, but then reconsidered. "What for? He'd probably say he hasn't had time to submit it yet."

"Yeah, you're right," Maya agreed, draining the last of her wine. She imitated Noggins next: "Come to my office at midnight tonight and I'll hand you a copy," laughing as she said it.

"It's okay," Sandusky wrote next. "It doesn't matter anymore because I'm taking steps to end it."

"What do you mean?" I wrote.

"Oh God, you think maybe she quit?" Maya asked, all laughter gone.

I shrugged. "Stranger things have happened."

"Look," Sandusky wrote, "I appreciate all your advice, but I just can't discuss this anymore." On that cryptic note, the message ended.

"Samantha, please tell me you followed up on at least one of our suggestions with HR?" I texted. But she didn't answer.

Both Maya and I looked at each other with puzzled expressions. Neither of us had the faintest idea what Sandusky meant.

I checked the time: one-forty. "We better get a move on or we'll sit here and yak away the rest of the afternoon. I have to run to the bathroom first, though." With that I took off.

Maya was chatting into her iPad when I returned. At first, I thought maybe she had managed to contact Sandusky again. But then I heard her say: "If you're there, on duty, you'll turn up somewhere, either by signing into Omega's computer system or by swiping your ID to get into the airport's employee parking lot. Doesn't matter if some dimwit manager tells you not to punch the clock."

The reply that answered came from a male voice. "So, you always have to swipe your ID to get in and out of the parking lot? That means there should be a record of everyone's comings and goings, right?" I was fairly certain that voice belonged to Mr. Chanel 5 news guy: Bryce Williamson.

I saw Maya's head nod at the screen.

"They'd have to prove you swiped out and never returned while technically still 'on duty' and being paid for it, right?"

Again, Maya nodded. As an afterthought she added; "We're all but microchipped, just like they do dogs. Trackable wherever we go."

"And this applies to supervision as well?" Bryce asked.

Maya turned around and looked at me. Then she turned back to Bryce, making no attempt to hide what they were talking about. "Of course. It's probably a FAA rule . . . or CAB, or DOT. One of those alphabet agencies. Everyone—every one of us—uses their badge for every access point, period."

"Every badged employee?" he repeated. "Don't want to be redundant, but I want to be sure of all the facts . . . "

Maya moved in close to her monitor and lowered her voice. "Look, even if we get a discount for the pay lot, we still have to swipe our ID to verify eligibility."

She blew a couple of kisses at the monitor, in what sounded suspiciously like a girlfriend/boyfriend sign off, then closed up the iPad and hurried off to the restaurant's front door.

Minutes later she returned. "I took care of lunch!" she announced. "My treat." She took the lead heading out into the street, though she still wouldn't reveal our destination. "It's a ten-minute walk. You're gonna love this."

A couple of blocks later, we passed an ATM. "You need more euros?" Maya asked, looking over at me the minute she spotted it.

I shook my head. "I think I'm good for now. If I find anything that costs more than €120, I'll just put it on my card."

We walked through an archway just before arriving at the Palazzo Vecchio. As we turned the corner, we spotted two girls in formal dresses, each accompanied by men in suits. Behind them came another couple and a small child dressed in wedding regalia. All were carrying flowers. "My guidebook mentioned that more people get married in City Hall than in churches here because it's so much cheaper," explained Maya. We stood a short distance apart, watching the group have their pictures taken.

"Maybe it's faster," I commented. "You know, no mass."

As soon as the wedding party departed, Maya grabbed my arm. "Come on, we're here." She led me closer toward the front entrance of the Palazzo. The copy of Michelangelo's David stood on the left side of the doorway, while a statue of Hercules stood on the right side.

"The statue of Hercules," Maya explained "was sculpted by Michelangelo's chief rival in gaining Medici patronage: Baccio Bandinelli. The graffiti is on the wall behind Hercules, but down low."

"What graffiti?" I asked. I had no idea what she was talking about.

"It's supposed to be near the right-hand corner, and down low," Maya said, inching closer to the wall. "Easily missed," according to my guidebook."

We both closed in until, at last, she found it and pointed it out. "There! It's supposedly Michelangelo's graffiti." It was a face scratched into one of the bricks.

"Why would Michelangelo carve this behind a competitor's statue?" I asked.

"For the hell of it?" Maya answered. "Who knows? There's lots of theories. Some say it was an example of his need to constantly create. Others say it was a self-portrait, meant to taunt Bandinelli, because that way Michelangelo had an 'exhibit' on each side of the palace doorway. Another theory is that Michelangelo passed this way daily on his way to his workshop, and some street pest constantly waylaid him and talked his ear off, so he carved the man's likeness while the guy was droning on and on about nothing."

"I like the story of an everlasting taunt to Bandinelli better."

Maya laughed. "There's more. One idea is that Michelangelo witnessed an execution here, and after seeing the expression on the man's face, he etched that face on the wall as a tribute. Another theory is that the executed was indebted to Michelangelo, and so he decided to leave his own condemnation since he never collected on the debt."

"Fascinating," was my summary, staring at the small face carved into the wall.

"Good surprise, no?" Maya asked.

I nodded. "One of the best. Thanks."

From the palace, it was a short walk to the Arno River, and from there to the Ponte Vecchio bridge. Along the way, Maya confessed that Bryce was working on some kind of investigation about Omega's management misdeeds.

"Hope you don't mind, but I've been passing him some background information."

"Like about Sandusky?" I asked.

She nodded. "Had to be done. Those bastards need to be stopped."

The bridge appeared directly ahead. Shops covered the bridge, with antique wooden shutters decorating their windows, high above the river.

"Did you know these used to be butcher's shops? They tossed so much garbage from their butchering into the river that the city finally ran them out. Guess the whole area stunk to high heaven. That's how these all became specialty shops. Tourists came next."

"I think I read that," Maya said, sounding like she didn't care. "I do know that this was the only bridge in Florence to survive WWII bombings."

Once on the bridge, we walked past several jewelry stores, each one pricier than the next, it seemed. We stopped in front of another's display window mid-way down the bridge. Maya fell in love with one of the rings in a corner grouping. The ring she selected had a wide gold band, but with a slight wavy curvature to it. Inset into the top of the band were six different colored gem stones.

"What do you think?" she asked, unable to make up her mind whether to go inside or not, probably because it was priced €370.00

"It looks like one of those mother's rings," I answered. "You know, with birthstones of your children. Only problem is that you don't have any kids, so who's stones do you put in it?"

"I'd just leave it the way it is."

We ended up turning and walking away. "You ought to get the store's name, in case you change your mind later," I suggested a few steps later. "Why don't you go get one of their cards? That way at least you'll have their phone number, too."

We turned around, intending to go back. Maya raised her phone to take a picture of the store's front. That's when the lettering over the store's display hit us: Bertani's.

We both stood frozen for a long minute. Then we looked at each other in open-mouthed surprise. "Bertani's" Maya mouthed. "You think this is the same place? The store that guy on the train was talking about?"

"It has to be!" I announced. "My God, it all makes sense now, doesn't it?"

Maya nodded. "I'm going to go inside and ask for Luigi and see if I can get the discount."

I grabbed her arm to hold her back. "Hang on, Maya. You can't just go rushing in there halfcocked. If you're going to do this, you have to do it right, like you really are the daughter's friend. What if, God forbid, she's already been here?"

Maya took a deep breath and nodded. "If this discount deal is even the slightest illegal, I doubt they'd call the cops."

"Yeah, but the Luigi guy might try to detain you. He'll want to know who the hell you are."

Maya shrugged. "True. Either way, I'll insist I'm . . . what was his name again?"

"Who?" I asked, confused.

"The guy on the train! I'll insist I'm his daughter's friend. It was all arranged."

"Bartolo. I think that's who it was."

"Worse comes to worse, I'll have to run, which means you'll have to hang on to my backpack."

I wouldn't admit it to Maya, but I was more than happy to remain behind with her backpack. "First things first: we need to make sure you have enough money to get the ring. Cash only, remember?" I pulled out my phone and opened the calculator. "How much was it again?"

"€370."

I calculated the 40% discount. "So, less €148 euros means you'll need €222 cash in hand. How much do you have on you?"

"€100," answered Maya. "That's the extra I got at the ATM this morning."

I opened my wallet and dug out a €100 note. Along with it, I pulled out a twenty-euro coin. "So, there's two-twenty. Now all you need are two one-euro coins."

"But I don't have any more," Maya wailed, sounding pitiful. "I can't believe you don't have any more. You always have plenty of cash!"

"God, Maya, for the life of me, I don't understand how can you go walking around Europe with no cash at all! How were you going to pay for a gelato here, with a stupid credit card?" I continued ranting as I searched through all the pockets inside my purse. You look again," I insisted, looking at the time, feeling panicky.

"We don't have time to go searching for an ATM. We have to have this finished in the next fifteen minutes or else forget the whole idea. We barely have time to get to the hotel and make it to the train station as it is."

Maya searched her backpack again. Nothing. She stuck her hand in one of her jean pockets, and came up with a single one-euro coin.

Finally, I found my last remaining euro coin and handed it over. "You so owe me!"

Maya recounted all the cash inside her open palm, nodding as she did so. Then she handed me her backpack, took a deep breath, and marched up to the store's front door.

I retreated to the safety of solid ground off the bridge, looking wistfully at a nearby gelato stand. I couldn't help but pull out my phone repeatedly to check the time.

Less than ten minutes later, Maya walked out of the store. I stared at her face, looking for some kind of sign indicating success or failure. Once she got closer, I spotted a broad smile stretching all across her face. She held up her right hand in anticipation of joining me, but I didn't wait for her to catch up. Not while we were still in sight of Bertani's front window.

Instead, I turned and half trotted the next two blocks, to the corner where we were turned away from the river, onto the street that would take us straight back to the cathedral. My heart pounded as I ducked around the corner and waited for Maya.

"Yee-haaaa" Maya shouted the minute she rounded the building. She held up her hand so that we both could admire her shiny new purchase. "Now this is what I call almost free!"

We didn't linger, however. We took off at a fast pace, retracing our steps past the Palacio, through the stalls of leather goods near the cathedral, laughing and rehashing the events leading up to this memorable buy all the way back to the hotel.

We were still laughing and congratulating ourselves as we turned the corner to our hotel, grabbed our bags from behind the unmanned desk, and took off again. Ten minutes later, we arrived at the train station leaving us with mere minutes in which to buy our tickets and find the loading platform.

Chapter 15

After our experience on the previous train ride, it was understandable that both Maya and I felt a twinge of apprehension as this one began. Well, to be honest, maybe it was more expectation than apprehension. At any rate, we both knew lightening wouldn't strike twice. But still we held our breath wondering what lie ahead as we validated our tickets and climbed onboard the train bound for Termini station in Rome.

Since we bought cheap seats on a *Regionale,* we had no illusions about what to expect onboard: the car would no doubt be full; there would be plenty of short stops along the way, with lots of commotion up and down the aisle until the moment we pulled out; there would be no WiFi. Again, seating was the standard double occupancy of two bench seats facing each other from opposite sides of a table.

Maya, knowing the WiFi situation ahead of time, had at least downloaded all her messages before we boarded, so she could sort through them at her leisure during the three-hour ride. She therefore plunked her iPad on the table in front of her the minute we sat down, then wrapped her stylishly long sweater around her and waited for the train to pull out.

Two oriental girls had rudely claimed all four seats on the opposite side of the aisle. There they sat, each facing the other in the middle of a seat having filled the rack above with two oversized wheelies. Between each of their legs was one of those upright, long-haul backpacks. I'm not exaggerating when I say that each of those packs must have been 3' high. God, I couldn't imagine traveling that way.

On our side of the aisle, opposite Maya and I, a youngish twenty-something female wearing jeans filled with stylishly frayed holes, a zip-up hoodie sweatshirt and untied high-top tennis shoes slid in, jarring the table as she got comfortable. Her hair was a bright burgundy color, liberally streaked with do-it-yourself copper highlights, making her look ready for Halloween—over two weeks away yet. She constantly adjusted her wire rimmed glasses while using the train window as a mirror to apply a fresh layer of red lip gloss. I couldn't help but notice that she wore no other makeup, so was puzzled as to why she bothered so much with her lips. Maybe she was practicing to look like a vampire.

"Do they even celebrate Halloween here?" I whispered over to Maya.

"Not the way we do," she answered back, opening her iPad just as the train slid into motion.

I watched the countryside go past as our speed increased. It was quiet now inside the car. Most everybody had snuggled down into their seats and were either reading a book, a newspaper, or glued to their phones. I turned and watched as Maya read a full screen single-spaced memo. When she finished, she closed the cover and stuffed it inside the backpack on her lap. She then moved the backpack to her other side, placing it next to the window. Finally, she turned to me.

"Remember how I told you in Florence that I've sorta been helping Bryce with his Omega investigation?"

I nodded, wondering where she was going with this.

"Well, I thought I'd ask you to share some of your stories with me. I mean, I have lots of bits and pieces—all the usual gossip that everyone talks about. But I don't know anyone actually involved, or if any of it is even true."

I snorted. "It's probably all true. Our management ranks are filled with unethical bastards, in my humble opinion."

"So, you'll help me, then?"

I stiffened. "Help you?" I repeated. I'd been very careful through the years to keep my nose clean. Sure, I knew plenty. But it was stored in my memory to protect me if and when I needed it, not to become a martyred whistleblower. Years of experience had taught me that when the internal bureaucracy is so thoroughly corrupted, a single person is useless to go up against them. Their network is too protected.

Maya sensed my hesitation. "I just want to pass along a few items. You know, give Bryce the big picture. I mean, it's his investigation, after all."

I knew that Bryce was investigating Omega. It was a favorite subject of his through the years. What would it hurt, I told myself. "Okay, but keep my name out of it, understood?"

Maya nodded. "I already have a couple of good leads."

"So do I. Tell Bryce to snoop around the ticket counter. Different days. Different hours. Ask around about Dough Boy's extended absences after the morning briefing."

"Dough Boy?" Maya repeated.

"Daugherty. Marvin."

"The ticket counter manager?" Maya asked, clarifying.

I nodded. "Then tell Bryce to go out to East Lake mall and visit the Putt Putt Golf driving range. Tell him to take a camera."

Maya nodded. "Look Sabra, I'm not going to repeat everything chapter and verse. But you gotta give me the whole story. I'll pass along what I remember, but it's gotta make sense to me first."

I took a deep breath, wondering how much I should give her. But then I figured what the hell, let Bryce make the most of it.

"The whole damn bunch it seems are double dipping during their working hours while holding the rest of our feet to the fire, quoting company rules ad nauseum, Daugherty owns and operates Putt Putt Golf. It's a shooting range near East Lake Mall. He does morning shift briefings then ducks into his office and shuts the door. Only he doesn't always stay there. Oh, he gives a great appearance of being busy—on a conference call or writing performance logs, something like that. The only way to contact him is via cell phone, which no one ever does since he delegates everything to one of his two pet leads. The real secret is that two or three days mid-week, he takes off to the shooting range to manage his business all by himself."

"How long has this been going on?" Maya asked.

I shrugged. "As long as I can remember. It's a great gig: two paychecks and no payroll to meet. No one likes the guy anyway, so who cares if he's gone or not?"

"How did you find out about it?"

"By accident." I stared up at the ceiling, remembering the day. "My kids ran out of gas enroute to the mall. Guess where they parked while waiting for me? Funny, I didn't think anything of it at the time. I mean, we all work crazy hours. I just assumed Dough Boy did, too. I didn't work ticketing. Only later, when the counter folks kept bitching about his extended absences did a bell ring."

"So? What did you do?"

"I send my husband out to hit a few balls, what else?"

"And take a few pictures!" Maya interrupted gleefully. "Putt Putt Golf, who goes there anyway?"

"No Omega employees, obviously. Otherwise, his secret would have been blown long before this. My guess is he began filling in a day or so when he had to, but then when it got easy to double dip, he just stepped in and replaced the part-time help."

Maya nodded. "If time is money, then technically he's stealing from the company. What else you got?"

"One of the concourse managers used to brag about how he didn't have to pay for babysitters. I wondered why, since his kids were pretty young. Didn't take long to find out he does much the same thing as Dough Boy, only on the pm shift: he leaves right after briefing then comes back at the end of the shift in time to file the shift report, turn out the lights, and lock up. "

"I always thought one of the floor leads submitted the report."

I shook my head. "They each submit a portion . . . to him. All he has to do is cut and paste theirs into the master. That way it looks like he was out there managing the entire shift, staying on top of things."

"Bastard," Maya muttered.

"I used to watch the nightly lineup of young mothers calling home in order to say good night to their kids before rushing out to work their next flight. Every time I see that manager's face, I think of that lineup. I don't know how he looks himself in the mirror."

"He probably thinks he's smarter than everybody else. Crooks usually do."

"Yum Yum Yoghurt is another biggie," I began, winding down, feeling tired. It was exhausting dredging up all these old stories and the negative feelings that came with them.

"The one in East Lake Mall, right?" Maya asked, perking up. "I've heard rumors; some gate agent was given a whole weekend off to drive one of Omega's ramp trucks somewhere, supposedly."

"Yep, orchestrated by one of the big honchos upstairs: Sitterding. The fact that Sitterding used a gate agent at all is what started the gossip. The gates biggest brown-noser, too—Russell Pugh. You might know."

"Pee-U?" Maya laughed. "That creep?"

"Everyone watches him cuz he's such a brown-nosing little snitch. But especially when he refused to discuss his 'Special Assignment' after it was posted on the work schedule. So stupid of them to even put it there."

Maya agreed. "They'd have been smarter just showing him out sick."

"But then they would have had to dock his pay, because the work schedule is copied in to both HR and payroll. This way he got paid for all those hours not worked."

"What was he doing anyway?" Maya asked, frowning.

"Picking up a used yoghurt machine for Sitterding's Yum Yum business."

"So? How far did he drive it?"

"Turns out he drove it all the way to New Jersey."

"How in hell did you manage to get the details?"

"One of the ramp's ground equipment agents discovered the extra twelve hundred miles on the truck. Sitterding ordered him to ignore it. But he'd already told me."

"How? Why? You don't work the ramp!"

I snickered. "His kid was in karate with one of mine."

"Wow! Small world, huh?"

I nodded. "The truth always comes out in the end."

By now I was winding down in rhythm to the rocking motion of the train. The sun was in the final stages of setting in the distance. I leaned back and closed my eyes.

"Can I ask you just one more question?" I heard Maya ask as I nodded off.

I opened my eyes and looked over at her. "Why didn't you ever report any of this?"

"And get set up like Sandusky? Not me. I just collect my paycheck and pass go. They'll get caught eventually. Everything happens in its own good time, you'll see."

The train's rocking motion was such that I nodded off. Though I heard bells clanging whenever we approached the next city on our route, I never came fully awake unless the sounds were accompanied by steady braking. On second thought, even then I never fully awakened unless I heard the hissing of engines and the banging of cabin doors along with parting shouts on the platform outside.

On those occasions we did stop, I could hear grunts of passengers while they hoisted their luggage onboard, followed by footsteps. Most kept their voices to a whisper as they lumbered down the car's narrow aisle. Invariably, we pulled out again after what seemed like five minutes and I'd fall back into semi-consciousness again.

It was dark when we came to a silent sliding pause at a rail siding leading into Termini station. Just as on airplanes, the great majority instantly jumped to their feet and began hauling bags down from the overhead rack in order to race into position near the doorway. Like every train I'd been on thus far, at this point we'd lurch forward, causing bodies to brace their feet and grab the nearest seat back, until we came to a full stop alongside our assigned platform with a loud hiss of the engine .

Maya and I got off last, then headed up the walkway between a set of rails for nearly fifteen minutes just to get to the front of the terminal. It stunk inside. The air reeked of exhaust and stale smoke. The only light that managed to make it down here came from overhead lights, high above us, revealing dirty tiles that were littered with trash and cigarette butts. Nearly everyone we passed was walking and talking on their cells, or stooped over in order to read their screens. Or they were busy texting.

We circled around slow-moving people at our peril mainly because of swinging arms— many holding lit cigarettes, our wheelies bouncing behind us. Once, while passing a pair engrossed in an intimate conversation, the female's arm shot out to emphasize a point and nearly stabbed my leather jacket with her red-hot poker. Sorry, but her quick "Scuzie," wouldn't make up for a burn hole in my leather jacket.

Maya's wheelie, meanwhile, thanks to the fix-it girl in Bologna, continued to behave as it should, except now her handle wouldn't stay up. If she stopped and struggled and managed to force it down, then it refused to come back up again without stopping for another struggle.

Once we arrived at the front exit doors, we stood off to one side to study the paperwork from the hotel. "It says it's a ten-minute walk from here."

"You didn't email them for detailed directions?" Maya asked, pulling out her cell and tuning into Termini's WiFi. Meanwhile, a guy standing on the sidewalk out front, otherwise busy hawking for hotels and taxis, asked us if we needed a hotel.

"No thanks, we already have one," I answered, showing him my confirmation printout.

He walked over and studied the paper for a moment, then pulled out his own map. Using his index finger to trace the street out front, he studied it for long minutes before pointing off to the left, toward the lights in the distance. "Go straight. At zee Piazza, turn right," he said while motioning for us to go left. "Turn again at McDonalds."

I nodded, confused over the first right or left turn. Maya was still studying her phone's directions. Finally, she tucked it in her pocket and said, "Okay, let's go."

We walked the way the guy told us to go until we arrived at the Piazza. "None of these street names match those on the map," Maya grumbled.

"He said to go right, but pointed left," I told Maya. "I wonder if it was a mistranslation?"

"So we go left first, and then if we don't find any street names on the map we'll try going right," she asked, starting to walk toward the left side corner crossing.

"Right."

Maya stopped. "I thought we agreed to go left first?"

"Right. To the left."

Maya let out her breath in exasperation as though I was intentionally confusing the issue. We walked left, but couldn't find any recognizable street names after walking at least six blocks, so we doubled back to the Piazza and crossed the street to go right. Next thing I knew we'd entered a residential area. Other than passing one small hotel on a corner, the furthest point we walked to was dark and totally deserted. In frustration we doubled back to the hotel and went inside to ask for directions.

An elderly man sat behind the desk in a small office cubby stretching to the back wall. He took to our inquiry with gusto and seriousness. He pulled out a map and a yellow highlighter. Then he turned to his computer, twisting in his seat to view the street names on the screen. Finally, he turned to face us and summarized: "Go back the way you came from Termini. One block before, turn right."

We thanked him for his efforts and walked back out into the street.

"I know he's wrong," Maya insisted as we approached Termini station again.

So, there we ended, right where we began, standing out front studying our maps beneath the streetlight. Our second time walking toward the Piazza, we turned left on the far side. We continued walking until finally we came to one street whose name matched our map: Firenze. That was our street, so we followed it for one block, then uphill where we began following the numbers. We passed number 11 while looking for 38. We kept walking. We passed 25 and kept going. Next thing I knew, we spotted #55.

"What the hell?" we asked each other, pulling out the map again.

Half a block up were cement steps leading up to an open doorway. I headed that way, retracting my suitcase handle in order to carry it up to the desk inside.

The guy sitting there took one look at our address, grimaced, and scratched his head. Meanwhile a man wearing a white cable-knit button-up sweater, jeans, and a white neck scarf came inside to inquire about picking up a package. The doorman asked him if he knew where our #38 Firenze was.

He looked at us. "*Buona notte.* What's your hotel name?"

"Oceana," we answered.

The guy in the white sweater nodded and said, "Follow me. I show you."

He made no attempt at conversation as he led us downhill, retracing our steps past where we saw number 11 earlier. He continued two blocks further down the wide street. The pavement here was cobblestoned, causing both our wheelies to bounce and bobble. I noticed that Maya kept a wary eye on her back wheel, as though expecting it to break down again at any moment.

This section of the city was filled with old houses. All were large, multi-storied estates clearly from a bygone age. Many had ornate wrought-iron gates leading to double wooden entrance doors. The majority had private gated driveways that descended into underground garages. Autos came up from or turned into them constantly, with our leader holding his arms out wide to prevent Maya and I from walking in front of the neighborhood Mario Andretti's.

At number 38, he stopped and pointed. "There you go."

"Sorry to say this," Maya commented, "but your numbering system here is all screwed up."

"Sì," he replied with a smile. "That's Italia for you. Hard to believe we invented street numbering, isn't it?" With that he turned and walked away.

Still, we were grateful for his assistance. I doubt we would have ever found the place on our own.

Both Maya and I picked up our wheelies and climbed up the ten or so discolored steps leading up to the double wooden doors at the top. I tested one to see if it was unlocked in spite of the fact there was no light on to indicate anyone was home. It was.

I opened the door and wrestled my bag inside, making way for Maya to follow. The foyer of this building had the look of a 1920's big city walkup. Mid-way down the long entrance hallway was a black wrought-iron elevator cage. The-doors were pull-out glass half doors. These, in turned revealed another set of double doors . You might know, these two opened inward. A sign posted on the back wall declared: 'Max capacity 6 people.'

"Six people?" Maya repeated. "With or without bags?"

We crowded inside with our luggage. I went first, so I had to keep squeezing backward to make room for Maya's wheelie to clear the double doors. I ended up straddling her bag as she struggled to close both sets of doors.

I had to laugh after Maya managed to latch the inner doors, punched the #3 button and nearly toppled as the cage lurched before creeping slowly upward. "Two of us and two bags and no room to spare! Can you imagine what it would be like with six people in here?"

"I hate these kinds of elevators," she said, shuddering. "Always afraid it'll stop between floors and we'll be stuck. I mean, I don't see a single soul around here, do you?"

We both breathed a sigh of relief when the elevator came to a halt. We managed to open the doors and scramble outside where we faced an indoor courtyard square. Opposite the elevator cage, visible in the moonlight, was a small cast iron table with two chairs on each side, with an empty glass ashtray sitting in the center.

In the distance ahead was a large paneled wooden door with a small bronze name plate on it: "Oceana."

"Do we knock or just enter?" whispered Maya at the doorway.

In answer, I opened the door. Almost immediately a burly man with bushy black hair came barreling into the foyer. "Come in, come in," he insisted in heavily accented English. He held a round brass key ring filled with what looked like 4" long skeleton keys, which he jingled as he led us inside.

Even from the entranceway, it was obvious that this was a converted home. Thick carpeting lined the hallway beneath high ceilings. Antique wooden furniture accented every wall. We followed this hotel representative into a spacious sitting room off to the left, and to the back of the room. There, in a comfy-looking sitting room was a couch, a recliner chair, and a flat TV (currently muted) on the wall. Against the side wall was a desk which contained a copy machine and a wire rack filled with papers.

"Do you live here or just work here?" I asked.

"Only work here. Eez comfortable. I like."

He verified our names against the register, grabbed another key ring, and led us back out to the hallway, pausing just long enough to switch on a light before leading us to our room. We passed the breakfast room on the left. Tables lined the wall, with clean tablecloths awaiting the morning's chaffing dishes. A dual stack of plates and a silverware holder occupied one end. The dozen or so tables inside were also prepped with white tablecloths, ready and waiting for breakfast.

The desk clerk stopped at the next door on the right, and inserted one of those oversized keys. "And here's your room."

I took one look inside and spotted the double bed. "No," I said. "That's not right. I know I requested two beds." I pulled out a copy of our reservation to show him.

He held up his hand and smiled. "No problem. Let me see what else I have."

Neither Maya nor I said a word after he left. After everything we'd gone through just to get here, we didn't want to head out into the night and begin searching for somewhere new.

The clerk returned moments later. "If you did notify us of your sleeping requirements, we never received it. But you are in luck because we are not yet filled." With that, he turned and led us to the end of the hallway, where he opened another set of doors. They opened to reveal an annexed portion of the building.

Whatever it was, it defined old world style: oriental carpeting, wide crown molding trim, heavy wooden doors. This section of the house was obviously at one time a family residence. I couldn't help but wonder if the original owners had died off, or emigrated. Maybe they couldn't pay their taxes so ended up selling the property to a developer. Whoever bought it had turned it into a charming 3-star hotel instead of dividing it up into apartments.

The hotel rep inserted another skeleton key at the wooden door and pushed it open.

The room was small, but serviceable. It contained two twin beds—collegiate style: long and narrow. On the far wall were three glass windows bordered with white lace curtains. Each window had a large brass handle mounted in the center. I walked straight over to test them. The windows opened inward, allowing a gentle breeze to blow the curtains at me. A scenic view outside revealed a cathedral across the street. It occupied nearly all of the block.

To the right of the entrance door was a wall lined with wooden panels. One, I noticed, was ajar. I opened it up to find a narrow closet filled with heavy wooden hangars. There was also an electronic safe on a shelf on one side.

The bathroom had been squeezed into the far corner, with a large triangular step platform in front to access it. The door at the top turned out to be a pocket door. I slid it open and peeked inside, and nearly tripped over the toilet. Maya crowded in behind me.

"You can barely see in here," she complained, flicking the light switch before walking over to flush the toilet as a way of testing the water pressure.

That's when we heard the noise: a vibrating deep-throated grumble. I wasn't sure if it was the pipes or the hot water tank—wherever they might have been hidden inside such small quarters—making that much racket. The noise floated across the room.

"At least it has some storage space," I commented, noting the marble shelf running across the bottom of the mirror. It contained an oblong basket filled with miniature bottles of lotion, shampoo, and conditioner. The semi-circular shower stall took up the entire far corner of the room.

"Shit," was Maya's next comment, checking the time on her cell. "I'm starving. And it's already 8 p.m.

"You're right," I said, agreeing. "Let's go."

We left everything right where we'd dropped them, locked the door and headed out.

Chapter 16

The hotel clerk raced out into the hallway and halted us at the front door. "I need your passports before you leave."

"What for?" asked Maya, instantly alert.

"I forgot to make copies. Sorry."

We followed him back into the office and waited as he copied the picture pages of both our passports. "Any good recommendations for a nearby restaurant?" Maya asked while we waited for the last page to finish printing.

He thought for a moment, then inspiration struck and he dug around on the desk beside the copy machine for a map. He partially unfolded it and stuck it in the machine and hit 'copy.' On the localized copy that came out, he highlighted the street name out front, and marked an X a short distance away. Over the X he printed, 'Tarantola's.' "Eez three blocks away and very easy to find. Good food."

We thanked him, pocketed our passports, and headed to the doorway.

We had no difficulty in finding the restaurant. The only problem was that it was closed. So, we turned around and double backed past our hotel, then continued downhill toward a lit green hotel sign on the corner a couple of blocks away. It turned out to be the same place where we stopped to ask for directions the first time.

"I ought to go in there and tell that jerk where the Oceana is," Maya huffed.

"Why bother," I said, continuing down the sidewalk.

There were several places to eat just past the hotel. Maybe we didn't notice them before because they weren't open yet. Suddenly we came upon one of those squat upright chalkboard menus on the sidewalk. Steps led from the sidewalk up into an open restaurant doorway. The interior appeared to be jam packed with local families.

"If it's frequented by locals, it means good food," Maya stated, climbing the steps.

I tuned to study the menu. It showed tonight's menu options of spaghetti or pizza for 12 euros, and vino for 5 euros. On the other side of the street was a sidewalk eatery, partially enclosed with plexiglass panels decorated with red gingham curtains. Flickering lights of butane heaters sticking up toward the night sky were evenly spaced down the block, unnoticed before now.

"You want to go over there instead?" Maya asked, pausing just inside the doorway.

"No, no, it's okay. Let's eat here."

A single male worked the restaurant floor inside, and working he was. He wasn't elderly, but he looked past his prime just the same. He had a small table and chair in a corner in the rear, to where he retreated for small breaks or to write out the cheques. During all other times he was all over the floor. He took orders, then marched them into the kitchen. He delivered plates to the assigned table out front. As soon as patrons departed, he bussed their tables, sometimes even sweeping the floor after them. He stopped for an occasional chit-chat with some—neighborhood regulars if I had to guess—but not for long. He was too busy to stand around and chat.

He led Maya and I to a table toward the back, near his little desk area where I suppose he could keep a close eye on us. For all he knew, we might have been unscrupulous tourists who would eat and run before paying.

"*Prendi dal menu?*" he asked.

Maya answered, "Sì," before quizzing him about the wine.

A lone male entered, meanwhile, and stood off to one side holding a wrapped package in brown paper. As soon as our waiter spotted him, he gave us a quick "*momento*," and took off to greet the newcomer as though he were an old friend.

Maya turned in her chair to watch. I thought he looked familiar. That's when we noticed it was our white-sweatered guide from earlier this evening, the one who walked us to our hotel.

The minute he spotted us, he smiled and waved. He handed over the package he was carrying to the waiter, then took a seat at a table in the middle of the floor with what could only have been the rest of his family.

Our waiter rushed the package to the kitchen and returned minutes later. "Now, red or white? Glass or bottle?"

"I can't drink a whole bottle," I said to Maya. "Tomorrow is going to be a long day touring Rome. I sure don't want to end up sleeping the morning away because I got snookered tonight."

"Agreed," said Maya, requesting a bottle of white and the WiFi password. "It would cost 10 euros for two glasses each, but only 12 euros for the whole bottle, which should equal about the same amount. Smart, huh?"

I ordered a pizza *con prosciutto e funghi* (mushrooms). Maya got the 4-cheese special.

On his next pass, the waiter delivered our wine bottle and two empty glasses, along with the WiFi code printed out on a slip of paper. Maya brushed away his offer to pour the wine after he extracted the cork. I think he was relieved to be able to get away and take a few minutes for himself.

Both Maya's iPad and my phone sounded off with incoming emails the minute we entered the code. Before reading anything, however, we took a minute to toast each other and taste the wine. It was surprisingly good, and only mildly sweet.

"Maybe we should buy a second bottle to take back to the room with us," Maya suggested.

"Whatever you want," I answered absently, occupied with my phone, waiting while my emails downloaded.

One was from Sandusky, which brought me to full attention. Hoping she had good news, I zeroed in. The caption stated: "Remember when you said life is filled with choices?" The subject line, however, was blank. Nor was there anything written in the body of the message. "That's strange," I said, showing the cryptic message to Maya and the blank space beneath it.

"Must be she accidentally hit send before writing the rest of it," Maya said, shrugging. "No big deal. I do it all the time when I'm in a hurry."

"Oh wait, there's an attachment," I said, clicking on it.

The next thing I knew a photo of a newspaper flashed across my screen. I stared at it for a long minute, wondering what the hell? Why would Sandusky send me this? Then I spotted the circled text at the bottom and it all made sense. I leaned back in my chair and let out a shriek.

"What?" asked Maya looking up from her iPad.

I turned the phone around so she could see the page. But to tease her, I purposefully held my finger across the lower half of the screen.

Maya's initial reaction was the same "wth" as mine—actually hers was 'wtf.' Until I lowered my thumb and revealed the rest of the page. After she read the rest of it, her mouth fell open. "Oh my God," she mouthed.

Sandusky Gazette

October 12, 2018

www.sanduskygazette.com

U.S. WATCH

Project to dig up possible Mona Lisa

Florence, Italy - Italian researchers said Tuesday they will dig up bones in a Florence convent to try to identify the remains of a Renaissance woman long believed to be the "Mona Lisa."

The research might help ascertain the identity of the woman depicted in Leonardo da Vinci's masterpiece - a mystery that has puzzled scholars and art lovers for centuries and generated countless theories.

The project launched Tuesday aims to locate the remains of Lisa Gherardini, the wife of rich sailk merchant Francesco del Giocondo.

Tradition has long linked Gherardini to the painting. Georgio Vassari, a 16th century artist and biographer of Leonardo, wrote that de Vinci painted a portrait of del Giocondo's wife.

Scratch & Sniff Stamps Coming

Letter writers will soon be able to express their sentiments in words and smells.

The US Postal Service announced Monday that it would soon issue its first scratch & sniff stamps. They will feature illustrations of ice pops.

The agency said the 20 new stamps will depict watercolor llustrations by California artist Margaret Berg.

Molten Lava Creates Air-Quality Danger

White plumes of acid and extremely fine shards of glass billowed into the sky over Hawaii as molten rock from the Kilauea volcano poured into the ocean, creating yet another hazard from an eruption that began more than two weeks ago: a toxic steam cloud.

Authorities warned the public to stay away from the cloud that formed by a chemical reaction when lava touched seawater.

Further upslope, lava continued gushing out of large cracks in the ground in residential areas of the Big Island, where molten rock made rivers that bisected forests and farms as they meandered toward the coast.

The rate of sulfur-dioxide gas shooting from the fissures tripled, leading Hawaii County to repeat warnings about air quality.

At the volcano's summit, two explosive eruptions unleashed clouds of ash. Winds carried much of it toward the southwest.

U.S. District Court of Columbus

Workplace discrimination charges were filed this week against Omega Air supervisor, Richard D. Noggins by Sandusky's own Samantha Schlagenhaufen, former Miss Sandusky 2017.

The legal firm of Freiking, Lutz, & Schlagenhaufen will be handling the case.

Congolese Receive Vaccine For Ebola

Health officials in the Democratic Republic of Congo began administering an experimental Ebola vaccine, as the country battles to contain its ninth outbreak of the hemorrhagic fever.

The first people to receive the vaccine on Monday were staff at a 20-bed Ebola treatment center set up by medical charity Doctors Without Borders in the northwestern city of Mbandaka, said Jessica Ilungu, a spokesperson for Congo's public-health ministry.

An initial shipment of 4,000 dosis of the experimental vaccine, developed by Merck & Co., arrived in the inland port city of 1.2 million people on the Congo River on Saturday.

The vaccine is being administered for the first time since it showed promising results two years ago in Guinea, in the final stages of an Ebola epidemic that killed more than 11,300 people across West Africa.

If it proves effective in Congo, the vaccine could permanently alter how the world responds to the virus, which is passed on through bodily fluids such as saliva or blood.

Correction:

A picture caption on an article Sunday about search-and-rescue crews' efforts in the aftermath of Hurricane Michael misidentified a dog used by rescue workers. It is Dexter who is trained to sniff out human life, not Luna, who is trained to sniff out human remains.

Maybe our waiter thought my shriek was due to impatience, I don't know. All I know is that our pizzas arrived in the middle of our impromptu celebration. They were thin and hot, and delicious.

Over dinner we discussed possible repercussions of Sandusky's actions, wondering if we might have been the inspiration that set this particular wheel in motion.

"I don't care why she did it," I told Maya. "I just hope she doesn't get fired because of it."

When the bill arrived, I pulled out my wallet. But Maya stopped me.

"You paid for the train tickets. I'll get this. We can settle up the difference tonight before we get into our last translation session." With that settled, she pulled out her AMEX and held it up for the waiter on his next pass through to the kitchen.

He stopped, pursed his lips and shook his head. "Cash," was all he said, in English, waiving an index finger at Maya. "Euros," he added just to be sure we got the message.

"No credit cards?" Maya repeated, sounding incredulous.

"No," the guy repeated, shaking his head again.

"Good thing I never leave home without cash, isn't it?" I couldn't help but add.

Our waiter watched as I counted out thirty-six euros, after which I dumped the assortment of bills and coins in his hand. "*Ritorna domani,*" (Come back tomorrow) he said, taking the money to his desk in the back.

"So what's the best way to see Rome?" I asked Maya while walking back to the hotel.

"The Hop-on Hop-off bus, no doubt about it. We'll get a good overview of the city that way as well as be able to get off and take some time to really see the top venues: The Colosseum, The Spanish Steps, Trevi, and the Vatican. If we get started by nine, we should be finished by four, easy."

"Did you price the tickets?" I asked.

Maya nodded. "A twenty-four-hour ticket is €30. And they take credit cards."

Once in the comfort of our room I realized we'd left the windows open. There was still a breeze blowing, and the curtains were flapping. Maya retreated to the bathroom while I closed the windows and lowered the shades. The pipes continued groaning and rattling overhead as we settled in for the night and began the last of the language lessons from my phone's recordings. However, this time there were no Prosecco-laden giggles like during our first session in Florence. This time there was much less fun in the exercise. Maya and I persisted though, plodding through the last sentence even though our hearts were no longer in it. Worse, I was half-way to slumberland before we finished.

At the same time, Maya received a facetime call from Bryce so she picked up her iPad and retreated to the privacy of the bathroom. I fell asleep to a hushed conversation that went on seemingly forever. I didn't wake up until the church bells rang out at 6 a.m. the next morning.

I hopped in the shower the minute I woke up, thus managing to destroy Maya's slumber in louder ways than any church bells ever could. The pipes rattled away long after I exited the bathroom and greeted Maya's morning frown.

"Do you want me to wait for you or head out to breakfast alone?" I asked.

"You might as well go eat. I'll get there eventually," she answered, grabbing some clothes from the top of her wheelie and heading to the bathroom.

The dining room was only half full, but there was enough food laid out for double that amount of people. There was a selection of jams and marmalades beside the breads; a choice of fried or scrambled eggs; ham slices filled one chafing dish, and potato wedges speckled with parsley another. In addition, there was an assortment of juices, milk, tea and coffee. I grabbed a coffee first, then went back and loaded up a plate with a little of everything. Who knew when we'd eat next?

I brought my city map with me, so I spread it out on the free half of the table and studied the layout of the city as I ate, noting where our targeted sights were. When the hotel's on-duty assistant entered the room, I caught her eye and asked her to show me on the map exactly where we were. She agreed and dug a pen out of her apron before leaning over the map. She circled *Piazza Repubblica.*

"From zee Piazza you need only walk to light. Two, three streets you are at Termini." She drew the line as she talked, showing me the 'ten-minute walk' route between the station and the hotel.

About this time Maya made her appearance. She was wearing those God-awful tight leggings again. I leaned sideways to give them a more thorough once over, but kept my comments to myself.

She must have read my thoughts. "Oh God, don't start. I'm dressed just like one of the locals, you'll see."

Once she claimed food at the buffet and returned to the table, her mood improved. "We need to decide how we want to handle our baggage. We either need to store them here or at Termini. Termini is more convenient, since we'll need to catch a bus from there to the airport hotel . . . "

"There's no way I want to walk through that humongous cavern looking for the baggage storage."

The hotel clerk heard us, and approached our table to join the discussion. "Sì, sì, better to leave bags here. Much safer. They'll be locked up. Also free. Is only 10-minute walk, so no problem."

So that's what we decided to do. That meant doubling back to our room after breakfast in order to pack up, then haul our bags to the office and turn in our key before heading out to greet the city.

Once done, we felt amazingly free. We walked down the street—following the route the clerk had mapped out—until we spotted McDonalds (the same one the guy outside Termini had mentioned when we first arrived), and from there walked straight to the Piazza. It truly was a 10-minute walk this time.

The Hop-on Hop-off bus stop was at the next corner. The red double decker bus had already arrived and was parked at the curb in front of their ticket booths. Several representatives of the company, all wearing red aprons with pockets filled with brochures, paraded back in forth all around the Piazza, handing out brochures and stopping pedestrians in order to drum up business. I didn't see an ATM anywhere close or I would have picked up a few more euros.

It was a cool yet sunny Rome day; 55 degrees and not a cloud in the sky. In spite of the chill, Maya and I boarded the bus and headed topside. Each seat back contained a headset in order to listen to taped information accompanying our route while driving through Rome's ungodly bumper-to-bumper traffic. The smell of exhaust mixed with the wetness of recently washed streets was everywhere.

As soon as we pulled out, the prerecorded message began:

"Rome is the heartland of the ancient Roman Empire. It's the seat of the Catholic church as well as a repository of many of the greatest cultural treasures in human history. Rome, the seat of the ancient empire's government, was home to both the ruling Caesars and the church's Pope. It's home to the Colosseum, the Pantheon, and the ancient forum. The city is packed with museums, filled with works of the greatest names in history: Bernini, St. Peters Basilica with its centerpiece, La Pietà, carved by a 19-year-old Michelangelo, who later painted the Sistine Chapel inside the Vatican."

Suddenly the recording ended and a twenty-something athletic-looking male stood up, microphone in hand. "Buongiorno everyone. My name is Nikau," he said in a rich Aussie accent. He had black curly hair and a dark tan which accentuated the white of his teeth in a near constant smile. He brought to mind images of Hawaiian surfers or those Polynesian boat rowers you see on Hawaii 5 O reruns. Nikau's eyes, meanwhile, focused on Maya and never looked away.

"Italy is famous, and not just because of Roma. Michelangelo's David still inspires artists from all over the world to come to study him. Brunelleschi's cathedral dome in Florence dominates its skyline.

Venice, the unique city of canals and bridges, surrounded by churches decorated by Titan and Tintoretto. The Leaning Tower in Pisa. Da Vinci's Last Supper in Milano. The vineyards of Tuscany. From the ghost town of Pompeii to the hiking trails of Cinque Terre, all the way to the ski villages of the Alps. There is more to see in Italy than in any other country."

"I'm surprised there's not a lot of cars honking," I said to Maya.

"Honking cars like what they show in the movies," Nikau said without breaking stride, "is what you find in France, not Italia."

I took the hint not to interrupt Nikau while he was holding center stage, so focused on the scenery instead. But not Maya.

"And yet this once great civilization self-destructed in the end. Just like ancient Greece," she continued. "And for the same reason: they got so big they couldn't effectively manage their resources. They ended up with internal corruption, ruling elites all fighting for control. Their workers died off in endless wars. And for what, power and profit for a few?"

"Sort of applies to corporations too, doesn't it?" I asked Maya, thinking of Omega.

Next thing I knew Nikau stored his microphone and walked back to us, where he dropped down into a free seat beside Maya. "Where are you from, *bella*?"

"Deep in the heart of Dixie," she laughed, faking a southern accent, flirting outrageously.

Poor Nikau, he didn't understand the accent or the meaning of Dixie. He just stared at her with that flashy smile of his. "I'm Mauri, from down under."

"Mauri?" Maya repeated.

Nikau nodded and smiled even wider. "Yes, Mauri, as in Native People. My people were originally Kiwis. Cannibals, too."

"No shit?" Maya exclaimed. A few minutes later, she questioned, "Kiwis?"

At the same time, I repeated, "Cannibals?" But no one was listening to me.

Nikau laughed, delighted at Maya's response. "New Zealanders," he clarified.

"So which are you, Kiwi or Aussie?" I asked.

He looked away from Maya only long enough to glance at me. "Aussie, through and through."

"How long have you been here, doing this?" Maya asked.

"Oh, I've been in the tourism industry for over ten years now, here in Italy mostly. So you could say I know Italy inside out. Before that I served a tour in Iraq."

Maya cocked a head at that bit of news. "As part of the Australian army?"

"Yes, something like that." His eyes never left Maya's face.

About that time a middle-aged female's head popped up at the top of the stairwell at the mid-point of the bus. The minute she spotted Nikau, she frowned and began clawing her way back to us, grabbing seatbacks row-by-row while fighting the constant motion. Once she got within earshot, she pointed at Nikau. "Hey, aren't you the one who's supposed to be guiding us?"

Reluctantly, our Aussie got up and resumed his position at the front with his microphone.

The bus passed a long field of grass speckled with patches of sand then turned to begin a long uphill journey. One side of the roadway was bordered with huge oak trees, each with long branches extending out over the road. Downhill, behind the field we just passed, stretched a line of brownish Roman ruins framed by a row of Cypress trees.

"The field you see at the bottom of the hill is known as Circus Maximus. It's where they filmed the famous chariot scene in Ben Hur," Nikau explained, pointing with his free hand.

"Ben who?" asked Maya, looking confused.

"Tell you later," I whispered.

But Maya's attention had already been diverted. She jabbed me with her elbow as our bus continued uphill into the path of a row of those arching three branches.

We both watched and held our breath as Nikau, his back to the trees, continued talking about the historical aspects of this section of town. We sat on the edge of our seats, expecting him to get decked any second. As luck would have it—for him anyway—he ducked in the nick of time in what was undoubtedly a well-practiced move.

Soon the bus pulled into the curb. "Colosseum is our first stop," Nikau announced, stashing his mic and standing just past the stairwell, offering comments to everyone as they departed. When Maya and I reached him, Nikau handed Maya a piece of paper. "Dinner tonight?" he whispered. "Text me where to meet you. *Ciao, bella,*"

Off the bus and on firm ground again, Maya stuffed Nikau's note in her backpack then shifted its position to her chest instead of her back. "Watch for pickpockets," she warned, heading out.

The whole area from the bus stop to the Colosseum was packed with people. There were lots of families walking about, taking in the sights. A great majority we passed were speaking Italian, many with small children in tow or pushing strollers.

"Strange that there's more locals out than tourists," was Maya's comment.

We walked past armed guards as well as tour groups. Some of the guards wore bright red 'Polizia del Stadie' vests indicating they patrolled only the stadium while others wore blue bibs proclaiming a more general 'Polizia.' Still others wore yellow vests labeled 'Carabinieri.'

"What's the difference?" I asked Maya, indicating the different insignias.

She thought for a minute. "Polizia are the state police, while the Carabinieri are military members . . . part of the army, I think."

We worked our way closer to the Colosseum ticket office, with the slow-moving crowds becoming thicker the closer we came to the ancient structure. "I know this place has a pretty dark history, what with gladiators fighting each other to the death just for entertainment . . . "

"I thought they fought lions, not each other?"

Maya just shrugged. "Still, it's pretty impressive, isn't it?"

I nodded and looked up at the top tier, now crawling with people. "Wonder how many spectators managed to get in here for the day's entertainment?" It was more of an observation than a question, but Maya answered anyway.

"Fifty thousand. Fifty-thousand bloodthirsty citizens. Can you imagine?"

We finally made it to the ticket window. The clerk inside the booth wasn't the least bit friendly. When Maya asked him, "How much?" he just pointed to the sign posted on the window above his head outside the booth. We both looked up at it: 2-3 hours guided, €34 each.

"Two to three hours?" I groaned. "I don't want to spend two to three hours here!"

At the same time, Maya huffed, "thirty-four euros?" She grabbed a brochure from the stand next to the ticket booth and stepped away. "I'll wait out here and read about it myself. Screw paying that much for someone to tell me what's inside!"

I stayed at the ticket booth window. "How much for an hour?"

He let out a sigh of exasperation. "€21 euros for self-guided." Then he pointed to the brochure stand. "That's what brochures are for."

"*Grazie*, you've been most unhelpful," I said, stepping away to join Maya.

"I don't know about you, but I don't want to spend the next hour fighting all these crowds just to see crumbling ruins." Maya replaced the brochure in irritation.

I looked at the long line standing at the entranceway, and then at the wall-to-wall lineup slow walking their way past the second-floor windows. "Me either. I'm not that much of a tourist."

We retraced our steps back to the Hop-On bus stop and waited until the next bus pulled in. No Aussie surfer boy onboard this time, but Maya didn't seem to care. Next thing we knew, we heard "Vatican City next" announcement and pulled in to the curb.

As soon as we got off the bus, we could see the avenue that led toward the Vatican. Even from this distance I recognized the Roman obelisk in the center of St. Peter's Square. We adjusted our backpacks and headed out.

Again, the sidewalk was crowded with Italian adults and children as well as tourists. We passed group of men assembling a nativity hut. Another group was hauling strings of Christmas tree lights from boxes stacked on a dolly nearby.

"Pretty early for Christmas, don't you think?" I asked Maya.

Maya shrugged. "Gets earlier every year, it seems. Even here."

We finally arrived at St. Peter's Square. A metal barricade made up of small gates stretched all the way across the square, completely blocking its entrance. On the cobblestoned courtyard side stood a loitering mass of humanity, just standing around waiting. Oversize TVs had been mounted on tall poles on each side of the square, slightly away from the staircase leading up to the Vatican's main entrance.

Maya and I trailed behind the slow-moving line until we finally arrived at the barricade. The opening was bordered by two tables, each side manned by security personnel. Naturally they all wore vests proudly proclaiming *Sicurezza Vaticana* (Vatican Security). Italians so love their officialdom. Maya and I dutifully dumped our backpacks on the table and waited as every zipper was unzipped, and every square inch inside was inspected.

"What in hell is going on?" Maya snapped.

"Not sure, but my guess is the Pope must be out and about today."

"Sì, sì, il Papa," answered the *Sicurezza* inspector, looking up from my bag. "Eez a great day when to hear il Papa *personalmente*, no?"

Maya snorted. "Not this Papa. He's too political for my taste. He should limit his comments to God and religion . . . "

I tried to shush Maya, especially in light of the ongoing stare the Sicurezza was giving her. But she brushed me aside.

" . . . instead of lecturing humanity in favor of controversial political topics of the day."

Surprisingly, the Sicurezza inspector said nothing in reply.

～ Chapter 17 ～

"Oh my God, look!" Maya exclaimed, pointing at one of the oversized TV monitors in the front corner of St. Peter's square. Tall speakers had been positioned all along the sides of the square, and everyone inside stood watching and listening to Pope Francis as his broadcast began. "All that security for a TV monitor!"

At first, I thought he was giving a mass. His voice sounded high-pitched and nasally, but with a pronounced accent.—Argentine, I already knew. I kept hearing him say "*immigrantes*," and knew that wasn't part of any mass I'd ever heard. I looked around at the crowd's reaction. There was no overt response, but I sensed a general stiffening of bodies despite of an overall attitude of respectful silence.

"You understand any of it?" I asked Maya.

She shrugged. "Probably as much as you. His accent is really thick."

I returned my attention to the screen. Il Papa was looking directly at us, using his hands for frequent emphasis. Then I looked up at the Vatican building. There, in one of the second story windows, I could just barely make out the red and white of his garments. I looked back at the teleprompter. By now it seemed that every other sentence included something about "*immigrantes*." Again, I looked around to see the reaction of the crowd.

I saw plenty of people listening intently, taking it all in. But I saw no nodding of heads in agreement anywhere in that huge crowd. I felt sure I wasn't imagining the tension in the air or the overall silence, and a general bristling of bodies at every mention of the word "*immigrantes*."

As soon as the speech was over, everyone began walking off in different directions. The barricade panels at the square's entrance were already being removed. Maya and I wasted no time in advancing to the front steps and, moments later, found ourselves inside St. Peter's Basilica. We spotted Michelangelo's Pietà in a room off to the right as soon as we entered.

The actual statue had been encased in a plexiglass cage to protect it from vandals. There was a display of brochures next to it, in all European languages as well as English. I took one and paged through it; nothing new inside, so I returned it.

Two elderly nuns stood a short distance away discussing the statue. I made my way over beside them in hopes of hearing what they had to say.

"It's the only one of his works he ever signed," one informed the other.

"But to carve his name across Mary's sash?" quizzed the other. "It seems disrespectful somehow."

The first one had either studied art or Michelangelo himself, because she began explaining how the autograph that extending the length of the sash came to be . . . "In his later years' rumors spread that this work was actually a product of Michelangelo's main competitor, a Cristoforo Solari. In anger, Michelangelo broke into the Basilica one night and added his name to the only site large enough to contain his name—the sash running across Mary's body."

I looked over at Mary, then at the sash and studied the bold letters. "MICHAELANGELVS BONAROTVS FLORENTINVA FACIEBAT." I knew from my own art history studies that the signature translated as: 'Michelangelo Buonarroti, the Florentine, made this.'

The first was quick to add: "Supposedly, he later regretted his outburst of pride and swore to never again sign a work of his making. And, do you know, he never did."

The second nun shook her head and made 'tsk tsk' sounds while cocking her head to decipher the engraving. "It was meant to capture the moment Christ was taken down from the cross, no?"

The other nun nodded. "When he was given to his mother, sì. Artistically, the work represents Renaissance ideals of classical beauty combined with naturalism. Michelangelo gave it an unprecedented aesthetic interpretation, supposedly inspired by Dante's Divine Comedy, which opened the door into what the art world now calls the High Renaissance.

Maya wanted to take a closer look at the chapel in the back of the building, but returned soon after leaving. "Couldn't get anywhere near it," she grumbled. "They were doing a private mass or baptism or something."

"We done here then?" I asked, happy to have received a free art history lesson while checking the time. It was getting close to lunch, and we still had Trevi and the Spanish Steps to see.

Maya nodded and made for the door. I followed.

The square out front had been almost completely vacated while we were inside. Not a single one of those barricade gates remained in sight. We shrugged it off and headed across the street toward the broad avenue leading away from Vatican City. One block later I spotted an ATM on the sidewalk in front of a row of Vatican souvenir stores. I made a mad dash across the street, shouting at Maya to follow me.

"Right behind ya," I heard. "Don't forget to get a bottle of holy water for Noggins. You'll pay big time if you forget."

In truth I didn't mind picking one up for him. It's just the way he turned a personal request into a command that didn't sit right. And the fact that he never offered to reimburse any of us for our efforts once we got home.

It took me less than thirty seconds to withdraw €100 and enter the store. No wonder St. Peter's was empty, the majority of the locals were now here shopping for Vatican souvenirs. And no one seemed in any hurry.

A young girl and her mother walked around the store blocking my progress. The little girl kept fingering merchandise, while her mother continually chastised her for doing so. Moments later I saw the girl pick up one of the glass bottles and play with its screw cap. The mother spotted her actions about the same time I did and grabbed the girl's arm to pull her away. In the process the girl dropped the bottle. The mother and I both froze and watched a growing pool of holy water seeping out onto the floor.

Suddenly one of the store clerks rushed over shouting. For once I understood every word. "You should keep a closer eye on your child. You'll have to pay for the broken merchandise, you know."

The little girl began crying. The mother apologized over and over, pleading with the clerk not to charge her the fifteen euros for the bottle. "I was paying close attention," she explained. "But I was also trying to select a gift. Take pity, please, after all my girl is only six. You know how these little ones are? Accidents do happen."

The clerk stopped yelling, but couldn't seem to decide what to do about the bottle still lying in a pool on the floor.

I bent over and picked the bottle up. It wasn't broken, just leaking from the loose twist-off cap. "It's okay," I said to the clerk. "I'll buy it."

That's when Maya showed up beside me. She must have been standing at the doorway waiting for me to make my purchase and leave. She made straight for the store's clerk. "Aren't you going to discount the price? You should, since it no longer contains a full allotment of holy water?"

"Ten euros," the clerk snapped without hesitation.

I handed over a ten note and made for the door accompanied by grateful benedictions from the girl's mother.

"Why in hell do you want that one for?" Maya asked the minute we reached the sidewalk.

"What do you mean? It's for Noggins, remember?"

"Yeah, but it's half empty!"

"So? I'll fill it up at one of those public drinking fountains. Noggins will never know the difference." With that, I screwed the cap on tight and tossed the bottle in my backpack, and led the way to the Hop-On bus stop.

Maya went over the rest of our itinerary while we waited for the bus to arrive. "We'll do the Spanish Steps next and explore around there a bit. There's a ton of name-brand stores nearby. I'd love to check out the prices. After that, we'll walk up to Trevi, maybe get a bite to eat nearby before heading back to the Piazza Republicca. From there we just need to walk to our hotel and pick up our bags."

I nodded in agreement. "Sounds good to me."

"Then from the hotel, we walk back to Termini."

"Back to the train station?" I asked. "I thought we were taking a bus to the airport?"

"We are. The bus leaves from the station. From the airport, we catch the Marriott hotel shuttle. The airport and the hotel are way the hell out in the boonies. With any luck at all we'll get to the hotel in plenty of time to get a good night's sleep before the rat-race of checking in for the flight tomorrow."

I felt tired just hearing about all the steps yet to do, but I didn't have time to dwell on it because just then the red double-decker bus pulled up.

There was no grinning Aussie tour guide on this one. I checked. No guide at all, in fact. We rode around the city for about fifteen minutes when we heard: "Spanish Steps next." The bus then pulled in to the curb on the high side of the steps, about a block away.

"That's weird," I heard Maya say as we joined the disembarking line up.

"What?"

"Usually they drop us down below in front of the steps and you have to climb up."

It proved to be a royal cluster to get close to the steps at all. There was no way forward, and no reason to go back since the bus had already pulled out. A throng of people blocked the street as far as the eye could see. Everyone seemed to be moving the same direction. We had no choice but to follow, until finally we got a glimpse of the famous steps in the distance.

Unfortunately, the top of the steps had been barricaded with those same small metal panels like we'd seen earlier at the Vatican. Again, there was a small table set up for the many security Polizia hovering nearby. Some waived hand metal detectors over people one-by-one—including baby strollers—while others examined everyone's bags and purses. It took us over an hour just to get to the front of the barricade entrance.

"Look at that," Maya insisted, pointing toward the bottom of the steps. The street running across it teemed with a slow-moving crowd. It was literally wall-to-wall people. All pedestrians. Not even a moped in sight.

"I can't see anything," I complained.

"That's the point. This is awful."

When our turn came for the security screening, Maya asked, "What's going on?"

"Il Papa," was all the officer said.

"Friggin Pope," was Maya's comment.

Finished with the screening, the fastest progress we made thus far was to the bottom of the Spanish Steps. There was no one loitering on them today. At the bottom we had no choice but to fall in line behind everyone else walking up a slightly uphill street that eventually terminated at Trevi. Along the way we passed countless high-end shops, but most were closed. Some owners stood in open doorways, but wouldn't let anyone inside.

All forward movement stalled a couple of blocks up. We tried cutting across a side street so as to find an unblocked parallel road, but there was no getting through. Polizi blocked all side streets by standing across them with their arms outstretched. No cycles, no pedestrians. No way.

Tired, hungry, and unwilling to continue walking uphill like this, Maya finally approached one of the guards. "What the hell is going on?" she asked, explaining that we just wanted to get to Trevi, or find the nearest Hop-On bus and go back to our hotel.

"*Il Papa viene*," he answered. "The pope's coming."

"Well, no wonder! Will you please let us get past to go find the Hop-On bus?"

The Polizi had a sense of humor. He grinned. "Nice try, *bella*. But no. Il Papa will be here any minute. After that you can pass."

"No way," Maya told him. "He just finished mass at the Vatican."

The guard shook his head. "No mass there. He did speech to celebrate Madre Maggiori."

"What's that?" Maya asked. "Never heard of it."

"National holiday. No schools. No work—except us. Everyone free to celebrate."

"Crap!" we both said in unison.

"I would have bypassed Rome altogether and gone home this morning had I known today's a friggin national holiday."

What should have been a leisurely one-to-two-hour excursion turned out to be a four-hour pedestrian traffic jam. We never did see the Pope's motorcade go past. Eventually though, we realized that the side streets were no longer blocked. We detoured through countless side streets just to out-maneuver the crowds, zig-zagging our way through the maze of streets until we finally got to within a block of Trevi. None of the streets went straight from A to B in this older part of the city. It was very confusing. And very Italian. It took nearly an hour before we arrived at the café-fronted street opposite the Trevi Fountain. Unfortunately, that was as close as we got. It was just too crowded.

We looked for an open spot at any number of nearby cafes. All, it seemed, were full and no one looked the least bit ready to leave. Every available seat was occupied. Over by the fountain, everyone that wasn't seated was either pushing strollers or taking pictures, thus blocking our view.

The minute I spotted a group standing up at a small café across the street, looking as though preparing to leave, I poked Maya. We rushed over before they'd vacated intending to commandeer the table. We managed to claim their seats before they cleared the sidewalk.

"*Scusi,* do you take credit cards," Maya asked a passing waiter. He ignored her.

She repeated the question to the next waiter. This one at least answered, "Sì," was all he said as he rushed to the kitchen, but never paused to ask what we wanted.

No one came out to wait on us, either.

We sat there for about fifteen minutes before we gave up, got up, and left. If we wanted to eat, we knew we needed to search elsewhere.

"Let's just head over to the main street and look for a Hop-On sign. There's got to be one somewhere near here. We'll just ride the bus for one or two stops. . . long enough to get out of this mess here. We'll look for a restaurant there instead."

"We can always double back here later, after the lunchtime crowds have gone home," I said, agreeing to the plan.

"If we still feel like it," Maya added. "I'm about done with this tourist shit."

We only had to walk for a half-dozen blocks before we came to a Hop-On sign. And, fortunately, we didn't need to wait long before the next bus appeared. We watched the streets outside, waiting to make our exit as soon as we cleared this crowded section of town, when the bus suddenly pulled over. Next thing I knew a heavy accented voice boomed from the speakers.

"Ladies and gentlemen, we must now take our one hour fifteen-minute lunch break. Another bus will come along shortly and continue your tour of Roma. Please wait here."

Some woman at the front stood up and shouted: "Hey, you can't just dump us here like this." But they did. As soon as the last person stepped off, the bus took off.

We all stood curbside for about fifteen minutes pondering what to do. Neither of us saw any restaurants nearby. No other bus pulled in, although an empty bus was parked a couple of blocks ahead of us. It was empty.

The same irate woman from earlier pulled out her cell and tried calling the Hop-On office—the number broadcasted across every one of their brochures. Minutes later she snapped her phone shut in irritation. "Out to lunch," was her only comment to the half-dozen or so of us watching expectantly.

Our entire group ended up walking to the parked bus. Maya was the one who looked up at the open top tier first. "Oh look, someone's up there," she said, pointing at a pair of black shoes dangling out into the aisle.

Sure enough, once she pointed them out, everyone knew there was a body up there. The person they belonged to must have been sound asleep because our shouts and pounding on the bus wall never caused those shoes to so much as twitch. The irate woman tried calling the Hop-On office again. Someone must have answered this time, because a profane-laden shouting conversation soon followed. Not long after she hung up, a hyena ring tone could be heard floating down from the open top tier. Finally, the shoes moved. A yawning dark-haired man came into view. Looking embarrassed, he came down to the main level and opened the door.

"This is more like it," Maya grumbled the minute we pulled out into traffic. She checked the time.

"Trevi fountain next," the driver announced.

"Huh?" we both said at once.

You might know this bus was going the opposite direction from the way we wanted to go.

"Well, at least we're closer to Trevi than the steps," I said, suggesting we might as well get off and try it again. The streets were still crowded, however, so we walked another couple of blocks searching for a Hop-On stop whose route went the opposite direction. It was there we spotted a small patio restaurant a block off the main street. It was situated in a small plaza where four streets came together, although there were no cars moving on any of these streets. The area was surrounded by residential buildings. The closer we got to the restaurant, the more we could see open tables with unfurled umbrellas, surrounded by lit upright butane heaters.

"Cash or credit card, I don't even care anymore," Maya announced, plunking down in a chair.

"If they only take cash, I'll pay. Otherwise, it's on you," I said with a laugh, not really meaning it. But Maya agreed so I offered to cover the tip.

The waiter was cute and started flirting with Maya before taking our order.

"Better we split the tab," Maya said after he left for the kitchen. "I don't want him thinking I'm here with my mother."

I didn't care either way. I just wanted to eat.

We ordered lasagna and wine, and summarized our lousy Roman adventure while we waited for our food. We didn't even remember to ask for the restaurant's WiFi password until we were well into our second glass of wine.

You might know, the first email I received was from Noggins, notifying the two of us our time to have our fingerprints taken on our first scheduled day back to work.

"What the hell is he talking about?" Maya asked.

I had no clue. Worse, at that moment, especially after the day we'd had, I didn't care. I shot him a quick reply. "What the hell for? We're on vacation, remember? Spare us any more of this stuff until after we get home."

"Ask him if he wants his holy water or not," Maya said. "He'll get the message." That caused a laugh-filled toast which emptied both our glasses. She was about to call the waiter over for another refill when I stopped her.

"We've still got a lot to do before we get to the airport hotel. Maybe we ought to call it quits while we're ahead."

Agreeing, we called for the cheque. We were in the middle of paying (cash this time!) when Noggin's reply came through, a cut and paste of the company's latest email announcement:

Omega Air has announced a systemwide upgrade to its current time & attendance tracking system to enhance employee support. The installation of hack-proof biometric time clocks will begin next week. Omega, like many other large corporations today, have turned to biometrics to automate attendance tracking for better accuracy, and to end "buddy punching" whereby one employee clocks in/out for another, thus causing one employee to get paid for hours they haven't worked.

Omega Air assures its employees that this new process will follow a comprehensive compliance program that meets all legal requirements in every state in which it operates. These new state-of-the-art biometric time clocks represent a sizeable investment in our people and will allow us to better manage costs. "For our employees it will mean no more manually clocking in and out each day," noted Omega's HR Rep Lakeisha Awasung. "What's not to like?"

All employees will need to complete and sign a written consent in order for their fingerprints to be collected. E-mails will be sent soon regarding the time and location of collection. Supervisors will oversee the collection process at their individual stations.

"What's the difference between swiping our ID to clock in and out versus pressing an index finger to a screen to do the same thing?" I announced after reading the announcement.

Maya, as usual, zeroed in to the heart of the issue. "Wonder if that means they eliminated the supervisor's ability to clock us in when we've been reassigned."

A light rain had begun falling when we left the restaurant. We needed to double back to the main street and from there go downhill until we came to the next Hop-On stop.

"Perfect," Maya complained. "Just friggin perfect." Meanwhile she started searching her pockets for her bus ticket. She found it at Hop-On stop #8.

I shook my head no and pointed to the sign on the post. "No stop on holidays."

"Crap," Maya said.

Like tourists, we continued trudging downhill with our maps open in front of us, until we finally came to stop #9. The only thing that indicated a change in our luck was the fact that the bus lumbered into sight moments later.

I checked the time. "It was 5 p.m. when we left the restaurant."

"So we should be at the airport hotel by 9," Maya predicted.

The ride to Piazza Republicca and the walk from there to our hotel went by in a blur. Once at the hotel, the same clerk was on duty as when we first arrived. He led us to a locked closet at the back end of the office to get our luggage.

"What's the best way to get to the airport?" Maya asked him.

I looked at her with a questioning look because I thought we already had a plan in place. But she ignored me.

"If you want best, is taxi. But very expensive."

"How expensive?"

The man wiped his brow as though the price alone brought on a headache. "Oh, 60 euros from here. From Termini, maybe 48."

"Forget that," Maya said, pulling up her suitcase handle and turning.

"Or you can take bus from Termini. Only costs 6 euros. Same time as taxi—about forty minutes, just more crowded. Best of all, buy ticket from driver."

Maya smiled at him. "Oh yeah, that's right. I'd forgotten about that."

"How could you have forgotten?" I asked her the minute we were out in the lobby waiting for the elevator. "We just discussed it not more than an hour ago."

"I was being nice," she said. "Italian men like believing they have all the answers."

∽ **Chapter 18** ∽

Our final walk down the long hill leading to Piazza Republicca took us some twenty minutes, probably because of Maya's baggage. Her wheelie was so lopsided it didn't want to roll in a straight line. Worse, she stacked her tote bag—also full and also lopsided—on top of it. All that weight pushing into her rear while walking downhill tended to force her on a leftward trajectory, thus causing constant course corrections. She had to stop frequently, turn and either kick or push her leaning tower so it was facing straight downhill again.

Before we actually arrived at Termini there appeared to be at least four or five busses lined up along the side of the building. Unfortunately, the first in line, the 6:30pm departure, was just pulling out. As soon as it left, the next bus in line rolled forward to take its place. That's when the crowd waiting on the sidewalk surged forward just like passengers at the airport, all trying to be the first onboard. Maya and I worked our way to the back of the crowd, prepared to wait.

"My turn to buy the tickets," I told Maya, once we finally approached the front of the line.

"*Fini,*" the driver announced. "Is full!" He turned and walked up the steps, leaving me standing one foot on the sidewalk and the other on the bottom bus step.

"When is the next?" I asked as he motioned for me to get off.

"7:30," he answered, attempting to close the door on me.

"Not for another hour?" I complained, grabbing the door and holding it open a crack. "You telling me there's only the one bus an hour to accommodate all these people?"

He just pointed up the street.

Maya and I had no choice but to walk up the street to investigate what he'd been pointing to. There was a bus sign there. According to it, the next airport bus would depart at 7:10 p.m.

"Ok, thirty minutes. That's better, I told Maya.

"You buy the tickets and watch the bags," she said. "I'll be right back."

She hung around until I purchased our tickets from the bus representative standing nearby, then helped me line up our wheelies alongside the station's cement wall. Then she raced inside Termini.

She returned carrying two plastic bags, one of which clinked with every step, just as the bus pulled in.

"What did you get?" I asked.

"Packaged dinner for the hotel. With drinks."

"Good thinking."

It was a marathon of pushing and shoving to load our own bags into the bus's underbelly storage bays before we could climb onboard. We had less than a five-minute window before the crowd left behind from the earlier departure realized this bus was also heading to the airport and came racing toward us.

Maya led the way onboard before everyone else arrived, claiming two vacant seats directly behind the driver. Then she leaned back and let out a long sigh. "I will be so glad to get to the hotel."

I had to agree. "I'm so tired of smelling like exhaust and cigarettes. I just want a long, hot shower."

"Hot shower and a bedtime Prosecco," Maya corrected, rattling the bag.

The drive to Fiumicino airport was a typical nighttime highway drive, except there wasn't much traffic heading out into the Italian countryside with us, and there were next to no highway lights either. The scenery reminded me of Nevada scrub land: dry, desolate, and deserted.

We pulled up at Fiumicino airport just before 8 p.m.

My Marriott hotel printout told us the pickup point for their shuttle was at Terminal 3, door #25. Incredibly, when we got off the bus, the pillar directly opposite was marked #23.

"This way," Maya said, piling her tote on top of the wheelie then leading the way.

The sign on the pillar indicated that pickup was at 2000 hours, leaving only one departure afterward, at 2100 hours.

"Think we have to call them or do they come here automatically?" I asked.

They should come automatically," Maya answered. "So you better call. This is Italy, after all. Sometimes logic gets lost here."

I checked the time. It was just now 8 p.m. "If they're not here by 8:15 I'll call."

At 8:20 I pulled out my cell and dialed the Marriott. I got a recording telling me all lines were busy, to continue to hold.

"Screw it," I said, hanging up.

Just then the Marriott bus rounded the corner . . . but not at door #25 exactly. Instead, it pulled in to a parking stall in front of the designated stop but one level below. A limo driver waiting nearby yelled up to us: "There you go!" He pointed at the Marriott van.

"I've never been so happy to see a hotel shuttle bus in my life," Maya said once we stowed our baggage and climbed onboard.

The drive from the airport to the hotel was silent, maybe because Maya and I were the only two passengers, or maybe the driver wasn't inclined to chit-chat. We drove out into more of the desolate countryside beneath a dark, starless sky for nearly fifteen minutes before we passed the exit sign—way off the highway and easily missed. We turned into a winding road leading to the hotel. There were no lights showing us the way, although a well-lit building was visible in the distance.

"You know, the smartest thing we did was to book this hotel tonight," Maya mused, watching the hotel come into view. Can you imagine going through all of this in the morning, during rush hour, just to get to the airport for a standby flight?"

The shuttle bus circled around to the front entrance and stopped. The driver waited for payment before walking around back to unload our bags. Inside, it was another story altogether and definitely something we weren't accustomed to: 4-star opulence at its finest.

"Oh my God," said Maya, standing frozen just inside the doorway, taking in the luxurious cavern stretching out in front of us. "What did you do, Sābra?"

I couldn't help but laugh. "What do you mean?"

"How much is this place costing us?"

"Relax," I said laughing again, delighted at her reaction to my little 4-star surprise. "I have a friend who works for Marriott. She let me use her discount."

"Does it come with a free breakfast?"

"Pretty sure it doesn't." I was so happy to get the discount that it never occurred to me to check.

The cavernous lobby-lounge and dining-room looked to be the size of a football field and was designed as an open concept, front to back, for maximum visual effect. Different sections had been partitioned off by using different flooring types, different seating configurations and with a strategic placement of assorted potted plants. A vaulted ceiling of arched wooden ribs covered the entire center section, extending out over a central sitting area. Muted lights hung everywhere, giving the area a private, seductive glow. The flooring, starting at the entrance and continuing as far back as the vaulted ceiling, consisted of a light-colored speckled marble. From there it switched to an thick oriental patterned carpet. A row of potted plants divided the marble from the carpet. Seating on the marble side was for semi-formal dining on padded wooden chairs at polished wooden tables. On the carpet side, the seating was thick cushioned chairs and love seats, with leather footstools inside each section.

The front desk had been positioned to the left of the main entrance. The bar was further back, facing the vaulted wooden ribs. Beyond that was more marble flooring, for an area set up for more casual dining . . . for breakfast maybe.

We got checked in and received our room keys in record time, in un-Italian-like silent efficiency.

"Is there WiFi in the room?" Maya asked.

The reception clerk shook his head. "No, not in rooms. Is free throughout lobby, however. Password is 'Marriott.'"

Maya stacked her bags and prepared to head for the elevator. "I'm going to sit down and check the flight loads before going upstairs," I said to her backside. "Because once I get in the shower and change clothes, I'm not coming out again."

I signed into the computer only long enough to check the flight. Relieved to see that we would definitely get cleared from standby, I stood and stretched and absorbed the surroundings, savoring the here and now for a quiet moment. I headed upstairs with a feeling of relief, knowing that this unbelievably long day was finally over with.

The minute I opened our room door, Maya said, "Don't tell me. I don't want to know."

"No worries," I announced in spite of what she said. "Flight's not showing full."

"Thank God. It's good to go, but better when you know you'll get home."

"Other than first class, that is. But it looks like we'll be able to grab a couple of seats in the back. Maybe three seats in the middle so we can get some sleep."

"I can live with that," Maya answered as she folded and stacked clothes. Everything she'd brought with her was now strewn out on top of her bed. She was in the process of repacking all of it, but in a more orderly fashion this go round. She was currently filling her backpack.

I left her to it and ducked into the bathroom. Our sandwiches and Prosecco could wait until I was clean and comfy.

The minute I came out, Maya picked up her iPad and headed for the door. "I'm going to head downstairs and check my email," she said.

"Tell Bryce I said hello," I answered, unwrapping my sandwich.

Maya paused in her tracks, opened her mouth to say something, then stopped. "Okay, I will," I heard as she shut the door behind her with a laugh.

I had just finished my first glass of Prosecco when Maya stormed back inside. "Oh my God, you won't believe it!" she announced, still slightly out of breath from her rush back up to our room. "Bryce told me the investigation report is finished and due to air last night. Or maybe it's tonight. I got confused because of the time change. Hell, maybe it's happening right now!"

"What all is in the report, did he say?"

Maya shook her head and headed to her side of the room to finish packing. "He told me to keep checking my email because he's going to send me a video feed of the newscast once it's aired."

"What if that doesn't happen till we're half-way across the Atlantic?" I asked.

"I'll just have to buy the onboard WiFi and keep checking. We have to see it. He said the story is big, so big that this time Omega won't be able to ignore it

Maya and I set both our cell alarms. In addition, we ordered a wake-up call for 8 a.m. You might know, all three went off at the same time. After that, it was a race to the bathroom.

Unlike Maya, who still hadn't finished packing, my suitcase had been ready to go since leaving the hotel yesterday. Maya simply had too much stuff. So much that she ended up dumping her wheelie on the floor and then had to climb on top of it on her hands and knees while I worked to get the bag zipped.

Downstairs at last, we made our way to the breakfast area of the lobby by following the scent of fresh-from-the-oven croissants. I picked up the entrance menu and gazed at the €30 per person price for the buffet.

"I'm going to pass," I said to Maya. "We'll get something to eat on the flight. If we eat here now, I doubt we'll be able to eat again in three hours."

"You do what you want," Maya said before making a beeline to a vacant table near the outer row where there was room to park her bags without blocking anyone. "If we were going to fly back in first class, I'd say you have a valid point. But this place is so special, don't you think we should take full advantage of it while we're here? Besides, if we eat now, we won't have to worry about getting one of those crappy coach TV dinners, or getting whatever's left after everyone else gets their choice of chicken or beef."

Her reasoning made sense. Plus, the fully stocked buffet beckoned. How could I sit there and not eat while Maya oohed and ahhed after loading up on a selection of just about everything?

Next thing I knew the hotel shuttle dropped us off at the airport right where we picked it up last night, except this time, rather than park on the downhill side of pillar #25, it pulled up outside the entrance across the street from the pillar. This was standard procedure. We were on familiar territory now.

Checking-in at any airport can be confusing and therefore stressful, but Rome's Fiumicino is in a class all by itself in this regard, in my humble opinion. Maybe I felt this way because it's so big it's intimidating. We wandered around the lobby for long minutes looking for Omega's signs. Thank God we had plenty of time to spare.

Once we finally found Omega's check-in counter, we followed the herding ropes toward the security posse. After answering the usual litany of stupid questions (Did you pack your own belongings today? Have they been with you the whole time? Would you admit it if you didn't?) we received a colored security sticker on the back of our passports and were then ushered to the check-in agent. I willingly surrendered my bag, not wanting to see it again until New York customs.

Not Maya, however. The agent motioned for her to set her wheelie on the platform leading to the conveyor belt. Maya shook her head. "I'm carrying it onboard."

The agent leaned over and eyed Maya's baggage. "No, you're not. Three items are too many."

"Three? My backpack is my purse."

"Yes but you have two baggages. One is too big. Two is too many. You must check one."

"But … "

Maya took a deep breath, ready to defend her position, but the agent held up her hand and threatened to call for a supervisor. "You especially, as a colleague, know the rules. You must abide by those rules. To be honest, I should charge you for excess weight. Why do you pack so much?"

"Go ahead and check it," Maya countered with a frown.

"It will make life better for you," the agent answered, reverting to friendly professionalism again.

What can I say? The rest of the check-in process went as smooth as glass. We walked through Italian passport control, where our passports were stamped, declaring us officially out of Italy. From there we walked to the gate, took a seat, and waited for the crew to show up. Thirty minutes later boarding got underway. Next thing I knew, I was hugging a pillow and a blanket alongside an empty seat.

We didn't receive the news feed from Bryce until the second half of the flight. It was after lunch, when the cabin was dark and the majority of passengers were either asleep, reading, or watching a movie. Against a background of droning engines, I heard Maya call me over to the empty seat beside her so I could watch the video feed with her.

Since her iPad only had one port for ear buds, I just watched and listened to her frequent comments. "Once I see it," she whispered, "I'll let you plug in and we'll play it again." I nodded and leaned closer to the screen.

The video opened to a closeup of Bryce sitting behind the Channel 5 podium holding several papers in his hand. The caption read: Omega Air Should Clean House.

"Several members of Omega Air's local management team, we have learned, are currently under internal investigation for double dipping employment hours while on duty at Omega," Bryce began. "One is being investigated for chronic unexcused absences while supposedly supervising dozens of charges . . . Let me begin by stating that names are being withheld for privacy purposes, as well as for legal concerns. But Channel 5 has learned much about the facts leading up to these investigations.

One manager, reportedly drawing a near six-figure salary at Omega, is the sole owner/operator of Putt-Putt Golf, located on the city's east side near East Lake Mall. Channel 5 has verified that there is only one part-time employee on duty at any given time during their ten-to-four operating hours."

A video clip then switched to the driving range. Several people could be seen swinging balls out into a green field. Next, the camera zoomed in to the sole employee. The minute he spotted the news crew, he raced to Putt Putt's office. The camera remained focus on the building until the same man slowly peeked around the corner of the doorway. He ducked back inside again, but not before the news crew had frozen the frame to reveal a somewhat blurry face.

The video feed then switched to Omega's ticket counter, with a close up shot of its manager in the same pose: peeking around the doorway, watching the employees as they worked. The camera zoomed in for a closeup of the manager's face and froze the frame. Next, the two frozen frames were laid out side-by-side. In spite of being somewhat blurry, the images left no doubt that they both belonged to the same man.

Bryce's voice began again. "Note the time and date inset into each of these video feeds. They were both shot the same day, hours apart. Omega's manager at that time was reportedly on-duty until 4pm. So was the Putt Putt operator. I ask you," Bryce asked, staring at the camera, "how is that possible?"

The next scene switched to inside the mall. "Another of Omega's managers is the sole owner of Yum Yum Yoghurt. But here's the thing . . . " continued Bryce. "While working at Omega Air, this 'leader of employees' reportedly borrowed one of the company's trucks and removed an employee from the work schedule for THREE DAYS in order to drive one of Omega's trucks to New Jersey to pick up a critical piece of equipment: a yoghurt machine! The employee who drove the truck was excused from duty, yet still got paid. The manager who authorized the use of Omega's truck never sought official permission to do so. Omega's own ground equipment logs reveal an increase of 1250 miles over a single weekend. Again, I ask, how is that possible?"

The newscast then switched back to Bryce seated at his podium. "Representatives of Omega Air vehemently deny all these allegations. In fact, in a statement issued earlier today, executives at Omega Air claim that all members of their leadership team have undergone a thorough and vigorous vetting process, establishing without a doubt that each and every one consistently demonstrate their core values of honesty and integrity. In addition, they claim these allegations are nothing but bogus misrepresentations by a handful of disgruntled employees."

As soon as the broadcast finished, I plugged in my earbuds and listened to it from the beginning. I kept glancing over at Maya throughout the examples, knowing full well how Bryce came to obtain the information. I wasn't quite sure how to react; should we celebrate or hide our heads?

"Well, what do you think?" Maya whispered when the video finished.

"He did a good job," I began. "And it needed to come out."

Maya agreed and rang her call button.

"What are you doing?"

"I'm going to order champagne. My treat!"

"Yeah, well let's see if anything comes of it. Knowing Omega, they'll try to sweep all of this under the rug."

"I doubt they'll be able to do that this time. Especially if those side businesses end up closing down for a couple of weeks due to lack of manpower."

We took turns watching the video two or three more times each, right up until we heard the announcement of our approach for landing in JFK.

We followed the line-up through customs, where we waited for what seemed like forever for our bags to arrive. After clearing customs, we dropped our bags on the other side on the connections belt, then headed straight to our connection gate for home. We were so focused on where we were going and what we were doing that I didn't remember to take my phone off airplane mode until we trekked half-way through the airport complex to get to our next gate and finally got the chance to sit down.

The first email I received came from a coworker friend. I nearly fell off my chair when I opened the attachment and read it. Maya must have received the same email, because I heard her scream before I saw her jump up out of her chair.

October 18, 2019

To All Employees:

After more than twenty years of dedicated service, Customer Service Supervisor Richard Noggins has announced his decision to retire to pursue other life options, effective immediately.

He will be greatly missed by his colleagues.

We wish Richard well in his future endeavors and would like to thank him for his many years of dedicated service as a member of Omega's leadership team.

I agree with Maya wholeheartedly when she says 'It's good to go, but better to get back home again.' For that reason alone, I was relieved when we finally boarded our last flight.

"Good evening, folks! We're going to have a smooth flight today, so strap in, sit back and relax," the pilot announced. "Oh, if you're superstitious you might want to close your window shade because there's going to be a spectacular full moon outside tonight. It will be visible on the right side of the aircraft all the way home."

I was about to put my cell on airplane mode, when another email came through, this one from Sandusky. "I'm almost afraid to look," I whispered over to Maya, leaning close to share the caption: "Private! For your eyes only!" Then I clicked on the link.

ΩA Omega Air
3466 North Seawall Road
Iliopolos, FL. 32920
www.omegaair.com

Lakeisha Awusung
Senior Vice president
Human Resources

October 20, 2019

To All Employees:

It is with great pleasure that we announce the selection of Miss Samantha Schlagenhaufen to join Omega's senior leadership team as the new Station Manager of Dayton, Ohio.

Sami, as she is known to friends and co-workers alike, has demonstrated unique talents and versatility during her short tenure at Omega, amassing a variety of job knowledge, from working gates and ticketing positions, to assisting in baggage service. Her skills as well as her connections throughout the upper Ohio business community, will prove to be valuable assets to Omega Air.

Samantha did her undergraduate studies at Bay College, in Sandusky, Ohio, where she majored in Business & Leadership.

She will assume her new duties in Dayton on November 1st.

~ FIN ~

Thank you so much for reading my latest book. I hope you enjoyed it. Please take the time to leave a review at your favorite eBook retailer or reading blog. I can't tell you how much I appreciate your helping me to spread the word.

**

Other works by Sābra Hunter:
From Word to eBook Made Easy
A Get-Acquainted Cruise
I'd Rather Eat Pizza than See Pisa
Praha: The Story Behind the Wedding Gift
CBP Hiring Process Explained